THE PHILOSOPHY OF STOICISM

ADVANCED STOIC TECHNIQUES FOR BUILDING RESILIENCE, INNER PEACE, AND WISDOM

ADRIAN COLE

CONTENTS

INTRODUCTION

Many years ago, I found myself at a crossroads. Life was moving fast, and the pressures of work and personal commitments seemed overwhelming. One day, while browsing a bookstore, I stumbled upon a worn-out copy of Marcus Aurelius's book, *Meditations*. Intrigued by the idea of a Roman Emperor reflecting on life, I bought the book. Little did I know this would start a transformative journey into Stoicism.

My book aims to offer you the same kind of transformation. Its purpose is to provide a guide to mastering advanced Stoic philosophy and practices. Stoicism is not just an ancient philosophy but a practical approach to living a balanced and meaningful life in our chaotic world. It teaches us to face challenges with wisdom, strength, and peace of mind.

This book is targeted at adults who are seeking to navigate life's challenges more effectively. Whether you are a professional striving for balance, a self-improvement enthusiast, or simply curious about philosophy, this book has something to offer. Stoicism speaks to the universal human experience—our struggles, resilience, and quest for meaning.

The structure of this is designed to be both comprehensive and practical. We will start by exploring advanced Stoic principles like virtue ethics and the dichotomy of control. Then, we will move into practical exercises for building emotional resilience, including cognitive reframing and *premeditatio malorum*. Daily meditation, reflection, and journaling practices will be covered to help you internalize Stoic teachings. Finally, we will discuss applying Stoicism to contemporary issues such as stress management and uncertainty.

What can you expect to gain from this book? First, you will develop emotional resilience. Life will still throw challenges your way, but you will be better equipped to handle them. You will also find inner peace, even amid chaos. Your decision-making will improve as you learn to focus on what you can control and let go of what you cannot, and personal growth will follow as you commit to a lifelong journey of self-improvement and wisdom.

The insights in this book are backed by extensive research. I have drawn from ancient texts, modern academic papers, and my experiences. My background as a scholar of philosophy and my years of studying Stoicism add credibility to the content. This is not just theory; it is a practical guide grounded in ancient wisdom and modern research.

By the end of this book, you will have a toolkit of practical, actionable guidance that you can integrate into your daily life. You will be able to face life's challenges with a new perspective and a sense of calm. The aim is not just to read about Stoicism but to live it.

I encourage you to engage with the content actively. Each chapter includes exercises, reflection questions, and journaling prompts to help you internalize and apply Stoic principles. Keep an open mind and commit to practicing these techniques. The more you engage, the more you will benefit.

As we embark on this journey together, remember that the path to wisdom and resilience is lifelong. There will be moments of challenge and moments of triumph. Through it all, Stoicism will be your guide. It will help you navigate the complexities of life with clarity and strength.

So, let's begin this journey. Let's explore the rich tapestry of Stoic wisdom and uncover how it can change our lives. The road ahead promises not just knowledge but profound, lasting change. Welcome to a life guided by Stoic principles.

FOUNDATIONS OF ADVANCED STOIC PHILOSOPHY

One evening, after a particularly grueling day at work, I found myself reflecting on the chaos and stress that seemed to dominate my life. I had been reading about Stoicism and was struck by a passage from Marcus Aurelius's *Meditations*. This Stoic philosopher wrote, "You have power over your mind—not outside events. Realize this, and you will find strength." This simple yet profound idea resonated deeply, and I began seeing the world differently. It was the first step in my journey toward understanding and applying Stoic philosophy.

In this chapter, we will explore the bedrock of Stoic philosophy: virtue ethics. We will delve into virtue, which, according to Stoicism, is life's highest good and ultimate aim. We will discuss the role of reason and rationality in achieving virtue and the belief in the universality of virtue. Practical exercises will be provided to help you cultivate virtue in your daily life.

VIRTUE ETHICS: THE CORE OF STOICISM

At the heart of Stoic philosophy lies the concept of virtue ethics. According to the Stoics, virtue is life's highest good and ultimate aim. Unlike other ethical systems prioritizing happiness or pleasure, Stoicism places virtue above all else. Virtue ethics is about developing a moral character and living according to nature. This means understanding and accepting the natural order of things and acting in a way that aligns with it. The Stoics believed that we can achieve a life of true contentment and purpose by cultivating virtues such as wisdom, courage, justice, and moderation.

Reason and rationality play a crucial role in achieving virtue. The Stoics thought that humans are rational beings and that our reasoning ability sets us apart from other animals. Using reason, we can understand the world and make moral decisions that align with nature. One of the most well-known Stoic philosophers, Marcus Aurelius, often reflected on the importance of rational thinking. He wrote in *Meditations*, "The happiness of your life depends upon the quality of your thoughts." He also emphasized the need for rational decision-making processes. By evaluating our actions and their consequences logically, we can ensure that we act virtuously.

The Stoic belief in the universality of virtue is another crucial aspect of their philosophy. The Stoics believed that virtue is accessible to everyone, regardless of social status or wealth. As one of the most prominent Stoic philosophers, Seneca often wrote in his letters about the equality of all humans in their capacity for virtue. He stated, "Virtue is that which is honorable and becoming, and is of profit to the possessor." This egalitarian principle is reflected in modern views on equality and justice. Everyone has the potential to cultivate virtue, and it is through our actions and choices that we demonstrate our moral character.

Practical Exercises to Develop Virtue Daily

Practical exercises are essential to help you develop virtue in your daily life. Begin by incorporating daily journaling prompts that encourage self-reflection. For instance, at the end of each day, write about a situation where you acted virtuously or could have acted more virtuously. Reflect on your actions and intentions, and think about how to improve. Another exercise is to ask yourself reflective questions throughout the day. When you have a choice, ask, Is this aligned with virtue? Am I doing this out of wisdom, courage, justice, or moderation? These questions guide you toward making more ethical choices.

When you understand and apply these virtue ethics principles, you will see positive change in your life. You will find that true contentment comes not from external circumstances but from living by your values and principles. This foundation of Stoic philosophy will serve as a guide as we explore more advanced techniques and practices in the chapters to come.

THE FOUR CARDINAL VIRTUES: WISDOM, JUSTICE, COURAGE, AND MODERATION

In Stoicism, the four cardinal virtues—Wisdom, Justice, Courage, and Moderation—form the backbone of ethical living. These virtues are not mere abstract concepts but practical guides for navigating life's complexities. Each virtue has its roots in the ancient philosophical tradition. Yet their relevance remains undiminished in modern times. Wisdom, or "Sophia," is the ability to make sound judgments and understand the world through reason. Justice, or "Dikaiosyne," emphasizes fairness and moral integrity in our interactions. Courage, or "Andreia," involves facing challenges with bravery. Moderation, or "Sophrosyne," advocates for balance and self-control in all aspects of life. These virtues collectively lead to a life of moral excellence and inner peace.

Wisdom (Sophia) is the cornerstone of Stoic philosophy. It involves discerning the right course of action in any given situation. Stoics believe that wisdom is achieved through the constant pursuit of knowledge and self-reflection. In *Meditations*, Marcus Aurelius often pondered the essence of wisdom. He wrote, "The object of life is not to be on the side of the majority, but to escape finding oneself in the ranks of the insane." This quote underscores the importance of independent, rational thought. In daily life, practical wisdom can manifest in various ways. For example, when faced with a difficult decision at work, gathering all relevant information and considering the long-term consequences aligns with the Stoic virtue of wisdom. It means not acting impulsively but thoughtfully ensuring our actions are grounded in reason and ethical principles.

Justice (Dikaiosyne) is another critical virtue in Stoicism. It is about treating others fairly and acting with moral integrity. Seneca's writings often highlight the significance of justice. In his letters, he stated, "Treat your inferiors as you would be treated by your superiors." This principle of reciprocity is fundamental to Stoic justice. In modern contexts, justice can be seen in actions that promote equality and fairness. For example, advocating for fair treatment of all employees in a workplace or standing up against discrimination reflects the Stoic commitment to justice. These actions uphold moral integrity and contribute to a more equitable society. Embodying justice ensures that our interactions are fair and contribute positively to our communities.

The Stoic virtue of Courage (Andreia) is essential for facing life's inevitable challenges. Stoics view courage as the strength to confront fear, pain, and adversity. It is about standing firm in the face of difficulties and maintaining moral integrity even when challenging. Personal stories of courage abound in Stoic literature. Consider the tale of Epictetus, one of the most renowned Stoic philosophers. He was born into slavery and endured physical suffering but remained steadfast in his philosophical convictions. His courage in adversity serves as an inspiration for us all. We can start with small acts of courage in our daily lives to cultivate bravery. Facing a problematic conversation head-on, standing up for what is right, or pushing through a challenging project at work are all ways to practice courage. These actions build our resilience and prepare us to face more considerable challenges with a Stoic mindset.

Moderation (Sophrosyne) is about finding balance and exercising self-control. It is the virtue that prevents excess and ensures that we live in harmony with our values and principles. The Stoics believed that moderation is crucial for maintaining physical and mental well-being. Practical tips for practicing moderation include limiting indulgences, whether in food, drink, or even work. For instance, having a balanced diet, regular exercise, and ensuring adequate rest are all ways to practice moderation. In ancient contexts, Stoics like Musonius Rufus, another prominent Stoic philosopher, emphasized moderation in all aspects of life, advising against excess and deficiency. This might translate to finding a healthy work-life balance in modern times, where neither work nor leisure is neglected. Practicing moderation creates a balanced life that aligns with our values and promotes long-term well-being.

By consistently practicing these four cardinal virtues, we can achieve a life of moral excellence and inner peace. Each virtue—Wisdom, Justice, Courage, and Moderation—guides our actions and decisions, ensuring that we live according to our highest principles. As we continue exploring Stoic philosophy, these virtues will serve as a base for understanding and applying Stoic teachings.

THE DICHOTOMY OF CONTROL: WHAT YOU CAN AND CANNOT CONTROL

A fundamental Stoic principle is the "dichotomy of control." It offers a straightforward, practical approach to many of life's uncertainties. This principle is rooted in the teachings of Epictetus. He asserted that some things are within our control while others are not. We gain mental peace and resilience by focusing on the factors we can influence and accepting those we cannot. Epictetus famously stated, "Some things are up to us and some things are not up to us." This simple yet profound distinction lies at the heart of Stoic thought, reminding us to direct our efforts where they will be most effective.

The dichotomy of control differentiates between internal and external factors. Internal factors include our thoughts, actions, desires, and aversions—essentially, everything that originates from within us. External factors encompass everything outside our control, such as other people's actions, external events, and circumstances. For instance, you can control your reaction to a colleague's criticism but not the criticism itself. This distinction has practical applications in modern life and not just theoretical ones. Focusing on our internal responses allows us to navigate external challenges more effectively and with better composure.

Understanding what we can control and cannot is crucial for maintaining mental peace. When we focus on controllable aspects, we reduce stress and anxiety. Take a busy professional facing a tight deadline. They cannot control their boss's workload or expectations, but they can choose their approach to the task, time management, and attitude. Concentrating on these controllable elements allows them to manage stress more effectively and perform better. This shift in focus promotes a sense of calm and confidence, even amid challenging circumstances.

Practical Exercises for Practicing the Dichotomy of Control

Practical exercises can be highly beneficial to internalize the principle of the dichotomy of control. One effective exercise is to create a two-column list. On one side, write down things within your control, such as your actions, attitudes, and reactions. Alternatively, list things outside your control, like the weather, other people's opinions, or global events. Reflect on this list daily to reinforce the distinction. Another helpful exercise involves thought experiments. When faced with a stressful situation, pause and ask yourself, "Is this within my control?" If not, focus your energy on what you can influence.

Real-world scenarios also help in practicing this principle. When you are stuck in traffic on your way to an important meeting, you can't control the traffic but can control your response. Instead of getting frustrated, use the time to listen to an educational podcast or practice deep breathing. This shift in focus transforms a potentially stressful situation into a productive one. Similarly, in personal relationships, you cannot control how others behave, but you can control your reactions. By focusing on your responses, you maintain your inner peace and contribute to healthier interactions.

We must emphasize the importance of focusing on what we can control. It empowers us to take ownership of our lives and reduces the emotional burden of worrying about uncontrollable factors. This focus leads to a more resilient mindset, enabling us to face life's challenges with even more fortitude. Whether dealing with professional setbacks, personal conflicts, or everyday annoyances, the dichotomy of control provides a clear framework for maintaining mental peace and resilience. It is a practical tool that, when consistently applied, transforms our approach to life's inevitable ups and downs.

THE STOIC VIEW OF FATE: AMOR FATI AND ACCEPTANCE

Amor fati, or "the love of fate," is a cornerstone of Stoic philosophy that invites us to embrace everything that happens to us, good and bad. This concept, deeply rooted in Stoicism, suggests that we should accept and love our fate. Stoics believed that everything happens for a reason and that every event is necessary for our growth. Marcus Aurelius captured this sentiment beautifully when he wrote, "A blazing fire makes flame and brightness out of everything that is thrown into it." This idea was later echoed by Friedrich Nietzsche, who described *amor fati* as his formula for human greatness, where one wants nothing to be different and loves what is necessary.

The benefits of accepting fate are profound. Acceptance leads to inner peace and reduces resistance to life's inevitable challenges. Consider the case of Viktor Frankl, a Holocaust survivor and psychiatrist who practiced *amor fati* during his time in concentration camps. Frankl found meaning in his suffering, which allowed him to endure unimaginable hardships. By embracing his fate, he discovered a sense of purpose and strength. Psychologically, acceptance helps us avoid the mental turmoil of fighting against what we cannot change. When we accept our circumstances, we free ourselves from the stress and anxiety of constant resistance. This acceptance does not mean we become passive; instead, it empowers us to face our challenges with a clear mind and a resilient spirit.

It is essential to differentiate between fate and fatalism. Accepting fate, or *amor fati,* is not about passivity or resignation. It is about actively engaging with life and making the best of every situation. For instance, an athlete who suffers a career-ending injury can either wallow in despair or embrace their new reality and find new ways to contribute, perhaps by coaching or mentoring young athletes. This proactive acceptance transforms obstacles into opportunities for growth. In modern life, this principle can be applied professionally and personally. Whether dealing with the loss of a job or a relationship, embracing fate allows us to move forward constructively rather than getting stuck in imagining what might have been.

Practical Exercises for Embracing Amor Fati

To practice *amor fati*, start by reflecting on past events with acceptance. Think about a difficult situation you faced and ask yourself how it contributed to your growth. Write about this experience in a journal, focusing on the positive outcomes that emerged from the challenge. This exercise helps reframe your perspective and fosters a sense of gratitude for the lessons learned. Another valuable exercise is visualization. Imagine a future scenario where things do not go as planned. Visualize how you would accept this outcome and your actions to adapt constructively. This mental rehearsal prepares you to face real-life challenges with a mindset of acceptance and resilience.

By embracing *amor fati*, we see every event as a stepping stone toward personal growth. This shift in perspective reduces our resistance to life's challenges and helps us find meaning and purpose in every experience. As we continue to explore Stoic principles, we will see how this attitude of acceptance and proactive engagement with life enriches our understanding and application of Stoicism.

UNDERSTANDING STOIC PHYSICS AND THEOLOGY

Stoic physics and theology are crucial to understanding the natural world and its divine order. The Stoics believed the universe operates according to a rational and purposeful design governed by a divine principle called "Logos." This concept, central to Stoic thought, posits that the universe is a coherent system where every event is interconnected and meaningful. We can trace the development of Stoic physics back to early Greek philosophers such as Heraclitus, who influenced later Stoics like Zeno of Citium, Chrysippus, and Epictetus. These thinkers built upon the idea that the cosmos is an orderly, living organism permeated by reason and purpose.

Logos is a term derived from Greek, meaning "word" or "reason." The Stoics believed Logos is imminent in all things, providing structure and coherence to the cosmos. This divine reason is not an external deity but an intrinsic aspect of the natural world, guiding its processes and ensuring harmony. Marcus Aurelius reflects on this in *Meditations* by stating, "All things are woven together and the common bond is sacred, and scarcely one thing is alien to another. For they are continuous and in sympathy with one another and all things are coordinated and combine to form the same universe." This highlights the Stoic view that everything in the universe is interconnected and part of a greater whole.

The concept of "cosmic sympathy" is also central to Stoic physics. This idea suggests that all parts of the universe are inextricably linked and that changes in one part affect the whole. The Stoics used the metaphor of a vast organism to describe this interconnectedness, where each part functions in harmony with the others. This perspective finds modern parallels in scientific theories such as the Gaia hypothesis, which views Earth as a self-regulating system, and quantum physics, which reveals the interdependence of particles across vast distances. These scientific parallels affirm the Stoic belief in the interconnectedness of all things, emphasizing that our actions have far-reaching consequences.

Stoic physics and theology remain relevant in contemporary discussions of science and philosophy. The Stoic understanding of the natural world as an interconnected system resonates with modern ecological and environmental ethics. Recognizing the interdependence of all life forms encourages a sense of responsibility toward the environment. For instance, the ethical implications of this view are evident in the principles of sustainability and conservation, which aim to protect the delicate balance of our ecosystems. The Stoic emphasis on living in harmony with nature aligns with contemporary efforts to address climate change and promote environmental stewardship.

In modern physics and cosmology, the Stoic idea of Logos echoes in the search for a unified theory that explains the universe's fundamental forces. Scientists strive to understand the principles governing the cosmos, much like the Stoics sought to comprehend the divine reason that orders everything. This pursuit of knowledge reflects the Stoic commitment to rational inquiry and intellectual curiosity. By relating Stoic physics to contemporary scientific endeavors, we can appreciate the timeless relevance of Stoic thought and its contributions to our understanding of the universe.

The ethical implications of Stoic physics and theology extend beyond environmentalism. They also shape our moral responsibilities toward one another. Believing in cosmic sympathy encourages us to recognize our fates' interconnectedness and shared humanity. This perspective fosters empathy, compassion, and a sense of social responsibility. In a world where individual actions have global repercussions, the Stoic view of interconnectedness reminds us that our choices matter and that we are part of a larger, interdependent community.

STOICISM AND COGNITIVE BEHAVIORAL THERAPY (CBT): A MODERN CONNECTION

In our exploration of Stoic philosophy, it is fascinating to note its profound influence on modern cognitive behavioral therapy (CBT).

This connection is not just historical but deeply practical, offering valuable insights for those seeking to manage emotions and behaviors through rational thought. CBT, a widely respected psychological treatment, focuses on identifying and changing negative thought patterns. Its roots can be traced back to Stoic principles, particularly the teachings of Epictetus and Marcus Aurelius. These ancient philosophers emphasized the importance of rational thinking in achieving emotional well-being, a cornerstone of CBT.

The historical development of CBT is a testament to the enduring relevance of Stoic philosophy. In the mid-20th century, psychologists like Albert Ellis and Aaron Beck pioneered CBT, drawing inspiration from Stoic ideas. As the founder of rational emotive behavior therapy (REBT), Ellis explicitly acknowledged the influence of Stoic philosophy on his work. He believed irrational beliefs and negative thinking patterns were the root causes of emotional distress, a view shared by the Stoics. Beck, the father of cognitive therapy, also incorporated Stoic principles into his approach, emphasizing the importance of challenging and reframing negative thoughts.

Both Stoicism and CBT focus on rational thought to manage emotions and behaviors. They teach that our interpretations of events, rather than the events themselves, determine our emotional responses. This shared emphasis on rational thinking is evident in techniques like cognitive restructuring, a core component of CBT. Cognitive restructuring involves identifying irrational beliefs, challenging them, and finally replacing them with more rational and balanced thoughts. This process mirrors the Stoic practice of examining and correcting false judgments, as described by Epictetus in his *Discourses*.

A common CBT technique called "thought records" illustrates the practical application of these principles. Thought records help individuals track their thoughts, identify cognitive distortions, and reframe them. For example, if you think *I always fail at everything*, a thought record would guide you to challenge this belief by examining the evidence. You might realize that while you have encountered failures, you also have many successes. This rational re-evaluation aligns with the Stoic practice of questioning and reframing negative thoughts.

Practical Exercises Combining Stoic and CBT Techniques

To help you integrate Stoic and CBT principles into your daily life, let's explore some practical exercises. Start with cognitive reframing exercises. When you encounter a distressing thought, pause and ask yourself if it is rational. Use a thought record to document the thought, challenge its validity, and reframe it. For instance, if you think, *I'm not good enough*, challenge this by listing your achievements and positive qualities. This exercise encourages a balanced perspective and reduces emotional distress.

Another effective exercise is the use of real-life scenarios. Imagine you are preparing for a job interview and feel anxious. Instead of succumbing to the anxiety, apply Stoic and CBT techniques. Identify the irrational belief driving your anxiety, such as, *If I don't get this job, I'm a failure*. Challenge this belief by considering other opportunities and reminding yourself of past successes. This rational approach helps manage anxiety and improves performance.

Case studies further demonstrate the effectiveness of integrating Stoic and CBT practices. Take, for example, a therapy session involving a client struggling with social anxiety. By combining CBT techniques with Stoic principles, a therapist can help clients identify and challenge irrational beliefs about social interactions. The client learns to reframe negative thoughts like *Everyone will judge me*, to more balanced ones like *Some people might judge me, but many others won't.* This shift in perspective reduces anxiety and enhances social confidence.

Therapists and practitioners often share success stories highlighting the transformative power of these combined approaches. One practitioner recounted a client who, through CBT and Stoic techniques, overcame a debilitating fear of public speaking. The client gradually built confidence and delivered successful speeches by challenging irrational beliefs and practicing rational reframing. Testimonials like this underscore the practical benefits of integrating Stoic wisdom with modern therapeutic techniques.

Understanding the synergy between Stoicism and CBT provides a robust framework for improving emotional resilience and mental well-being. Both approaches emphasize the importance of rational thought in managing emotions and behaviors. We can harness the wisdom of ancient philosophy and modern psychology through practical exercises and real-life applications to lead more balanced and fulfilling lives.

As we conclude this exploration, remember that the principles and techniques discussed here are not just theoretical. They are practical tools to integrate into your daily life, offering a pathway to greater emotional resilience and inner peace. The fusion of Stoic philosophy and CBT provides a rich, evidence-based approach to personal growth and well-being.

2

BUILDING EMOTIONAL RESILIENCE

Years ago, during a particularly challenging period in my career, I found myself overwhelmed by stress and anxiety. One evening, after a particularly difficult day, I recalled a technique I had read about in a book on cognitive behavioral therapy (CBT). It involved reframing my thoughts to alter my emotional responses. I decided to give it a try. To my surprise, this simple shift in perspective brought immediate relief and clarity. It was a revelation that led me to delve deeper into the practice of cognitive reframing, a method deeply rooted in Stoic philosophy, as we discussed in the previous chapter. This chapter will explore how changing your perspective can fundamentally alter your emotional landscape, providing you with tools to build mental toughness and resilience.

PREMEDITATIO MALORUM: PREPARING FOR ADVERSITY

The ancient Stoics had a unique way of preparing for life's inevitable challenges. One of their essential practices was *premeditatio malorum*, which translates to the "premeditation of evils." This Stoic exercise involves contemplating potential misfortunes before they occur. By doing so, you mentally prepare yourself for adversity, reducing the shock and emotional turmoil when those events happen. Seneca frequently practiced this technique. He once wrote, "He robs present ills of their power who has perceived their coming beforehand." Marcus Aurelius echoed this sentiment, advising, "Begin each day by telling yourself: Today I shall be meeting with interference, ingratitude, insolence, disloyalty, ill-will, and selfishness." These reflections are not meant to foster pessimism but to build resilience and mental toughness.

The psychological benefits of *premeditatio malorum* are well documented. By preparing for adversity, you increase your mental preparedness. When you expect challenges, you can develop strategies to cope effectively. This foresight reduces the impact of unexpected events. Instead of being blindsided by difficulties, you face them with a calm, composed mindset. This practice also diminishes fear and anxiety. When you envision worst-case scenarios, you realize that you can survive them. This realization fosters a sense of empowerment and reduces the fear of the unknown. As you become more accustomed to the idea of potential setbacks, you build a mental buffer against stress and anxiety.

To incorporate *premeditatio malorum* into your life, start with visualization exercises. Take a few minutes each day to imagine potential challenges you might face. For example, consider a scenario where you have to have a difficult conversation with a colleague. Visualize how the conversation might unfold, the possible objections or conflicts, and how you would calmly and effectively address them. This mental rehearsal prepares you for the event, making you more confident and composed when the time comes.

Let's look at another specific example. Imagine you are about to have a challenging performance review at work. Instead of dreading the meeting, practice *premeditatio malorum*. Visualize the possible criticisms your manager might offer. Think about how you would respond constructively, focusing on your strengths and the steps you plan to take for improvement. Preparing for this scenario reduces anxiety and increases your chances of having a productive conversation.

Reflective journaling is another powerful tool. Write about potential adversities and how you would handle them. For instance, if you are worried about a financial setback, describe the steps to manage your finances, seek additional income sources, and cut unnecessary expenses. This exercise not only prepares you mentally but also provides practical solutions. This preparation empowers you to face financial challenges with a clear and calm mind.

By mentally preparing for these scenarios, you reduce the emotional impact and increase your ability to handle them effectively. Incorporating *premeditatio malorum* into your daily routine will build resilience and mental toughness. By regularly contemplating potential adversities, you become better equipped to face life's challenges with a calm and composed mindset. This practice, deeply rooted in Stoic philosophy, offers a powerful way to reduce fear and anxiety while enhancing your ability to navigate life's inevitable ups and downs.

COGNITIVE REFRAMING: CHANGING YOUR PERSPECTIVE

Cognitive reframing is the process of changing the way you view a situation to alter its emotional impact. At its core, it involves recognizing and challenging negative thought patterns. Then, you replace them with more constructive alternatives. This practice is not about denying reality but seeing it from a different angle. The Stoics, particularly Epictetus, emphasized the power of perspective. He famously said, "It is not the things themselves that disturb people, but their judgments about these things." This quote encapsulates the essence of cognitive reframing. By changing our judgments, we change our emotional responses.

The importance of cognitive reframing in Stoic teachings cannot be overstated. Stoicism teaches that our attitudes and biases color our interpretations of events. These interpretations, rather than the events themselves, determine our emotional responses. For example, if you view a job loss as a catastrophic failure, you will likely feel despair and anxiety. However, if you see it as an opportunity for growth and new beginnings, your emotional response will be more positive. Cognitive reframing requires mindfulness and a willingness to question our automatic thoughts. Doing so can transform our emotional experiences and build greater resilience.

The benefits of cognitive reframing are numerous. First and most importantly, it reduces stress and anxiety. When we change our perspective on stressful situations, we can approach them with a calmer, more rational mindset. This shift not only alleviates immediate stress but also builds long-term emotional resilience. Improved emotional regulation is another significant benefit. By reframing negative thoughts, we gain better control over our emotional responses, leading to more balanced and stable moods. This mental toughness is crucial for navigating life's challenges, allowing us to respond to adversity with composure and clarity.

To begin practicing cognitive reframing, start by identifying negative thought patterns. Pay attention to moments when you feel stressed or anxious and note the thoughts that accompany these emotions. After you have identified these negative thoughts, challenge them with evidence and logic. Question if your thoughts are based on assumptions or facts. For example, if you think *I'll never be successful*, question the validity of this statement. Find evidence of past successes and remind yourself of your skills and qualities.

Replace the negative thought with a more balanced and constructive one, such as, *I've faced challenges before and succeeded; I can do it again.*

Let's consider a real-life example. Imagine a professional who feels overwhelmed by workplace stress. They might think, *I can't handle this workload; I will fail.* By practicing cognitive reframing, they can challenge this thought by recalling times when they successfully managed heavy workloads. They might reframe their thought to, *This is a challenging situation, but I've handled similar ones before and succeeded. I can break this task into manageable steps.* This new perspective reduces anxiety and fosters a sense of competence and control.

Exercise: Journaling Negative Thoughts and Writing Positive Alternatives

A practical exercise to reinforce cognitive reframing is journaling. Start by writing down a negative thought you frequently experience. Next, challenge this thought with evidence. Finally, write a more positive and balanced alternative. For instance, if you often think, *I'm not good enough*, challenge this by listing your achievements and positive qualities. Then replace the thought with, *I have many skills and accomplishments that prove my worth.* Regularly practicing this exercise will help you internalize the habit of cognitive reframing, leading to improved emotional resilience and mental toughness.

Integrating cognitive reframing into your daily life can change how you react to stress and adversity. This practice, deeply rooted in Stoic philosophy, empowers you to take control of your emotional responses and build lasting resilience. It is a powerful tool that, when consistently applied, can lead to profound changes in your mental and emotional well-being.

THE ART OF SELF-DISCIPLINE: STAYING FOCUSED AND COMMITTED

Self-discipline is a core tenet of Stoic philosophy, crucial for building resilience and achieving personal excellence. Within the Stoic framework, self-discipline involves controlling one's impulses, focusing on long-term goals, and acting according to rational principles. The Stoics viewed self-discipline as a critical component of virtue, fundamental to living a life of moral integrity and inner strength. In *Meditations*, Marcus Aurelius often reflected on the importance of self-discipline, noting that true freedom comes from mastery over oneself. By cultivating self-discipline, you strengthen your resolve and enhance your capacity to face life's challenges with composure and determination.

Cultivating self-discipline requires actionable strategies that you can incorporate into your daily routine. One effective technique is to set clear goals and priorities. Start by determining what is very important to you in the short and long term. Write your goals down and break them down into manageable steps. Clarifying your goals and steps will help you stay motivated and focused and give a roadmap for your actions.

Additionally, creating and adhering to routines is essential for developing self-discipline. Establish a schedule each day for work, exercise, and relaxation. Consistency is key. By following a structured routine, you build habits that support your goals and reduce the likelihood of procrastination.

Practical exercises can further enhance your self-discipline. Start your day with a morning routine that sets the tone for focus and productivity. This might include activities like a brief workout, meditation, or journaling. These practices help center your mind and prepare you for the day's tasks. Another valuable technique for overcoming procrastination is the "two-minute rule." Do a task immediately if it only takes you less than two minutes. This simple rule helps you tackle small tasks efficiently, preventing them from piling up and overwhelming you. For more significant tasks, break them down into manageable, small steps with specific deadlines for each one.

Consider a marathon runner preparing for a race who exemplifies the power of self-discipline. Training for a marathon requires unwavering commitment and rigorous preparation. This runner starts the day with a disciplined routine, including early morning runs, balanced nutrition, and adequate rest. Adhering to this regimen builds the physical and mental endurance needed to complete the marathon successfully. Similarly, a disciplined approach can lead to significant career growth in the professional realm. Take the example of a professional who sets clear career goals and consistently works toward them. They dedicate themselves daily to skill development, networking, and seeking new opportunities. Over time, this disciplined approach results in promotions, new job offers, and personal fulfillment.

Self-discipline also plays a crucial role in maintaining balance and avoiding burnout. By setting boundaries and prioritizing self-care, you ensure that your pursuit of goals does not come at the expense of your well-being. For instance, incorporating regular breaks and leisure activities into your schedule helps recharge your energy and maintain focus. This balance is vital to sustain productivity long-term and reach your goals without compromising your health.

The Stoic practice of voluntary hardship is another powerful technique for building self-discipline. This involves deliberately subjecting yourself to minor difficulties to strengthen your resilience. For example, taking cold showers, fasting, or engaging in challenging physical activities can help you build mental toughness.

By willingly facing discomfort, you train your mind to remain steadfast in adversity. This practice enhances your self-discipline and prepares you for unexpected challenges.

Incorporating these exercises and strategies into daily life can significantly enhance self-discipline. By setting clear goals, creating routines, and practicing voluntary hardship, you build the mental toughness and resilience needed to achieve your aspirations. The stories of successful individuals, from marathon runners to career professionals, illustrate the transformative power of self-discipline. As you cultivate this virtue, you will be better equipped to navigate life's challenges with focus, commitment, and unwavering determination.

MANAGING ANGER: STOIC STRATEGIES FOR EMOTIONAL CONTROL

The emotion of anger can quickly take over, leading to regrettable consequences. Stoic principles provide practical strategies for managing and dissipating anger, turning it from a destructive force into a manageable emotion. According to Stoicism, anger is a natural reaction that should be controlled through rational thought and self-awareness. Seneca offers extensive advice on anger management. He wrote, "The greatest remedy for anger is delay." This simple yet profound idea underscores the importance of taking a moment to pause and reflect before reacting in anger.

Uncontrolled anger can have significant negative impacts on various aspects of life. In personal relationships, anger can create rifts, breed resentment, and lead to misunderstandings. A single outburst can damage trust and intimacy, making it difficult to repair the relationship. The effects extend to physical and mental health as well. Chronic anger may increase stress levels, cause high blood pressure, and weaken the immune system. Concerning mental health, it can contribute to anxiety, depression, and a sense of constant agitation. These repercussions highlight why managing anger effectively and maintaining emotional balance is crucial.

Practical techniques for managing anger are essential for incorporating Stoic principles into daily life. One effective method is deep breathing exercises. If you begin to feel angry, take slow, deep breaths to calm your nervous system. Inhale deeply through your nose. Hold your breath for a few seconds. Then, exhale slowly through your mouth. This physiological response can help reduce the intensity of your anger, giving you time to think before you act. Another technique is cognitive reframing, which involves changing how you interpret and respond to anger-inducing situations. Ask yourself if the source of your anger is essential in the grand scheme. Often, the answer is no, and this realization can help diffuse your anger.

Reflecting on past instances of anger can also be a powerful tool for managing future outbursts. Take some time to think about a recent situation where you felt angry. What triggered your anger? How did you respond? What were the consequences? Consider alternative responses that could have led to a more positive outcome. This reflection helps you understand your triggers and develop strategies for responding more calmly in the future. For example, if you often get angry during heated work meetings, think about how you could handle these situations differently. You could take a moment to breathe deeply, remind yourself to stay calm and respond with a composed and measured tone.

Let's consider a real-life scenario. Imagine you are in a heated argument at work, and a colleague makes a comment that makes you mad. Instead of reacting impulsively, take a deep breath and count to ten. This brief pause allows you to calm down and think more clearly. Ask yourself if the comment is worth getting angry over. Is it possible that your colleague didn't mean to offend you? By reframing your perspective, you can respond in a constructive way instead of an aggressive way. This approach helps you manage your anger and sets a positive example for others.

Exercise: Reflecting on Past Instances of Anger and Alternative Responses

To reinforce these techniques, try an exercise in reflection. Consider a recent instance where you felt angry and write about it in detail. What triggered your anger? How did you respond? What were the consequences? Next, brainstorm alternative responses that could have yielded a more positive outcome. Write these down as well. This exercise helps you gain insight into triggers and brainstorm strategies for managing your anger more effectively in the future.

By incorporating these Stoic strategies for managing anger, you can transform this powerful emotion into a tool for growth and self-improvement. The principles of deep breathing, cognitive reframing, and reflective exercises provide practical and effective ways to maintain emotional control and improve your overall well-being. When managed well, anger can become a catalyst for positive change rather than a source of regret and harm.

OVERCOMING ANXIETY: STOIC TECHNIQUES FOR CALMNESS

Anxiety can be a persistent and overwhelming emotion, but Stoic philosophy offers practical techniques to help calm the mind. Stoics understood that anxiety often stems from our perceptions and judgments about events rather than the events themselves. Epictetus famously said, "Men are disturbed not by things, but by the views which they take of them." This insight lies at the heart of the Stoic approach to overcoming anxiety. By changing how we view and respond to situations, we can reduce our anxiety and regain a sense of calm.

The Stoic approach to managing anxiety involves several practices designed to improve mental clarity and enhance emotional stability. One of the primary benefits of Stoic techniques is the development of a calmer mind. We can think more clearly and make better decisions when we learn to see things as they are without attaching unnecessary judgments or fears. This mental clarity is crucial for navigating stressful situations effectively. Additionally, Stoic practices help stabilize our emotions. By focusing on what we can control and accepting what we cannot, we create a more balanced and resilient emotional state. This stability allows us to face challenges with confidence and composure.

To manage anxiety effectively, consider incorporating mindfulness and meditation practices into your daily routine. Mindfulness is paying attention to the present moment without judgment. Focusing on the here and now can quiet the mind and reduce anxious thoughts about the future. Meditation, primarily guided Stoic meditation, can help cultivate this mindfulness. Start with a few minutes each day. Sit quietly and focus on your breath. Breathe in and out and observe your thoughts without getting caught up in them. This simple practice can help create a headspace where anxiety can dissipate.

Another powerful technique for reducing anxiety is cognitive reframing. When you notice anxious thoughts, challenge them with evidence and logic. Determine if your thoughts are based on facts or assumptions. For example, if you are worried about an upcoming presentation, you might think, *I will fail, and everyone will judge me.* Challenge this thought by recalling past successes and reminding yourself of your preparation. Reframe thinking to something more balanced, such as, *I have prepared well, and I can handle this presentation.* This perspective shift can significantly reduce anxiety.

Exercise: Daily Mindfulness Meditation

To practice mindfulness meditation, do the following:

1. Pick a quiet space to sit comfortably.
2. Close your eyes and take some deep breaths.
3. Focus attention on your breath as it flows in and out.
4. Gently bring focus back to your breathing if your mind wanders.

Do this practice for five to ten minutes each day. Over time, this meditation will help calm your mind and reduce anxiety.

Let's consider a specific scenario where Stoic principles can help manage anxiety. Imagine you have an important presentation at work and feel anxious about it. Instead of succumbing to the stress, apply Stoic techniques. Begin with a few minutes of mindfulness meditation to calm your mind. Then, use cognitive reframing to challenge any negative thoughts. Remind yourself of your preparation and past successes. Visualize yourself delivering the presentation confidently and effectively. Combining mindfulness and cognitive reframing helps reduce anxiety and enhances your performance.

Integrating these Stoic techniques into your daily life can overcome anxiety and cultivate a sense of calmness. Mindfulness, meditation, and cognitive reframing provide practical and effective ways to manage anxious thoughts and emotions. These practices, rooted in ancient Stoic wisdom, offer powerful ways to navigate the complexities of modern life with greater ease and confidence.

DEALING WITH JEALOUSY: CULTIVATING CONTENTMENT

Jealousy, a familiar yet corrosive emotion, often stems from comparing ourselves to others. According to Stoic philosophy, jealousy is seen as a misjudgment of values. The Stoics believed true contentment comes from within, not external achievements or possessions. Marcus Aurelius advises us in *Meditations*, "The happiness of your life depends upon the quality of your thoughts." This underscores the Stoic view that jealousy is a result of misplaced focus. We can cultivate genuine contentment by shifting our attention from what others have to our inner virtues and achievements.

The adverse effects of jealousy are profound and far-reaching. In relationships, jealousy can breed resentment and mistrust, eroding the foundation of love and companionship. It can lead to low self-esteem and feeling inadequate as we constantly measure ourselves against others. This mental and emotional drain detracts us from appreciating our lives and achievements. The energy expended on jealousy could be better used for personal growth and self-improvement. Recognizing these detrimental effects is the first step toward overcoming jealousy and fostering emotional well-being.

Practical techniques rooted in Stoic philosophy can effectively overcome jealousy and cultivate contentment. One such technique is practicing gratitude. By focusing on what we already have and appreciating the positives in our lives, we shift our attention away from what we lack. Begin a daily gratitude journal by listing three things you are grateful for daily. This simple practice can change your mindset and help you see the abundance in your life. Reflecting on your achievements is another powerful tool. Take time to acknowledge your accomplishments, no matter how small. This reflection builds self-esteem and reduces the tendency to compare yourself to others.

Consider the story of a professional who struggled with workplace jealousy. This individual constantly compared their career progress to their colleagues, leading to feelings of inadequacy and frustration. Through self-reflection and practicing gratitude, they began to shift their focus. They started a gratitude journal and regularly reflected on their achievements. Over time, they noticed a significant change in their mindset. Instead of feeling envious of their colleagues, they felt content and proud of their progress. This shift improved their emotional well-being and enhanced their professional relationships.

Exercise: Daily Gratitude Journaling

To reinforce the practice of gratitude, try a daily gratitude journaling exercise. Each evening, write down three things you are grateful for. These can be as simple as a good meal, a kind word from a friend, or a personal achievement. Over time, you will find that this practice helps you focus on the positives in your life and reduces feelings of jealousy.

Practicing gratitude and reflecting on your achievements are potent ways to shift your focus from what others have to what you possess. Integrating these Stoic techniques into your daily routine can transform jealousy into contentment. This change in perspective fosters a sense of inner peace and satisfaction, allowing you to appreciate your life fully.

Recognizing the detrimental effects of jealousy and employing these practical strategies will help you build emotional resilience and contentment. As you continue to explore Stoic principles, you will find that these practices enhance your overall quality of life and improve your emotional well-being.

In this chapter, we have explored several Stoic techniques for building emotional resilience. From cognitive reframing to managing jealousy, these strategies provide practical tools for navigating life's challenges with more stability and peace. As we move forward, we will delve into daily practices that further solidify these concepts, helping you cultivate a Stoic mindset in every aspect of your life.

3

INNER PEACE THROUGH MEDITATION AND REFLECTION

Quite a few years ago, I struggled with daily life's chaos. One morning, I decided to try something different. Instead of jumping out of bed and diving into my hectic routine, I woke up early, found a quiet spot, and spent ten minutes meditating. This simple practice set the tone for the rest of my day. I felt more centered, focused, and ready to tackle whatever came my way. It was my first encounter with the transformative power of morning meditation, a practice deeply rooted in Stoic philosophy.

MORNING MEDITATION: SETTING INTENTIONS FOR THE DAY

Starting your day with morning meditation is like laying a solid foundation for a building. It aligns your mind with Stoic principles, setting a positive tone to influence your daily actions and decisions. Marcus Aurelius understood this well. He wrote extensively about his morning routines in his journal (*Meditations*). By beginning his day with reflection and intention-setting, Aurelius cultivated mental clarity and resilience, which guided him in personal and imperial matters.

The benefits of morning meditation are numerous. First, it enhances mental clarity. When you start your day with a calm and focused mind, you can approach tasks with greater concentration and efficiency. Morning meditation also reduces stress and anxiety, providing inner peace that carries you through the day's challenges. Moreover, it fosters a positive mindset, helping you respond to situations with composure and wisdom. This practice aligns with the Stoic belief in the power of rational thought and self-control. We will combine several ideas covered in the first two chapters to create a beneficial morning routine of meditation and intentions.

We reviewed a basic mindfulness routine in the previous chapter, but it is worth revisiting. To incorporate morning meditation into your routine, settle into a quiet space where you will not be bothered. Sit in a comfortable position, whether it is on a chair, cushion, or directly on the floor. Close your eyes and take a few deep breaths to center yourself. Focus on your breath, feeling the sensation of each inhale and exhale. Acknowledge that thoughts arise without judgment and gently bring your focus back to your breath. This simple breathing helps anchor your mind in the present moment, setting a calm and focused tone for the day ahead.

Once you are centered, set your intentions for the day. These intentions should align with the Stoic principles discussed in Chapter 1, focusing on virtue and character. Consider what kind of person you want to be and what values you want to embody. For example, you set the intention to practice patience, show kindness, or remain resilient in facing challenges. Setting intentions for personal growth and resilience helps you navigate your day purposefully and clearly. It provides a moral compass to direct decisions and actions so they align with your highest values.

In addition to setting intentions, you can enhance your morning meditation with visualization techniques. Visualize yourself moving through your day with grace and virtue. Picture how you will handle various situations, from mundane tasks to potential challenges, with composure and wisdom. This mental rehearsal prepares you for the day and reinforces your commitment to Stoic principles. Visualization helps you embody the virtues you aspire to, making them a natural part of your daily interactions. (We will review negative visualization a bit later in this chapter.)

Breathing exercises are another valuable component of morning meditation. Start with a simple practice like diaphragmatic breathing. It is when you breathe deeply into your belly rather than shallowly into your chest. This breathing practice activates the body's relaxation response, reducing stress and calming you. Alternatively, try the 4-7-8 technique:

1. Inhale for four counts.
2. Hold your breath for seven counts.
3. Exhale for eight counts.

This exercise can help center your mind and body, enhancing the overall effectiveness of your meditation. Integrating morning meditation into your daily routine sets a positive and intentional tone.

This practice, rooted in Stoic philosophy, offers numerous benefits, from enhanced mental clarity to reduced stress. It helps you align your actions with your values, fostering personal growth and resilience. Whether through visualization, breathing exercises, or simply setting intentions, morning meditation provides a powerful tool for cultivating inner peace and living a life guided by virtue.

GUIDED STOIC MEDITATIONS: AUDIO AND VIDEO RESOURCES

Guided meditations enhance the meditation experience by providing structure and support, especially for those new to the practice. Audio and video resources can make this process effective and even more accessible. Modern Stoic practitioners often emphasize the benefits of guided meditations, highlighting how these tools can help maintain focus and deepen the meditative state. For instance, listening to a soothing voice guide you through meditation can reduce distractions and help you stay present. Video resources add a visual element, which can be particularly helpful for guided visualizations and breathing exercises.

Several types of guided Stoic meditations align with Stoic principles. Breathing exercises for mindfulness are a common technique. These exercises involve focusing on your breath to anchor your mind in the present moment. A guided session might prompt you to pay attention to your breath entering and leaving your body, helping you cultivate mindfulness. Another valuable technique is guided visualization for resilience. This involves imagining yourself facing and overcoming challenges, reinforcing your mental strength and preparedness. For example, a guided meditation might take you through a scenario where you handle a difficult conversation calmly and with composure, helping you internalize these qualities.

Numerous audio and video resources are available to help you get started with guided Stoic meditations. Apps like Calm and Headspace offer a variety of guided meditation sessions that can be easily integrated into your daily routine. Websites such as Daily Stoic provide specific Stoic-themed meditations, often accompanied by reflections from ancient Stoic texts. YouTube is another excellent resource, with channels dedicated to Stoic philosophy offering guided meditations and visualizations. For instance, you might find a session focused on practicing gratitude or building resilience, each designed to align with Stoic principles.

Integrating guided meditations into your daily routine requires consistency and a conducive environment. Set a regular meditation schedule that fits your lifestyle. It could be first thing in the morning, during a lunch break, or before bed. The key is to make it a habit. Create a space that is quiet and free from distractions. It might be a corner in your bedroom, living room, or peaceful outdoor spot. Ensure that this space is comfortable and inviting, with minimal interruptions. Over time, this designated meditation space will become a sanctuary for your practice, helping you maintain consistency and focus.

Using guided meditations can also help you explore different techniques and find what resonates with you. For instance, you might start with a simple breathing exercise to calm your mind and then move on to a guided visualization for resilience. Experiment with different sessions and notice how they impact your mental and emotional state. Jot down your experiences in a journal, noting which techniques are most effective for you. This detailed approach ensures that your meditation practice remains dynamic and aligned with your evolving needs.

Incorporating guided Stoic meditations into your daily life can enhance your emotional resilience, mental clarity, and overall well-being. The structure provided by audio and video resources makes it easier to maintain focus and deepen your practice. If you are a beginner or an experienced meditator, these tools offer valuable support on your path to inner peace and personal growth. The variety of techniques available, from mindfulness breathing exercises to guided visualizations, lets you tailor your practice to your specific needs and goals. The key is to be consistent, create a conducive environment, and remain open to exploring different approaches.

VISUALIZATION TECHNIQUES: PRACTICING NEGATIVE VISUALIZATION

Negative visualization is a powerful Stoic practice that involves contemplating potential misfortunes to build resilience and appreciation for what you have. This technique, known as *premeditatio malorum* in Latin, was widely practiced by ancient Stoic philosophers like Seneca, who famously advised, "Set aside a certain number of days, during which you shall be content with the scantiest and cheapest fare, with coarse and rough dress, saying to yourself the while: 'Is this the condition that I feared?'" By imagining the worst-case scenarios, you mentally prepare yourself for adversity, making you less reactive and more grateful for your current circumstances.

The psychological benefits of negative visualization are substantial. First, it increases mental preparedness. When you regularly contemplate potential challenges, you become more adept at handling them when they arise. This mental rehearsal reduces the shock and stress associated with unexpected events. For example, if you imagine losing your job, you can plan how to manage your finances and seek new opportunities, making you more resilient if such a situation occurs.

Additionally, negative visualization fosters greater appreciation for your current circumstances. By contemplating the loss of things you often take for granted, you develop a more profound gratitude for them. This shift in perspective enhances your overall well-being and contentment.

To practice negative visualization effectively, find a quiet space to focus without distractions. Sit comfortably and close your eyes. Begin by taking a few deep breaths to center your mind. Once you are calm, visualize a specific challenge or misfortune. Imagine it in vivid detail, considering how it would impact your life. For instance, imagine a day without modern conveniences like electricity or running water. Picture yourself navigating this scenario and reflect on how you would cope. This exercise helps you appreciate the conveniences you currently enjoy and prepares you mentally for potential disruptions.

Visualizing potential obstacles in your personal and professional life can also be highly beneficial. Imagine facing a significant setback at work, such as a failed project or a missed promotion. Visualize how you would handle the disappointment and what steps you would take to move forward. This mental rehearsal equips you with strategies to manage real-life challenges, reducing anxiety and increasing resilience. Similarly, contemplate potential obstacles in your personal life, such as relationship conflicts or health issues. By preparing mentally for these scenarios, you become more capable of handling them with composure and wisdom.

Practical Application: Visualizing a Day Without Modern Conveniences

To make negative visualization a regular practice, schedule sessions once or twice a week. During these sessions, spend 5-10 minutes contemplating specific challenges. Start with simple scenarios, like imagining a day without modern conveniences. Picture yourself waking up without electricity, running water, or internet access. Think about how you would adapt to this situation. What alternative solutions would you find? How would you manage your daily tasks? This exercise helps you appreciate the conveniences you often take for granted and prepares you for potential disruptions.

Another practical application is to visualize potential obstacles in your personal and professional life. For instance, imagine facing a major financial setback. Visualize losing a significant portion of your income and consider how you would manage your finances. Think about the steps you would take to cut expenses, find additional income sources, and maintain your financial stability. This mental rehearsal prepares you for potential financial challenges and reduces the anxiety associated with uncertainty.

Incorporating negative visualization into your routine builds mental resilience and fosters a deeper appreciation for your current circumstances. This Stoic practice helps you navigate life's challenges with greater ease and composure, turning potential misfortunes into opportunities for growth and gratitude.

THE DISCIPLINE OF JOURNALING: DAILY STOIC PRACTICE

Journaling has long been a cornerstone of Stoic practice, a powerful tool for self-awareness and personal growth. By putting pen to paper, you can internalize Stoic teachings and reflect on your daily actions, thoughts, and emotions. This fosters a deeper understanding of your behaviors and helps you align them with Stoic principles. The benefits of daily journaling are numerous. It lets you track your progress, identify areas to improve, and cultivate a mindset of continuous growth. Moreover, journaling provides a safe space to explore your innermost thoughts and feelings, promoting emotional resilience and mental clarity.

Historically, Stoic philosophers like Marcus Aurelius and Seneca were avid journal keepers. Marcus Aurelius's *Meditations* is a prime example of Stoic journaling. In his writings, he reflected on his daily experiences, examined his thoughts, and reinforced his commitment to Stoic virtues. Seneca, too, used journaling as a means of self-examination, often writing letters to himself to explore philosophical ideas and moral dilemmas. These historical examples highlight the enduring value of journaling in Stoic practice. By following in their footsteps, you can harness the transformative power of reflective writing.

Setting aside dedicated time each day is crucial to maintain a consistent journaling practice. Choose a time that works best for you, whether in the morning, during lunch, or before bed. Consistency is vital, as regular journaling helps reinforce the habit and deepen its impact. Using prompts can also guide your journaling sessions and ensure they remain focused and purposeful. Prompts can range from questions about your daily actions and decisions to reflections on your emotions and thoughts. These prompts serve as a starting point, helping you delve deeper into your experiences and extract valuable insights.

There are various types of Stoic journaling that you can explore. Reflective journaling involves examining your daily actions and behaviors through the lens of Stoic principles. This type of journaling encourages you to assess how well your actions align with your values and identify areas for improvement. For example, you might reflect on a challenging interaction with a colleague and consider how you could have responded with more patience and understanding. On the other hand, gratitude journaling focuses on cultivating contentment by acknowledging the positives in your life. By regularly listing things you are grateful for, you shift your focus from what you lack to what you have, fostering a sense of inner peace and satisfaction.

To get started with your journaling practice, here are some practical prompts. Reflect on the four cardinal virtues—Wisdom, Justice,

Courage, and Moderation—and consider how they manifested in your actions today. Ask yourself questions like, "Did I act with wisdom in my decisions?" and "How did I practice justice in my interactions?" These prompts help you evaluate your day through the lens of Stoic virtues, reinforcing your commitment to ethical living. Another useful exercise is to reflect on daily challenges and learning experiences. Write about a specific challenge you faced and what you learned from it. Consider how to apply these lessons in the future to navigate similar situations with greater ease and wisdom.

Exercise: Reflecting on Daily Challenges and Learning Experiences

To reinforce your reflective journaling practice, try this exercise. At the end of each day, take a few minutes to write about a challenge you encountered. Describe the experience in detail and reflect on your response. What did you learn from this situation? Moving forward, how can you apply this lesson? This exercise helps you gain valuable insights from your daily experiences, fostering continuous growth and self-improvement.

Incorporating these journaling techniques into your daily routine can deepen your understanding of Stoic principles and enhance your personal growth. Reflective writing and gratitude journaling offer powerful tools for self-examination and contentment, helping you navigate life's complexities with greater clarity and resilience. The prompts and exercises serve as a starting point, guiding you toward continuous self-discovery and improvement.

Reflective Questions: Engaging with Stoic Wisdom

Reflective questions are a potent tool for deepening your understanding of Stoic philosophy and internalizing its teachings. By asking yourself thought-provoking questions, you can explore your actions, thoughts, and emotions, gaining insights that promote self-awareness and personal growth. The Stoics, including great philosophers like Epictetus and Seneca, often used reflective questioning to examine their lives and align their behavior with their values. This practice encourages you to engage actively with Stoic principles, making them a tangible part of your daily life rather than abstract concepts.

Engaging with reflective questions offers numerous benefits. One of the most significant is enhanced self-reflection. By regularly examining your actions and thoughts, you become more aware of your strengths and areas for improvement. This self-awareness is vital for personal growth, because it enables you to make conscious decisions that align with your values and goals. Moreover, reflective questioning improves decision-making. When you take the time to reflect on past decisions and their outcomes, you gain valuable insights that inform your future choices. This practice promotes emotional regulation by helping you understand your emotions' underlying causes, enabling you to manage them more effectively.

To help you incorporate reflective questioning into your routine, consider the following curated list of questions that align with Stoic principles. These questions guide your self-examination and foster a deeper understanding of your actions and emotions. Ask yourself about daily actions and decisions: "Did I act following my values today?" "How did I respond to challenges?" and "What could I have done differently?" These questions help you assess how well your actions align with Stoic virtues and identify areas for improvement. For personal growth and virtue cultivation, consider questions like: "What virtues did I embody today?" "How did I practice wisdom, justice, courage, and moderation?" and "What steps can I take to cultivate these virtues further?"

Reflective questions can be incorporated into your daily life through simple yet effective exercises. One practical way is to set aside time each evening for reflection. Find a quiet, comfortable spot to review your day. Then, use the provided questions to guide your reflection and write down your thoughts and insights. This practice reinforces your commitment to Stoic principles and helps you internalize the lessons learned. Another practical approach is to use reflective questions in your journaling sessions. As you write about your experiences, incorporate the questions to prompt deeper exploration and understanding. This combination of writing and reflection enhances the impact of both practices, fostering continuous growth and self-awareness.

Exercise: Setting Aside Time Each Evening for Reflection

Dedicate a few minutes each evening to this exercise to make reflective questioning a regular practice. Sit quietly and review your day, using the reflective questions to guide your thoughts. Write down your insights and observations. For example, consider a challenging interaction you had and ask: "How did I respond?" "What could I have done differently?" and "What did I learn from this experience?" This exercise helps you gain valuable insights from your daily experiences, promoting continuous improvement and alignment with Stoic principles.

Engaging with reflective questions can deepen your understanding of Stoic philosophy and enhance your personal growth. This practice promotes self-awareness, improves decision-making, and fosters emotional regulation. The curated list of questions is a starting point, guiding you toward continuous self-discovery and improvement. By asking these questions daily, you make Stoic principles a tangible part of your life, fostering a constant growth mindset and alignment with your values.

Evening Reflection: Reviewing Your Actions

As the day winds down, a moment of reflection can offer profound insights into your actions and thoughts. Evening reflection, a practice deeply embedded in Stoic philosophy, provides a structured way to review your day, fostering personal growth and self-awareness. The Stoics, including Seneca and Marcus Aurelius, emphasized the importance of this practice. Marcus Aurelius, in *Meditations*, often reflected on his behavior and decisions, seeking to align them with his values. In his letters, Seneca advised daily self-examination to understand one's progress and areas needing improvement. This nightly introspection was not just about self-criticism but learning and evolving.

The benefits of evening reflection go beyond mere self-assessment. It promotes a deeper understanding of your actions, thoughts, and emotions to help you identify patterns and areas for growth. This practice enhances self-awareness, allowing you to recognize your strengths and weaknesses. It also fosters a sense of accountability as you take responsibility for your actions and their consequences. By consistently reflecting on your day, you cultivate a continuous improvement mindset, aligning your daily actions with your long-term goals and values.

To practice evening reflection effectively, follow a structured approach. Start by going to a quiet spot where you can sit comfortably without distractions. Reflect on your actions, thoughts, and emotions throughout the day. Consider moments of success and areas where you could have acted differently. Identify specific actions that aligned with your values and those that did not. This reflection helps you recognize positive behaviors to reinforce and negative ones to address. Write down these observations, as writing can deepen your understanding and commitment to change.

Self-compassion plays an essential role in this process. It is vital to see the difference between constructive criticism and self-judgment. Constructive criticism involves acknowledging areas for improvement without harsh self-criticism. It is about learning and growing, not punishing yourself for mistakes. Marcus Aurelius, a master of balance, wrote, "When you arise in the morning, think of what a privilege it is to be alive, to think, to enjoy, to love." This quote underscores the importance of self-compassion. Reflect on your day with kindness, recognizing that everyone makes mistakes and each day is an opportunity to learn and improve.

Incorporate specific reflection prompts to guide your evening reflection. Ask yourself, "What did I do well today?" and "What could I have done better?" Consider how your actions align with your values and identify areas for growth. Reflect on your emotional responses and how they influenced your behavior. Did you react with patience and understanding, or were there moments of frustration and anger? These questions help you better understand your behavior and its impact, paving the way for positive change.

Exercise: Writing a Nightly Summary of Challenges and Successes

To reinforce your evening reflection, try writing a nightly summary. Each evening, take a few minutes to write about the success you had and the challenges you faced. Focus on specific actions and their outcomes. Think of what you learned from these experiences and how you can apply these lessons. This exercise helps you internalize your reflections and commit to continuous improvement. Over time, you will notice patterns in your behavior and identify strategies for overcoming recurring challenges.

Integrating evening reflection into your nightly routine creates a powerful tool for self-improvement. This practice, rooted in Stoic philosophy, helps you align your actions with your values. It fosters personal growth and self-awareness. The structured approach, guided by reflection prompts and self-compassion, ensures you learn from each day and strive to improve.

In this chapter, we have explored various practices for cultivating inner peace through meditation and reflection. From morning meditation to evening reflection, journaling, and negative visualization, each technique offers unique benefits for personal growth and self-awareness. As we continue, we will dive into practical applications of Stoic principles in modern life, helping you navigate today's challenges with wisdom and resilience.

4

PRACTICAL APPLICATIONS IN MODERN LIFE

A few years ago, I found myself endlessly scrolling through social media, comparing my life to the curated highlights of others. Each swipe deepened my sense of inadequacy. It was not until I stumbled upon the teachings of Epictetus that I realized how much control I had relinquished to my screen. He said, "It is not the things themselves that disturb us, but our judgments about these things." This wisdom prompted me to reassess my relationship with social media and to apply Stoic principles to regain my mental well-being.

MODERN MINDFULNESS: INTEGRATING STOICISM INTO DAILY LIFE

Modern mindfulness and Stoicism share a deep connection, emphasizing the importance of presence and awareness in daily life. In the Stoic context, mindfulness involves a heightened awareness of one's thoughts, actions, and surroundings. Marcus Aurelius often reflected on the importance of living in the present. He wrote, "Confine yourself to the present" and "The happiness of your life depends upon the quality of your thoughts." These quotes underscore the Stoic belief that true contentment comes from focusing on the present moment and maintaining a vigilant awareness of our internal states.

Incorporating Stoic mindfulness into daily life can significantly enhance your mental well-being. One practical approach is mindful breathing. This involves focusing solely on your breath for a few moments each day. Sit in a comfortable position, close your eyes, and breathe deeply. Pay attention to the sensation of the air entering and leaving your body. This simple practice helps anchor your mind in the present, reducing stress and promoting a sense of calm. Another effective technique is reflective meditation. At the end of each day, take a few minutes to reflect on your actions and decisions. Consider how they align with your values and Stoic principles. This reflection fosters greater self-awareness and helps you make more intentional choices.

The benefits of Stoic mindfulness for mental well-being are profound. Practicing mindfulness improves focus and concentration. When you train your mind to stay present, you become more attentive and engaged in your tasks. This heightened focus leads to greater productivity and a sense of accomplishment. Mindfulness also reduces stress and anxiety. You can nurture a more balanced and peaceful mind by staying present and not getting lost in worries about the future or regrets about the past. This emotional stability is crucial for navigating life's challenges with resilience and grace.

To illustrate the practical application of Stoic mindfulness, consider the story of an individual who struggled with chronic anxiety. They decided to integrate mindful breathing and reflective meditation into their daily routine. Each morning, they spent five minutes focusing on their breath, which helped them start the day with a calm and clear mind. In the evenings, they reflected on their actions and decisions, considering how to improve. Over time, these practices significantly reduced their anxiety and improved their overall well-being. They felt more in control of their emotions and better equipped to handle stress.

Exercise: Practicing Mindful Walking and Reflecting on Sensory Experiences

A practical exercise to deepen your mindfulness practice is mindful walking. Find a quiet location where you can walk without distractions. As you walk, pay close attention to each step. Notice the rhythm of your breathing, your feet touching the ground, and the sounds and sights around you. This practice helps you stay present and fully engage with your surroundings. After your walk, take a few minutes to reflect on your sensory experiences. Write down what you noticed and how it made you feel. This exercise enhances your awareness and appreciation of the present moment.

Integrating Stoic mindfulness into your daily life allows you to grow a more profound sense of awareness and presence. Mindful breathing, reflective meditation, and mindful walking are practical techniques that help you stay grounded and focused. These practices improve mental clarity and emotional stability and foster greater inner peace. Whether you are dealing with stress, anxiety, or the demands of daily life, Stoic mindfulness offers powerful tools to enhance your well-being and live more intentionally.

BUILDING EMOTIONAL INTELLIGENCE: STOIC PRINCIPLES IN RELATIONSHIPS

Emotional intelligence is a crucial aspect of Stoic philosophy, particularly in the context of relationships. It involves recognizing, understanding, and managing our feelings and other's emotions.

Epictetus emphasized this when he said, "It's not what happens to you, but how you react to it that matters." This quote encapsulates the essence of emotional intelligence within Stoicism. Emotional intelligence includes self-awareness, self-regulation, empathy, and social skills. These elements are vital for maintaining healthy relationships and navigating social interactions with grace and wisdom.

Enhancing emotional intelligence through Stoic practices involves several actionable steps. One key strategy is practicing empathy. Empathy lets us understand and share the feelings of others. To develop empathy, try to view situations from another person's perspective. Ask yourself how they might feel and what they might be experiencing. This practice fosters deeper connections and reduces conflicts. Another critical step is reflecting on your emotional responses and triggers. Take time to identify what situations or behaviors elicit strong emotional reactions. Understanding these triggers helps you manage your responses more effectively, preventing unnecessary conflicts and misunderstandings.

Self-awareness and self-regulation are foundational to emotional intelligence. Self-awareness involves recognizing your emotions and understanding their impact on your behavior. One technique for increasing self-awareness is keeping an emotion journal. Regularly write down your feelings and reflect on the events that triggered them. This practice helps you identify patterns and gain insights into your emotional landscape. Self-regulation, on the other hand, is about controlling your emotional responses. Stoicism teaches us to pause and reflect before reacting. When faced with an emotionally charged situation, take a moment to breathe and assess your feelings. Ask yourself if your reaction aligns with your values and long-term goals. This pause allows you to respond thoughtfully rather than impulsively.

Real-life examples can illustrate the power of these practices in building emotional intelligence. Consider a couple who struggled with frequent arguments and misunderstandings. They decided to practice Stoic empathy by genuinely trying to understand each other's perspectives. Additionally, they reflected on their emotional triggers and worked on self-regulation techniques. Their relationship significantly improved over time. They communicated more effectively, resolved conflicts quickly, and felt more connected. This story demonstrates how Stoic principles can transform relationships by fostering empathy, self-awareness, and emotional control.

Exercise: Reflecting on Recent Interactions and Identifying Emotional Triggers

To apply these principles in your own life, try this exercise. Reflect on a recent interaction that elicited a strong emotional response. Write down the details of the interaction, including what was said and how you felt. Identify the specific emotions you experienced and the triggers that caused them. Consider how you reacted and whether it aligned with your values. Reflect on how you could have responded differently to achieve a more positive outcome. This exercise helps you gain insights into what triggers you emotionally and develop strategies for managing them more effectively.

Integrating these Stoic strategies into daily interactions can enhance emotional intelligence and improve relationships. Practicing empathy, reflecting on your emotional responses, and developing self-awareness and self-regulation are potent tools for navigating social interactions with wisdom and grace. These practices help you build deeper connections, resolve conflicts more effectively, and maintain a sense of inner peace amid the complexities of human relationships.

HANDLING LIFE TRANSITIONS: STOIC GUIDANCE FOR CHANGE

Life transitions can be some of our most stressful and disorienting experiences. Whether it is a career change, moving to a new city, or navigating a shift in a personal relationship, these significant changes disrupt our routines and challenge our sense of stability. The psychological impact of such transitions is substantial. They can evoke uncertainty, fear, and a loss of control. For instance, switching careers often brings anxiety about new responsibilities and the fear of failure. Moving to a new city can lead to loneliness and the daunting task of building a new social network. Relationship changes, such as a breakup or a new partnership, come with emotional upheaval and adjustment.

Stoic philosophy offers practical strategies for navigating these transitions with grace and resilience. As previously mentioned, one fundamental concept in Stoicism is *amor fati*, or the love of fate. This principle encourages us to embrace everything that happens, seeing it as necessary for our growth. Instead of resisting change, Stoicism teaches us to welcome it as an opportunity. Reflect on past experiences where change led to personal development. This reflection can help you see current transitions as part of a more extensive, joyous journey. For example, recall when a career shift opened new doors and brought unforeseen benefits. By embracing *amor fati*, you learn to love and accept life's unpredictability.

Maintaining a sense of purpose is crucial during life transitions. A clear understanding of purpose provides stability and direction, even when everything else seems uncertain. To identify and reaffirm your purpose, start by reflecting on what truly matters to you— your core values. Consider what drives you and brings you fulfillment. Quotes from Stoic philosophers can offer inspiration. Marcus Aurelius wrote, "The impediment to action advances action. What stands in the way becomes the way." This quote emphasizes the importance of purpose in overcoming obstacles. By focusing on your purpose, you can navigate transitions with a sense of direction and confidence.

Practical exercises can help you apply Stoic principles during life changes. One effective exercise is writing a letter to your future self about your current transition. Describe your hopes, fears, and plans to navigate the change. This exercise helps you articulate your thoughts and create a roadmap for the future. Reflect on how you want to grow and what you hope to achieve.

Another practical example is the story of a professional who navigated a career change using Stoic principles. Faced with the uncertainty of a new job, they embraced *amor fati*, seeing the change as an opportunity for growth. They maintained a clear sense of purpose by focusing on their long-term career goals and values. They successfully adapted to their new role through reflection and purposeful action and found fulfillment.

Exercise: Writing a Letter to Your Future Self About Current Transitions

To deepen your engagement with this practice, set aside time to write a letter to your future self. Describe the transition you are experiencing and how you plan to navigate it. Include your goals, fears, and strategies for maintaining a sense of purpose. Reflect on how you hope to grow through this change. This exercise provides clarity and a motivational tool, reminding you of your resilience and capacity for growth.

Applying these Stoic strategies allows you to navigate life transitions more easily and resiliently. Embracing *amor fati*, maintaining a sense of purpose, and engaging in reflective exercises can transform your approach to change. These practices help you see transitions not as disruptions but as opportunities for personal growth and self-improvement. Through purposeful action and a positive mindset, you can face life's inevitable changes with confidence and composure, turning challenges into stepping stones for a brighter future.

WORKPLACE STRESS: STOIC SOLUTIONS FOR PROFESSIONAL RESILIENCE

Workplace stress is a common issue that many of us face. High workloads and tight deadlines are two significant contributors to this stress. The pressure to meet deadlines often can lead to long hours, sacrificing personal time and well-being. The constant demand to deliver results can be overwhelming, causing anxiety and burnout. Interpersonal conflicts with colleagues also play a significant role in workplace stress. Misunderstandings, differing work styles, and competition can create a tense environment. These conflicts can drain your energy, making it difficult to focus on your tasks. Additionally, the fear of making mistakes or not meeting expectations can add to the stress. This combination of high demands and interpersonal friction creates a challenging work environment that many need help to navigate.

Stoic philosophy offers valuable techniques for managing workplace stress. One of the fundamental Stoic principles is focusing on what is within your control. This means concentrating on your actions, efforts, and attitudes professionally rather than external factors like colleagues' behaviors or company policies. By directing your energy toward what you can influence, you reduce feelings of helplessness and gain a sense of empowerment. Another effective Stoic practice is gratitude. Reflect on the positives in your job, such as learning opportunities, supportive colleagues, or meaningful projects. This shift in focus can help balance the negatives and foster a more positive outlook. It has been proven that gratitude improves mental well-being and resilience, making it a powerful tool for managing stress.

Maintaining composure under pressure is crucial in a high-stress work environment. Stoic principles can help you stay calm and focused during challenging situations. One technique is deep breathing. When you feel overwhelmed, take a moment to breathe deeply. Inhale air through your nose and exhale air through your mouth. This simple breathing practice can clear your mind and calm your nervous system. Visualization is another helpful method. Imagine yourself handling the stressful situation with confidence and ease. This mental rehearsal can prepare you to face the event with more composure. Stoic leaders like Marcus Aurelius exemplified calmness under pressure. As a Roman emperor, he faced numerous challenges but remained steadfast and composed, relying on Stoic principles to guide his actions. His ability to maintain his poise in the face of adversity is a testament to the power of Stoicism in managing stress.

Real-life examples and exercises can illustrate Stoic practices in the workplace. Consider the case of a manager who faced a major crisis at work. A critical project was behind schedule, and the team was under immense pressure. Instead of panicking, the manager applied Stoic principles. He focused on what was within his control, such as organizing the team and prioritizing tasks. He practiced gratitude by acknowledging the team's hard work and dedication. He successfully navigated the crisis by maintaining his composure and guiding the team with a clear and calm mind. This example demonstrates how Stoic techniques can help manage high-stress situations effectively.

Exercise: Reflecting on a Stressful Workday and Identifying Controllable Factors

To apply these principles to your own work life, try this exercise. At the end of a stressful workday, take a few minutes to reflect on the day. Identify the factors that caused stress and categorize them into two lists: those within your control and those outside your control. Focus on the actions you can take to address the controllable factors. For example, if a tight deadline causes stress, consider how to manage your time more effectively or seek colleague support. Reflect on how you handled the stress and think about ways to improve your response in the future. This exercise helps you gain clarity and develop strategies for managing workplace stress more effectively.

Incorporating these Stoic strategies into your daily work routine can build resilience and maintain your well-being in a high-stress environment. Maintaining composure under pressure, practicing gratitude, and focusing on what you can control are potent tools that can transform your professional experience. Whether you are dealing with tight deadlines, interpersonal conflicts, or high demands, Stoic principles offer practical solutions to easier and with more confidence.

MANAGING FINANCIAL STRESS: STOIC APPROACHES TO MONEY

Financial stress is a common struggle. It can significantly impact your mental and emotional well-being. Several factors contribute to financial anxiety, including job instability and economic uncertainty. The fear of losing your job or facing an economic downturn can create a constant undercurrent of stress. This anxiety is compounded by debt and financial obligations. These financial burdens, whether a house mortgage, credit card bills, or student loans, can feel overwhelming. The pressure to meet financial commitments while managing day-to-day expenses can lead to sleepless nights and chronic stress.

You can find practical ways to alleviate this stress by applying Stoic principles to financial challenges. One core tenet of Stoicism is the dichotomy of control, which teaches you to focus on what you can control and accept what you cannot. In financial situations, this means concentrating on your spending habits, saving strategies, and financial planning while accepting that market fluctuations and economic conditions are beyond your control. Reflecting on what is necessary for a fulfilling life is another Stoic practice that can help manage financial stress. Marcus Aurelius often wrote about the importance of distinguishing between needs and wants. By focusing on what you genuinely need, you can reduce unnecessary spending and find contentment in simplicity.

Financial planning and mindfulness are essential components of managing financial stress. Creating a realistic budget is a practical step providing clarity and control over your finances. Start by tracking your income and spending to understand where your money is going. Identify areas where you can cut back and allocate funds toward savings and debt repayment. This proactive approach helps reduce financial anxiety by providing a clear plan for managing your money. Mindful spending and saving are also crucial. Before purchasing, ask yourself if it aligns with your values and long-term goals. This reflection helps you make more intentional financial decisions, reducing impulse buys and unnecessary expenses.

To illustrate these principles, consider the story of an individual who overcame financial stress through Stoic budgeting. They decided to apply Stoic principles to their finances because of significant debt and economic uncertainty. They began by practicing the dichotomy of control, focusing on their spending habits and saving strategies. They created a detailed budget, tracking every expense and identifying areas for reduction. By reflecting on what was necessary for their happiness, they cut out non-essential spending and found contentment in a simpler lifestyle. Over time, their financial situation improved, and their stress levels decreased. This example demonstrates how Stoic principles can provide practical solutions for managing financial stress.

Exercise: Reflecting on Financial Goals and Aligning Them with Stoic Values

To apply these principles to your finances, try this exercise. Begin by making time to reflect on your financial goals. Write down your short-term and long-term objectives, such as paying off debt, building an emergency fund, or saving for retirement. Next, reflect on how these goals align with your values. Consider what is truly necessary for your happiness and fulfillment. Are your financial goals driven by external pressures or by genuine needs? This reflection helps you prioritize your spending and saving in a way that aligns with your values and reduces financial stress.

Integrating Stoic strategies into your financial management can build resilience and reduce anxiety. Practicing the dichotomy of control, reflecting on what is necessary, and creating a realistic budget are powerful tools for managing financial stress. Mindful spending and saving further enhance your financial well-being, helping you make intentional decisions that align with your values. Through these practices, you can navigate financial challenges with greater ease and confidence, finding contentment in simplicity and control in planning.

NAVIGATING SOCIAL MEDIA: STOIC STRATEGIES FOR DIGITAL WELL-BEING

In our digital age, social media has become an essential part of our lives, but its impact on our mental health is a growing concern. Too much social media use can lead to higher levels of anxiety, stress, and a pervasive sense of inadequacy. Studies show that prolonged exposure to the curated lives of others often results in unfavorable self-comparisons. According to a study published by the National Center for Biotechnology Information, social media use can aggravate mental health problems, with factors like time spent and type of activity playing significant roles. The study reviewed multiple papers and found a connection between prolonged social media use and adverse mental health outcomes like depression and anxiety. Modern psychologists emphasize that humans require meaningful social connections for mental well-being, and superficial interactions on social media often fall short.

Stoic strategies offer practical guidance to help you healthily navigate the digital landscape. One of the core Stoic principles is the dichotomy of control, which teaches us to focus on what we can control and accept what we cannot. Apply this principle to your online interactions. You cannot control what others post or how they react, but you can control your response and time on these platforms. Setting boundaries is crucial. Set aside specific times for social media use and stick to them. For example, you may check your accounts only during lunch breaks and avoid them entirely in the evenings. This practice helps create a healthier balance and reduces the compulsive urge to check your phone constantly.

Mindful social media use is another effective strategy. Practicing mindfulness means being present and intentional in your actions. Before you open a social media app, ask yourself why you are doing it. Are you looking for entertainment, information, or validation?

Reflecting on the purpose and value of your interactions can help you make more conscious choices. When you do engage, stay present. Avoid mindlessly scrolling and, instead, focus on meaningful interactions. Comment thoughtfully, engage in discussions, and share content that aligns with your values.

To further enhance your digital well-being, consider regular digital detoxes. Taking breaks from social media can help reset your mind and reduce dependency. Start with short detox challenges, such as a 24-hour break, and gradually extend the duration. During these detoxes, pay attention to your feelings and experiences. Note any changes in your stress levels, mood, and overall well-being. Journaling about these observations can provide valuable insights. Write about how you felt before, during, and after the detox. Reflect on any positive changes and consider incorporating regular detoxes into your routine.

Exercise: Digital Detox Challenge and Journaling

To implement a digital detox, choose a day when you can step away from social media. Inform your friends and family in advance if necessary. During the detox, engage in off-line activities like hiking, spending time with loved ones, or reading. Write in a journal about your experience. Write about any challenges you faced and how you felt without the constant presence of social media. Reflect on the benefits you noticed and consider how to incorporate more mindful and balanced social media use moving forward.

By applying Stoic strategies to your digital life, you can mitigate the negative impacts of social media and enhance your mental well-being. Practicing the dichotomy of control, setting boundaries, and engaging mindfully are actionable steps that help create a healthier relationship with technology. Regular digital detoxes and reflective journaling further support this process, allowing you to navigate the digital world more easily and resiliently.

5

INSIGHTS FROM STOIC PHILOSOPHERS

I magine standing on a balcony overlooking the vast city of Rome, the weight of an empire resting on your shoulders. This was the daily reality for Marcus Aurelius, who ruled the Roman Empire and sought wisdom through Stoicism. His life's work, captured in *Meditations*, offers a window into his inner life and the principles that guided him. These writings are not mere philosophical musings; they are practical reflections born out of the struggles and responsibilities of leadership. Beginning with Aurelius, we will review several Stoic philosophers, past and present, who paved a path for us to follow.

MARCUS AURELIUS: MEDITATIONS ON LEADERSHIP AND PERSONAL GROWTH

Marcus Aurelius was born into a prestigious family in 121 AD and became the Roman emperor in 161 AD. Despite the immense power at his disposal, he is remembered not for tyranny but for his wisdom and virtue. His *Meditations*, written as personal notes to himself, reflect his efforts to live a life of virtue, justice, and wisdom. These writings have become a cornerstone of Stoic philosophy, offering timeless insights into personal growth and leadership.

One of the central themes in *Meditations* is the importance of self-reflection. Marcus Aurelius believed that introspection was crucial for personal growth and ethical behavior. He often used his writings to examine his thoughts, actions, and motivations, asking himself whether they aligned with his values and principles. This practice of self-reflection is not just an exercise in navel-gazing; it is a powerful tool for developing self-awareness and integrity. By regularly examining our inner lives, we can identify areas for improvement and cultivate virtues such as wisdom, courage, and justice.

Another critical theme in *Meditations* is the balance between power and humility. Despite ruling one of the most powerful empires in history, Marcus Aurelius constantly reminded himself of the transient nature of power and the importance of humility. He wrote, "Do not waste what remains of your life in speculating about your neighbors, unless with a view to some mutual benefit. To wonder what so-and-so is doing and why, or what he is saying, or thinking, or plotting, is a waste of time." This focus on humility and self-improvement, rather than gossip or envy, is a lesson that resonates in both personal and professional contexts.

Stoic principles profoundly influenced Marcus Aurelius's approach to leadership. He believed in handling crises calmly and rationally, setting an example for others. The Roman Empire faced numerous challenges during Aurelius's reign, including plagues, wars, and political turmoil. Yet, Marcus Aurelius remained steadfast, applying his Stoic training to navigate these crises with composure. He understood that while he could not control external events, he could control his reactions and decisions. This attitude helped him maintain his sanity and inspired confidence and stability in those he led.

Justice and fairness were also central to Marcus Aurelius's leadership. He believed that a leader should act with the good of the community in mind rather than seeking personal gain. In his *Meditations*, he frequently reflected on the importance of acting justly and treating others with respect and fairness. This commitment to justice is evident in his governance, where he sought to implement equitable and beneficial policies for the empire. His leadership style emphasizes the importance of moral integrity and ethical decision-making, which are relevant today.

To apply Marcus Aurelius's teachings in your own life, consider starting a practice of reflective journaling. Each evening, take a few minutes to write about your day. Reflect on your actions, thoughts, and emotions, and ask yourself whether they align with your values and principles. Use prompts inspired by *Meditations* to guide your reflections. For example, you might ask, "Did I act with wisdom and fairness today? How did I handle challenges? What can I learn from my experiences?" This practice can help you cultivate wisdom, courage, and justice and develop greater self-awareness.

Another practical exercise is to cultivate humility and self-awareness through daily actions. Consciously try to speak less, listen more, and consider others' perspectives before forming judgments. Practice gratitude for your opportunities and responsibilities rather than focusing on what you lack. By incorporating these small, daily practices, you can develop a mindset of humility and continuous self-improvement, much like Marcus Aurelius.

His life and writings offer a wealth of wisdom for anyone seeking to grow as an individual and a leader. By embracing self-reflection, balancing power with humility, and applying Stoic principles to our actions, we can navigate life's challenges with greater wisdom, strength, and peace of mind.

EPICTETUS: THE ENCHIRIDION AND PRACTICAL STOICISM

Epictetus's life story is a testament to the transformative power of Stoic philosophy. Born into slavery in ancient Rome around 50 AD, Epictetus experienced the harshest conditions. Yet, his spirit remained indomitable. After gaining his freedom, he dedicated himself to philosophy, becoming one of the most influential Stoic teachers. His teachings, compiled by his student Arrian in *The Enchiridion*, offer practical advice for living a life of virtue and resilience. Unlike other philosophical texts that may seem abstract or theoretical, *The Enchiridion* is a handbook designed for everyday use, making it accessible and relevant for anyone seeking to improve their life.

One of the cornerstone teachings in *The Enchiridion* is the dichotomy of control. Epictetus emphasized that some things are within our control, such as our opinions, desires, and actions, while others, like our body, property, and reputation, are not. This simple yet profound distinction helps us focus our energy where it can be most effective. For instance, you cannot control whether it rains tomorrow, but you can decide to carry an umbrella. By accepting this fundamental principle, you can significantly reduce your stress and anxiety. You learn to let go of what you cannot change and concentrate on what you can influence, making your life more manageable and peaceful.

Another critical teaching from Epictetus is the importance of accepting events as they happen. Life is full of unexpected twists and turns, and our natural tendency is to resist or wish things were different. Epictetus advised against this. He taught us to accept whatever comes our way, not as passive resignation but as an active engagement with reality. For example, if you lose your job, instead of lamenting your fate, you could see it as an opportunity to find a better-suited position or even start a new career. This mindset fosters resilience and adaptability, letting you face challenges with strength and grace.

Epictetus placed a strong emphasis on personal responsibility. He believed that we cannot control external events, but we can control how we respond to them. Taking ownership of one's actions and reactions is pivotal in Stoic philosophy. By focusing on your responses, you reclaim your power and agency. If someone insults you, it is not the insult that hurts but your interpretation. By choosing to remain unfazed, you maintain your inner peace. You can apply this practice of self-discipline and resilience in various aspects of life, from personal relationships to professional settings, enhancing your emotional well-being and overall quality of life.

To integrate Epictetus's teachings into your daily routine, start with daily reflections on control and acceptance. Each evening, take a few minutes to review your day. Reflect on situations where you felt stressed or anxious. Ask yourself whether these situations were within your control. If they were not, practice letting go. If they were, consider how you could have handled them differently. This exercise helps you internalize the dichotomy of control and trains your mind to focus on what truly matters. Over time, you will find that this practice reduces your stress and enhances your sense of well-being.

Another practical exercise is to cultivate self-discipline. Begin with small, manageable tasks. Set a specific goal, like waking up early or completing a daily workout, and commit to it. The key is consistency. Regularly practicing self-discipline builds mental resilience, making it easier to tackle more considerable challenges. Look at using a journal to track your progress. Write down your goals, note your achievements, and reflect on any setbacks. This process not only keeps you accountable. It also provides valuable insights into your habits and behaviors, enabling you to make more informed choices.

Epictetus's teachings offer a wealth of practical wisdom for navigating the complexities of modern life. By embracing the dichotomy of control, accepting events as they happen, and taking personal responsibility for your actions, you can cultivate a life of virtue, resilience, and inner peace. These principles are philosophical ideals and actionable strategies that can transform your daily experiences and enhance your overall quality of life.

SENECA: LETTERS FROM A STOIC AND HANDLING ADVERSITY

Seneca, a towering figure in Stoic philosophy, wore many hats during his life—statesman, playwright, and philosopher. Born around 4 BC in Córdoba, Spain, Seneca was a highly influential adviser to Emperor Nero. His philosophical writings have endured despite his political entanglements, offering timeless wisdom on navigating life's challenges. His most famous work, *Letters from a Stoic*, is correspondence written to his friend Lucilius. These letters delve into Stoic principles, providing practical advice for living a virtuous and fulfilling life amid adversity.

In *Letters from a Stoic*, Seneca explores several key themes, most notably the importance of mental preparation and cultivating inner peace amid external chaos. He believed life consists of unpredictable events, and mental readiness is the best way to handle them. Seneca often emphasized the value of preparing the mind for potential difficulties. He advised, "He who suffers before it is necessary, suffers more than is necessary." By mentally rehearsing possible challenges, we can mitigate their impact when they do occur. This practice does not mean we should live in constant fear but build resilience by anticipating possible hardships.

Another central theme in Seneca's letters is cultivating inner peace regardless of external circumstances. He argued that true tranquility comes from within and is not dependent on external factors. Seneca wrote, "True happiness is... to enjoy the present, without anxious dependence upon the future." This mindset allows us to maintain calm and composure even when the world is in turmoil. By focusing on our inner state rather than external events, we can achieve a sense of peace that remains unshaken by life's inevitable ups and downs.

Seneca's practical wisdom for handling adversity is evident in his letters and life. One of his key strategies for overcoming personal challenges is to see adversity as an opportunity for growth. He wrote, "Difficulties strengthen the mind, as labor does the body." Seneca viewed hardships not as obstacles but as occasions to build resilience and wisdom. This perspective can be incredibly empowering. For instance, if you face a professional setback, instead of viewing it as a failure, consider what lessons it can teach you and how it can contribute to your personal development.

Seneca also embraced the idea that adversity can be a growth path. He believed that facing and overcoming challenges makes us stronger and more resilient. This is not just theoretical; Seneca's life was marked by political intrigue, exile, and personal loss. Yet, he used these experiences to deepen his understanding of Stoic principles and cultivate a sense of inner strength. His life serves as a testament to the power of Stoic philosophy in navigating adversity.

To apply Seneca's teachings, start with reflective journaling on past adversities. Take time to write about your challenges and how you dealt with them. What did you learn from these experiences? How did they shape your character? By reflecting on past adversities, you can gain vital insights about your strengths and areas for improvement. This practice helps you process past events and prepares you mentally for future challenges.

Another practical exercise inspired by Seneca is mental preparation. Each day, take a few minutes to anticipate potential challenges you might face. Visualize how you would handle these situations with calm and resilience. For example, if you know you have a difficult meeting at work, mentally rehearse how you will respond to various scenarios. This practice helps build mental toughness and reduces anxiety. It lets you approach challenges with a composed and proactive mindset.

Seneca's wisdom offers valuable guidance for handling adversity. By preparing your mind for potential difficulties, cultivating inner peace, and embracing adversity as a path to growth, you can navigate life's challenges with greater resilience and tranquility. These practices, rooted in ancient Stoic philosophy, provide practical tools to achieve a balanced and fulfilling life.

MUSONIUS RUFUS: STOIC TEACHINGS ON ETHICS AND VIRTUE

Musonius Rufus may not be as well-known as Seneca or Marcus Aurelius, but his contributions to Stoicism are profound and enduring. Born around 30 AD, Musonius Rufus was a Roman philosopher who dedicated his life to teaching Stoic principles. He believed philosophy was a theoretical exercise and a practical guide to living virtuously. His teachings focused on ethics and daily conduct, emphasizing that virtue is the only true good. Musonius Rufus saw philosophy as a way to correct errors in thinking and behavior, advocating for a life of simplicity and moral integrity.

One of the critical themes in Musonius Rufus's teachings is the importance of virtue in everyday life. He argued that living a virtuous life was not just for philosophers or scholars but for everyone. According to Musonius, virtue should guide all actions at work, home, or social settings. He believed that ethical living was the foundation of a good life and that by practicing virtue, we could achieve true happiness and fulfillment. This focus on practical ethics set Musonius apart, as he provided concrete advice on incorporating virtue into daily routines.

Musonius Rufus also strongly emphasized ethical living as a Stoic practice. He believed that moral behavior should be the norm, not the exception. For Musonius, this meant living a life of self-control, moderation, and simplicity. He advocated for a modest yet nutritious diet, believing overindulgence weakened the body and the soul. He also emphasized the importance of frugality, arguing that excessive wealth and luxury were detrimental to one's moral character. By living simply and ethically, Musonius taught us to focus on what truly matters—developing our virtues and contributing to the common good.

Education and self-improvement were also central to Musonius Rufus's philosophy. He believed education was essential for cultivating virtue and that learning should be a lifelong pursuit. Musonius argued that education should not be limited to formal schooling but should include practical lessons in ethics and daily conduct. He believed that everyone, regardless of gender or social status, should have access to education. This progressive view extended to his belief in equal education for women, a radical idea for his time. Musonius argued that women possessed the same rational capabilities and virtues as men and should receive the same education.

To embody Musonius Rufus's teachings, start with daily reflections on virtuous actions. Each evening, take a few minutes to reflect on your day. Consider the choices you made and whether they were guided by virtue. Ask yourself questions like, "Did I act with integrity today? Was I kind and just in my interactions?" This practice helps you become more aware of your actions and encourages you to make more ethical choices in the future. By regularly reflecting on your behavior, you can identify areas to improve and develop a more substantial commitment to living virtuously.

Another practical exercise inspired by Musonius Rufus is ethical decision-making. When you are faced with a decision, pause and consider the moral implications. Ask yourself whether the choice aligns with your values and principles. For example, if you are tempted to cut corners at work to save time, consider whether this action upholds your commitment to honesty and integrity. By reflecting on your choice's ethical implications, you can ensure your actions are consistent with your values. This practice helps you make better decisions and strengthens your moral character.

Musonius Rufus's teachings offer valuable insights into ethical living and self-improvement. By focusing on virtue, practicing ethical conduct, and committing to lifelong learning, you can cultivate a life of moral integrity and true happiness. His emphasis on practical ethics and daily conduct makes his teachings accessible and relevant, providing a roadmap for anyone seeking to live a virtuous life.

HIEROCLES: THE CIRCLE OF CONCERN AND COMMUNITY

Hierocles, a Stoic philosopher from the 2nd century AD, made significant contributions to Stoicism, particularly in his focus on community and relationships. While less known than his contemporaries, his ideas have had a lasting impact on the way we understand our social responsibilities. Hierocles believed that our well-being is deeply connected to our relationships with others and that a strong sense of community is crucial for a fulfilling life. His philosophical focus was on how individuals can cultivate empathy and compassion within their social circles, enhancing personal and communal well-being.

One of Hierocles's most influential ideas is the concept of the "circle of concern." This model helps us understand our relationships and community by visualizing them as concentric circles. At the center is the self, followed by circles that include immediate family, extended family, friends, fellow citizens, and humanity. The goal is to expand our circle of concern, moving from self-centeredness to a broader, more inclusive view that encompasses all humanity. By doing so, we develop empathy and a sense of social responsibility, recognizing that our actions have far-reaching impacts. Hierocles's model encourages us to consider how we can support and nurture these relationships, ultimately contributing to a more harmonious and interconnected world.

In Stoicism, community and social responsibility are paramount. Stoics believe that we are all interconnected and that our well-being is tied to the well-being of others. This philosophy promotes mutual support and compassion, encouraging us to act in ways that benefit the community. Practicing empathy within the circle of concern involves actively listening to others, understanding their perspectives, and offering support when needed. It is about looking beyond our immediate needs and seeing the humanity in every person we encounter. This approach fosters stronger community bonds and creates a mutual support network that withstands life's challenges.

To strengthen community bonds, consider integrating strategies that promote empathy and compassion. Start by actively engaging with those around you through small acts of kindness or more significant contributions to communal projects. Volunteering your time and skills can have a profound impact, not just on those you help but also on your sense of purpose and connection. Building strong relationships within your circle of concern also involves open and honest communication. Share your thoughts and feelings with others, and encourage them to do the same. This openness fosters trust and deepens connections, creating a supportive and resilient community.

Reflective journaling is a powerful tool to apply Hierocles's teachings to your relationships. Take time each day to write about your interactions with others. Reflect on how you contributed to these relationships and consider ways to expand your circle of concern. Ask yourself, "Did I act with empathy and compassion today? How can I better support those in my community?" These questions help you stay mindful of your social responsibilities and encourage continuous relationship growth. It also provides a space to process your thoughts and emotions, helping you navigate complex social dynamics more easily.

Practical exercises can further help you embody Hierocles's teachings. One effective exercise is to expand your circle of concern consciously. Start by focusing on your immediate family and close friends. Aim to understand their needs and offer support. Gradually extend this focus to include neighbors, colleagues, and even strangers. Look for opportunities to connect with others and contribute to their well-being. This might involve simple gestures like offering a listening ear or more substantial actions like organizing community events. By actively working to expand your circle of concern, you cultivate a more inclusive and compassionate mindset.

Hierocles's emphasis on community and relationships offers valuable insights for enhancing our social connections. We can build stronger, more supportive communities by understanding and expanding the circle of concern, practicing empathy and compassion, and engaging in reflective journaling and practical exercises. These practices enrich our lives and contribute to the well-being of people around us, creating a ripple effect of positive change.

MODERN STOIC THINKERS: CONTEMPORARY INTERPRETATIONS

In recent years, a resurgence in Stoic philosophy has been led by modern thinkers who have adapted ancient teachings for today's world. Among these influential figures are Massimo Pigliucci and Ryan Holiday. Massimo Pigliucci, a professor of philosophy, has dedicated much of his career to making Stoic principles accessible to a broader audience. His book *How to Be a Stoic* blends classical wisdom with modern scientific insights, providing practical advice for living a virtuous life. Ryan Holiday, a best-selling author and marketer, has popularized Stoicism through books like *The Daily Stoic* and *The Obstacle Is the Way*. His work emphasizes the relevance of Stoic principles in overcoming modern challenges and achieving personal growth.

The importance of their work lies in their ability to help bridge that gap between ancient philosophy and contemporary life. By interpreting Stoic teachings through the lens of modern psychology and self-help, they have made these principles more relatable and actionable. Pigliucci, for instance, integrates cognitive-behavioral techniques with Stoic practices, demonstrating how both can complement each other in managing emotions and enhancing mental well-being. On the other hand, Holiday uses historical anecdotes and practical exercises to illustrate how Stoicism can be applied to achieve success and resilience in various aspects of life, from career to personal relationships.

Contemporary interpretations of Stoic principles have shown how these ancient teachings can be adapted to address the complexities of modern life. For example, the Stoic idea of focusing on what we can control has been integrated into stress management techniques. In today's fast-paced world, external pressures make it easy to feel overwhelmed. Modern Stoics advise practicing mindfulness and setting boundaries to maintain focus on what truly matters. They also highlight the importance of self-discipline and intentional living, encouraging people to set clear goals and align their actions with their values. These adaptations make Stoic principles relevant and practical for navigating contemporary challenges.

The impact of modern Stoic literature has been significant, influencing both the self-help genre and personal development practices. Books like *How to Be a Stoic* and *The Daily Stoic* have become essential for those seeking to improve their lives through philosophy. *How to Be a Stoic* offers a step-by-step guide to incorporating Stoic practices into daily routines, making it accessible to seasoned practitioners and beginners. *The Daily Stoic*, structured as a daily devotional, provides bite-sized wisdom and practical exercises for each day of the year, fostering a consistent practice of Stoicism. These works have broadened the appeal of Stoicism, making it a valuable tool for anyone looking to enhance their emotional resilience and mental clarity.

To apply the teachings of modern Stoics, consider incorporating daily readings from Stoic texts into your routine. Start your day with a passage from *The Daily Stoic*, reflecting on its relevance to your life and how you can apply its lessons. This practice establishes a positive tone for the day and reinforces a Stoic mindset. Another practical exercise is to integrate Stoic principles into your daily life. For instance, practice the dichotomy of control by listing things you can and cannot control each morning. Focus your efforts on what you can influence, and let go of what you cannot. This simple exercise can significantly reduce stress and improve your overall well-being.

Massimo Pigliucci and Ryan Holiday have shown that Stoic philosophy is not just an ancient relic but a living, breathing practice that can enhance our modern lives. Adapting Stoic teachings to contemporary contexts has provided valuable tools for achieving personal growth, resilience, and inner peace. Their work underscores the timeless relevance of Stoicism, demonstrating that its principles can guide us through the complexities of modern life with wisdom and grace.

As we progress, these insights from modern Stoic thinkers will serve as a foundation for exploring more advanced techniques and practices. Integrating their teachings into our daily lives allows us to navigate life's challenges with greater wisdom, strength, and peace of mind.

6

CULTIVATING VIRTUES AND OVERCOMING ADVERSITY

A while ago, I found myself standing at the edge of a quiet lake, pondering the complexities of life. The water was perfectly still, reflecting the sky above with pristine clarity. It struck me that wisdom, like the lake's calm surface, offers a clear and undistorted worldview. This moment of reflection led me to delve deeper into the Stoic virtue of wisdom, understanding its profound impact on making rational decisions and leading a virtuous life.

CULTIVATING WISDOM: PRACTICAL STEPS FOR EVERYDAY LIFE

Wisdom in Stoic philosophy is the cornerstone of rational decision-making and living a virtuous life. Defined as the ability to discern the true nature of things, wisdom guides us in understanding what is good, bad, and indifferent. Marcus Aurelius eloquently captures this when he says, "The happiness of your life depends upon the quality of your thoughts: therefore, guard accordingly, and take care that you entertain no notions unsuitable to virtue and reasonable nature." This quote underscores the importance of wisdom in shaping our thoughts and actions, highlighting its role in achieving a fulfilling and balanced life.

Developing wisdom requires consistent effort and deliberate practice. One effective strategy is continuous learning and self-education. Start by reading and reflecting on philosophical texts. Works by Marcus Aurelius, Seneca, and Epictetus offer timeless insights into human nature and ethical living. As you read, take notes and reflect on how the principles can be applied to your life. This reflective practice deepens your understanding and helps internalize the teachings. Additionally, seek out diverse sources of knowledge. Attend lectures, participate in discussions, and explore different perspectives. This broadens your intellectual horizons and enhances your ability to think critically.

Reflection and critical thinking are essential components of wisdom. They enable us to analyze situations objectively and make informed decisions. Practicing critical thinking involves questioning assumptions and evaluating evidence before forming conclusions. For instance, when faced with a complex problem at work, take a step back and consider all possible solutions. Weigh the good and the bad and consider each option's long-term implications. This analytical approach helps you arrive at a rational and well-thought-out decision. Reflective journaling is another powerful tool. At the end of each day, take a few minutes to write about your experiences, challenges, and the decisions you made. Ask yourself questions like, "What did I learn today?" and "How could I have handled that situation better?" This practice enhances self-awareness and promotes continuous improvement.

Real-life examples illustrate how wisdom can guide us through challenging situations. Consider the case of a business leader navigating a crisis. During a significant downturn, they faced pressure to make quick decisions that could impact the company's future. Instead of reacting impulsively, they took the time to gather information, consult with experts, and reflect on the best course of action. By applying wisdom, they made decisions that stabilized the company and positioned it for long-term success. This example demonstrates how wisdom enables us to navigate crises with clarity and composure.

On a personal level, wisdom can guide everyday decisions. Imagine you are faced with a difficult choice, such as whether to move to a new city for a job opportunity. Instead of focusing solely on the immediate benefits, consider the long-term impact on your happiness and well-being. Reflect on your values and goals and how the decision aligns with them. This thoughtful approach ensures your choices are grounded in wisdom and aligned with your aspirations.

Exercise: Reflective Journaling Prompts

To cultivate wisdom through reflection, try incorporating these journaling prompts into your daily routine:

- What significant decision did I make today, and what factors influenced it?
- How did I apply wisdom in handling a challenging situation?
- What can I learn from today's experiences that will guide me in the future?

By consistently practicing this, you can develop and enhance your wisdom, leading to more rational decisions and a virtuous life. Wisdom, as the foundation of Stoic philosophy, empowers you to navigate the complexities of life with clarity, integrity, and purpose.

PRACTICING JUSTICE: STOIC ETHICS IN ACTION

Justice within the Stoic framework is more than a legal or societal concept; it is a moral virtue that embodies fairness and integrity. The Stoics believed that justice is about treating others with the respect and fairness they deserve. Seneca emphasized this when he said, "Treat your inferiors as you would be treated by your superiors." This idea highlights justice's reciprocal nature and the importance of moral integrity. Justice, for the Stoics, is about ensuring that our actions are fair and that we contribute positively to the community.

To practice justice in everyday life, treat others fairly and respectfully. This means recognizing the worth and inherent dignity of every individual you encounter. Whether it is a colleague at work, a family member, or a stranger, fairness demands that you consider their perspectives and act with kindness. Advocating for ethical practices in the workplace is another way to embody justice. This could involve standing up against unfair treatment or ensuring that company policies are equitable and inclusive. By advocating for justice, you create a fairer and more respectful environment.

Empathy and compassion are integral to practicing justice. Empathy lets you understand and share others' feelings. It fosters a sense of connection and concern. Compassion, on the other hand, motivates you to act on that empathy, striving to alleviate the suffering of others. Developing empathy can be as simple as active listening, where you genuinely focus on what someone else is saying without interrupting or judging. Compassionate actions include helping a colleague with a challenging task or supporting a friend through a tough time. These small acts of kindness and understanding contribute to a harmonious and just community.

One compelling example of justice in action is a whistleblower's story exposing unethical practices in their organization. Despite the personal and professional risks, this individual was morally obligated to ensure justice was served. Their actions led to significant organizational changes, promoting transparency and fairness. This story illustrates the power of standing up for what is right, even under challenging circumstances. Another example is community service initiatives. Individuals who volunteer their time and resources to support those in need embody the Stoic principle of justice. Whether it is organizing a food drive, mentoring youth, or advocating for social justice causes, these actions reflect a commitment to fairness and moral integrity.

Reflection Exercise: Empathy Building

To cultivate empathy, try an exercise in perspective-taking. Think about a recent interaction where you disagreed with someone. Reflect on their point of view and consider what might have influenced their perspective. Write about this experience, focusing on understanding their feelings and motivations. This exercise helps build empathy, which is crucial for practicing justice.

As envisioned by the Stoics, justice is a guiding principle for ethical living. It calls for fairness, respect, empathy, and compassion in all our interactions. Integrating these values into daily life upholds moral integrity and contributes to a more just and equitable society. The stories of individuals who have practiced justice in various contexts can serve as powerful reminders. Our actions can make a significant difference.

DEVELOPING COURAGE: FACING FEARS WITH STOIC STRENGTH

Courage is a pillar in Stoic philosophy, providing the strength to face life's challenges and uncertainties. Courage is confronting fear, pain, and adversity with bravery. It is indispensable for personal growth and resilience. Epictetus emphasized the necessity of bravery by stating, "It's not what happens to you, but how you react to it that matters." This quote underscores the importance of our response to difficulties, advocating for courage in adversity.

To cultivate courage in everyday life, start by setting and pursuing challenging goals. These should push you out of your comfort zone and test your limits. For instance, if public speaking terrifies you, set a goal to present at work or join a local speaking club. You build confidence and resilience by gradually exposing yourself to your fears in controlled settings. This method, known as graduated exposure, involves facing your fears incrementally, starting with less intimidating scenarios and progressively tackling more challenging ones. Over time, this practice reduces fears and enhances your courage to confront difficult situations.

Resilience and mental toughness are closely tied to courage. They enable you to withstand adversity and bounce back from setbacks. Building resilience includes developing a positive mindset and focusing on what you can control. Stress management exercises and mindfulness help maintain mental equilibrium during tough times. For example, practicing deep breathing exercises when you feel overwhelmed can calm your mind and body, allowing you to approach challenges with clear thinking. Maintaining a growth mindset—believing you can improve through effort and learning— fosters resilience. You build mental toughness and perseverance by viewing challenges as avenues for growth instead of insurmountable obstacles.

Consider the story of an athlete who overcame significant adversity to achieve greatness. This individual faced a career-threatening injury that required extensive rehabilitation. Instead of succumbing to despair, they viewed the setback as a challenge. They recovered and returned stronger through relentless training, mental conditioning, and unwavering determination, achieving new personal bests. This story exemplifies how courage and resilience can transform adversity into triumph.

Another powerful example is a professional who decided to take a bold career step by leaving a stable job to start their own business. Despite the uncertainties and risks, they pursued their passion with courage and conviction. They faced numerous challenges, from securing funding to building a client base, but their unwavering determination and resilience kept them moving forward. Today, their business thrives, serving as a testament to the power of courage in achieving one's dreams.

By adding these practices into your daily life, you can develop the courage to face life's challenges head-on. Setting challenging goals, practicing graduated exposure, and building resilience and mental toughness arm you with the tools to confront fear and adversity with bravery. The stories of individuals who have demonstrated courage in various situations serve as inspiring reminders that bravery is not being without fear but the strength to move forward despite it.

EMBRACING MODERATION: BALANCING DESIRES AND NEEDS

In Stoic philosophy, moderation is the virtue that ensures balance and self-control in all aspects of life. It is about finding the middle ground between excess and deficiency and maintaining a harmonious state. Musonius Rufus emphasized the importance of self-control by stating, "He who has self-control is moderate; he who is moderate is in the right state of mind." This quote captures the essence of moderation, highlighting its role in achieving mental and emotional equilibrium.

Practicing moderation requires actionable strategies that can be integrated into daily life. One effective technique is mindful consumption. This involves being aware of your desires and making deliberate choices about what you consume, whether it is food, media, or material possessions. For example, when it comes to eating, pay attention to when your body is hungry and savor each bite. Avoid mindless snacking and opt for nutritious meals that nourish your body. Similarly, practice mindful media consumption by limiting screen time and choosing content that adds value to your life.

Setting boundaries and maintaining them is another crucial aspect of moderation. This means knowing your limits and respecting them. For instance, clear work-life boundaries should be established to prevent burnout. This could involve setting specific work hours and sticking to them, ensuring you have time for rest and leisure. Additionally, practice saying no to commitments that do not align with your priorities. Doing so protects your time and energy, allowing you to focus on what truly matters.

Self-awareness plays a pivotal role in practicing moderation. It involves understanding your desires and recognizing when they become excessive. Techniques for increasing self-awareness include regular self-reflection and mindfulness practices. For example, take a few minutes daily to check in with yourself. Ask questions like, "Am I overindulging in any area of my life?" and "What can I do to restore balance?" Reflective journaling can also enhance self-awareness. Write about your experiences, noting any tendencies toward excess or deficiency. This practice is a way to identify patterns and consciously maintain balance.

Consider the story of a professional who successfully managed work-life balance through moderation. This individual was initially overwhelmed by work commitments, leading to stress and burnout. They regained balance and improved their well-being by setting clear boundaries and prioritizing self-care. They established specific work hours, took regular breaks, and made time for hobbies and family. This approach enhanced their productivity and contributed to a more fulfilling life.

Mindful eating is another practical example of moderation in action. Imagine someone who struggled with overeating and weight gain. Adopting mindful eating practices taught them to listen to their body's hunger cues and make healthier food choices. They savored each bite, ate slowly, and avoided distractions during meals. This shift in behavior led to improved health and a better relationship with food. It also fostered a sense of gratitude and enjoyment in their daily meals.

Reflective Journaling Prompts

To cultivate self-awareness and practice moderation, consider incorporating these journaling prompts into your routine:

- In what areas of my life do I tend to overindulge or neglect?
- How can I create and maintain boundaries to ensure balance?
- What small changes can I make today to practice mindful consumption?

You can embrace moderation and achieve a balanced life by consistently engaging in these practices. Moderation, as envisioned by the Stoics, ensures that our desires and needs are in harmony, leading to greater well-being and inner peace.

RESILIENCE IN THE FACE OF ADVERSITY: REAL-LIFE EXAMPLES

In Stoicism, resilience is the ability to withstand and recover from life's challenges and adversities. Defined as mental toughness and emotional strength, resilience is vital to navigate life's ups and downs. Seneca emphasized the importance of resilience by stating, "Difficulties strengthen the mind, as labor does the body." This quote underscores the idea that facing hardships can fortify our mental and emotional capacities, making us more robust and capable individuals.

Building resilience involves developing mental fortitude and emotional regulation. One effective strategy is practicing stress management techniques and mindfulness. Mindfulness helps you remain present and focused, lessening the impact of stressors. Try engaging in deep breathing exercises when you feel overwhelmed. Inhale deeply through your nose. Hold your breath for a few seconds. Exhale slowly through your mouth. This simple act calms your nervous system and clears your mind. Another practical approach is to create a support network. Surround yourself with people who uplift and encourage you. Share your struggles and seek their guidance. Their support can provide you with the strength to persevere.

The role of mindset and perspective in resilience cannot be overstated. A positive attitude helps you view challenges as opportunities for growth rather than insurmountable obstacles. Cultivating a resilient mindset involves practicing gratitude and focusing on what you can control. Write three things you are thankful for daily in a gratitude journal. This practice shifts your focus from what is going wrong to what is going right to foster a positive outlook. Reflective journaling is another powerful tool. At the end of each day, write about the challenges you faced and how you responded to them. Ask yourself, "What did I learn from this, and how can I apply this lesson in the future?" This reflection helps you gain insights and build resilience over time.

Real-life examples of resilience offer powerful lessons and inspiration. Consider the case of a business leader who faced significant financial challenges. During an economic downturn, their company struggled to stay afloat. Instead of succumbing to despair, they took proactive steps to stabilize the business. They implemented cost-cutting measures, sought new revenue streams, and engaged with their team to find innovative solutions. Their resilience and determination saved the company and positioned it for future growth. This story illustrates how mental fortitude and a positive mindset can turn adversity into opportunity.

On a personal level, resilience can be seen in the story of someone recovering from a major setback, such as a severe illness or injury. Imagine an individual diagnosed with a chronic disease that impacted their ability to work and enjoy life. Instead of giving in to hopelessness, they focused on what they could control. They adopted a healthier lifestyle, sought support from loved ones, and pursued hobbies that brought them joy. Over time, their health improved, and they found new ways to lead a fulfilling life. This personal story demonstrates how resilience and a positive outlook can help overcome even the most daunting challenges.

Reflective Journaling Prompts

To cultivate resilience through reflection, consider incorporating these journaling prompts into your routine:

- What challenges did I face today, and how did I respond?

- What lessons can I learn from today's experiences?
- How can I put these lessons into practice to build resilience in the future?

By consistently doing these practices, you can enhance your resilience and better navigate life's adversities. Resilience, as envisioned by the Stoics, empowers you to face challenges with strength and determination, transforming obstacles into opportunities for growth.

STOIC STRATEGIES FOR DEALING WITH FAILURE

In Stoic philosophy, failure is not seen as a defeat but as a valuable learning opportunity and a growth path. The Stoics believed that experiencing failure helps us understand our limitations, refine our strategies, and ultimately become better individuals. Epictetus captured this sentiment when he said, "It is impossible for a man to learn what he thinks he already knows." This quote highlights that authentic learning often comes from recognizing mistakes and failures. Viewing failure through this lens can transform setbacks into personal and professional development springboards.

Analyzing and reflecting on the experience is crucial to deal with failure effectively. Start by identifying what went wrong and why. Break down the situation into specific components and assess each aspect critically. This detailed analysis helps you pinpoint the exact reasons for the failure, whether it is a lack of preparation, poor decision-making, or external factors beyond your control. Once you have identified the causes, reflect on what you can learn from them. Ask yourself questions like, "What could I have done differently?" and "How can I apply this lesson in the future?" This reflective practice turns failure into a powerful learning tool.

Another effective strategy for managing failure is developing a growth mindset. A growth mindset, made famous by psychologist Carol Dweck, is the idea that abilities and intelligence can be developed through effort and learning. Embrace that failure is not an indicator of your worth but a way to grow and improve. When faced with a setback, remind yourself it is a temporary obstacle and focus on your progress. Celebrate small victories along the way and use them as motivation to keep pushing forward. This mindset shift fosters resilience and perseverance, helping you bounce back stronger from failures.

Resilience and perseverance play a crucial role in overcoming failure. They enable you to face setbacks with determination and continue striving toward your goals. Building resilience involves developing mental toughness and emotional strength. Techniques like mindfulness and stress management exercises can help you be focused and calm during challenging times. For example, practice deep breathing exercises to reduce stress and maintain clarity. Perseverance, on the other hand, requires a steadfast commitment to your goals. Set specific, achievable targets and break them down into smaller, manageable steps. This approach helps you track progress and keep motivated, even when faced with obstacles.

Consider the story of an entrepreneur who experienced a significant failure in their business venture. After years of hard work, a sudden market shift led to the company's collapse. Instead of giving up, they took the time to analyze what went wrong. They identified areas where they could have been more adaptable and resilient. Armed with these insights, they started a new venture, applying the lessons they had learned. This time, their business thrived, becoming a success story built on the foundation of past failures. This example illustrates how resilience and a growth mindset can turn setbacks into opportunities for success.

Another inspiring example is a student who faced academic setbacks. Struggling with poor grades and self-doubt, they could have easily given up. Instead, they sought help from tutors, developed better study habits, and remained committed to their goals. Over time, their efforts paid off, and they achieved academic success. This personal story demonstrates how perseverance and wanting to learn from failure can lead to significant achievements.

Integrating these Stoic strategies into your daily life lets you effectively manage and learn from failure. Analyzing and reflecting on setbacks, developing a growth mindset, and building resilience and perseverance equip you with the tools to turn failures into valuable learning experiences. The stories of people who have successfully overcome failure are potent reminders that setbacks are not the end but the beginning of new opportunities for growth and success.

In this chapter, we have explored various Stoic virtues and strategies for overcoming adversity. From cultivating wisdom and practicing justice to developing courage and resilience, these principles provide practical tools for navigating life's challenges. As we move forward, we will delve into daily practices that further solidify these concepts, helping you cultivate a Stoic mindset in every aspect of your life.

7

PERSONAL GROWTH AND PROFESSIONAL SUCCESS

A few years ago, I attended a workshop on goal setting. The seasoned executive speaker shared his personal story of how he transformed his career by setting clear, actionable goals. He spoke about his journey from a struggling middle manager to a successful CEO. What struck me was his emphasis on aligning goals with personal values and virtues, a concept deeply rooted in Stoic philosophy. This experience was a turning point for me, highlighting the power of purposeful living and the importance of setting goals that resonate with one's core principles.

GOAL SETTING: STOIC METHODS FOR ACHIEVING SUCCESS

In Stoic philosophy, goal setting is not just about achieving external success but about aligning your actions with your inner values and virtues. Seneca often wrote about the importance of purposeful living. He stated, "If one does not know to which port one is sailing, no wind is favorable." This quote underscores the necessity of having clear, defined goals. Without them, you drift aimlessly, at the mercy of external circumstances. Stoic goal setting involves identifying what truly matters to you and directing your efforts toward those objectives.

Setting Stoic goals requires discipline and self-awareness. Begin by defining clear, actionable goals. Break them down into specific, manageable steps. This approach makes the goals less daunting and provides a clear roadmap. For example, to improve your physical fitness, start with small, achievable milestones like committing to a 30-minute workout three times a week. Over time, you can build on these smaller steps to achieve larger fitness goals. The key is to make each step specific and attainable, ensuring steady progress toward your ultimate objective.

Aligning goals with personal values and virtues is crucial in Stoic goal setting. Reflect on what is truly important to you. Does external validation drive your goals, or do they resonate with your inner values? Ensure that your goals reflect virtues such as wisdom, courage, and justice. For example, if you value wisdom, set goals that involve continuous learning and self-improvement. If courage is vital to you, challenge yourself to step out of your comfort zone and take on new opportunities. By aligning your goals with your values, you ensure your actions are fulfilling and meaningful.

Perseverance and resilience play a vital role in achieving goals. The Stoics believed that true success comes from persistent effort and overcoming obstacles. Techniques for staying committed to long-term goals include regular self-reflection and maintaining a positive mindset. Reflect on your progress periodically and celebrate small victories. This practice keeps you motivated and helps you stay focused on your objectives. Additionally, develop a growth mindset by viewing setbacks as learning opportunities rather than failures. This perspective fosters resilience and keeps you moving forward, even when you face challenges.

Overcoming obstacles and setbacks is integral to goal setting. The Stoics taught that obstacles are inevitable. However, how you respond to them defines your character. When faced with a setback, take a step back and analyze the situation. Identify what went wrong and what you can learn from it. Develop a plan to address the issue and move forward. For instance, if you miss a deadline at work, reflect on the factors that contributed to the delay and implement strategies to manage your time more effectively. This proactive approach helps you navigate challenges with grace and determination.

Exercise: Writing a Personal Mission Statement

To solidify your goals, try writing a personal mission statement. This statement should encapsulate your core values, long-term objectives, and the virtues that guide your actions. Reflect on questions like, "What do I want to achieve in life?" and "How do my goals align with my values?" Write a concise statement that constantly reminds you of your purpose and direction.

Consider the story of a professional who successfully achieved their career goals using Stoic methods. Initially working mid-level, this individual aspired to become a senior executive. They began by setting clear, actionable goals aligned with their values of wisdom and courage. They pursued continuous learning, sought mentorship, and took on challenging projects that pushed their limits. Despite facing numerous obstacles, they remained resilient, viewing each setback as an opportunity for growth. Over time, their consistent efforts paid off, and they achieved their goal of becoming a senior executive. Their journey illustrates the power of Stoic goal setting in achieving personal and professional success.

DECISION-MAKING: RATIONAL CHOICES IN PROFESSIONAL LIFE

In professional life, decision-making can often feel like navigating a dense fog. The Stoic approach to decision-making brings clarity and focus, emphasizing rational and thoughtful choices. Rational decision-making in Stoicism involves using reason to evaluate situations objectively, free from the distortions of irrational emotions. Epictetus asserted, "It is not things themselves that disturb us, but our judgments about these things." This highlights the importance of rationality in making decisions. We can navigate complexities with a calm and clear mind by grounding our choices in reason.

Making rational decisions starts with evaluating options and outcomes. Begin by gathering all relevant information, considering various perspectives, and weighing the potential consequences of each option. This comprehensive analysis helps identify the best course of action. One effective technique is the decision-making matrix, where you list your options along one axis and criteria for evaluation along the other. Rate each option based on these criteria; the option with the highest score is often the most rational choice. This structured approach minimizes the influence of emotions and ensures a balanced evaluation.

Minimizing emotional influence is crucial in Stoic decision-making. Emotions cloud judgment and can lead to impulsive choices. To manage this, practice mindfulness and emotional regulation techniques. For instance, if you feel overwhelmed by a decision, take a moment to breathe deeply and calm your mind. This pause allows you to approach the situation with a clear head. Another method is cognitive reframing, where you challenge and reframe irrational thoughts. Ask yourself, "Is this emotion driving my decision, or is it based on reason?" By questioning your emotional responses, you can ensure that your choices are grounded in rationality.

Aligning decisions with Stoic values such as wisdom and justice is essential. Wisdom involves making choices that reflect a deep understanding of the situation, while justice ensures that your decisions are fair and ethical. To practice value-based decision-making, reflect on your core values and how they apply to the decision. For example, if you value honesty, ensure your choices are transparent and truthful. In professional settings, ethical decision-making is paramount. Consider a business leader faced with a dilemma involving financial gain versus ethical practices. They choose the ethical route by prioritizing justice and integrity, even if that means sacrificing short-term profits. This decision upholds moral standards and builds long-term trust and credibility.

Exercise: Decision-Making Matrix for Evaluating Options

To aid in rational decision-making, try using a decision-making matrix. List your options in the top row and evaluation criteria in the side column. Rate each option based on these criteria and sum the scores to identify the most rational choice.

The story of a business leader exemplifies the application of Stoic principles in decision-making. Faced with a challenging situation where they had to choose between cutting executive bonuses or laying off employees, they turned to Stoic values for guidance. Reflecting on justice and fairness, they cut executive bonuses, ensuring that financial constraints were shared equitably. This decision, though difficult, was rooted in ethical considerations and demonstrated a commitment to fairness. By aligning their choices with Stoic values, they navigated the dilemma with integrity and maintained the trust of their team.

In professional life, rational and thoughtful decision-making is a crucial skill. By evaluating options and outcomes, minimizing emotional influence, and aligning decisions with Stoic values, you can navigate complexities with clarity and confidence. The practical steps and real-life examples here offer actionable strategies to enhance decision-making. Embrace these principles and let Stoic wisdom guide your choices, ensuring they are rational, ethical, and aligned with your inner values.

TIME MANAGEMENT: STOIC STRATEGIES FOR PRODUCTIVITY

Time management is a core principle in Stoic philosophy, reflecting the value placed on purposeful living. Seneca emphasized the fleeting nature of time. He famously wrote, "It is not that we have a short time to live, but that we waste a lot of it." This underscores the importance of using our time wisely and effectively. Efficient time management aligns with Stoic teachings, ensuring every moment is spent pursuing meaningful and virtuous goals. You can reach your goals and live a life of purpose by managing your time well.

Begin by prioritizing tasks to manage your time effectively. Identify what matters and zero in on those activities. One practical technique is the Eisenhower Matrix, which categorizes tasks into four quadrants: urgent and important, important but not urgent, urgent but not necessary, and neither urgent nor essential. This helps you prioritize tasks that align with your long-term goals while minimizing distractions from less critical activities. Another method is to break down larger tasks into smaller, manageable steps. This approach reduces overwhelm and ensures steady progress. For instance, divide it into daily or weekly tasks if you are working on a significant project to make tracking progress and staying motivated easier.

Minimizing distractions is another crucial aspect of effective time management. In our digital age, distractions are everywhere, from social media notifications to constant emails. To maintain focus, create a dedicated workspace free from distractions. Use website blockers to limit access to distracting sites during work hours. Additionally, practice time-blocking, where you allocate specific time slots for different tasks. This not only helps you stay focused but also ensures that you dedicate adequate time to each task. For example, set aside specific hours in the morning for deep work and reserve afternoons for meetings and administrative tasks.

A vital aspect of time management is self-discipline. It enables you to stick to your schedule and resist procrastinating. Building and maintaining self-discipline involves setting clear boundaries and consistently adhering to them. One effective technique is the Pomodoro Technique. It is when you work for a set period—typically 25 minutes—followed by a short break. This method enhances focus and productivity. It creates a sense of urgency and provides regular intervals for rest. Overcoming procrastination requires a shift in mindset. Begin by identifying what lies behind your procrastination. Is it a lack of motivation, feeling overwhelmed, or fear of failure? Address these underlying issues and implement strategies to counteract them. For instance, if you procrastinate for fear of failure, remind yourself that every task is an opportunity to learn and grow.

Creating a daily schedule aligned with Stoic principles can significantly enhance your productivity. Begin by writing down your goals and priorities for the day. Allocate time for each task, ensuring that you include breaks and time for self-reflection. Reflect on your progress at the end of each day and adjust your schedule as needed. This practice keeps you on track and fosters a sense of accomplishment and continuous improvement. Consider the story of a professional who struggled with time management and productivity. By implementing Stoic principles, they transformed their approach to work. They began by prioritizing their tasks, focusing on what truly mattered. They minimized distractions by creating a dedicated workspace and practicing time-blocking. Over time, their productivity soared, and they achieved their professional goals more quickly and efficiently.

Exercise: Creating a Daily Schedule Aligned with Stoic Principles

To create a daily schedule aligned with Stoic principles, list your top priorities for the day. Set up specific time slots for each task to ensure breaks and time for self-reflection. Use the Eisenhower Matrix to prioritize tasks and the Pomodoro Technique to maintain focus. Reflect on your progress at the end of the day and adjust your schedule as needed.

Integrating these time management strategies into your daily routine can significantly improve productivity. By prioritizing tasks, minimizing distractions, and maintaining self-discipline, you can make the most of your time and achieve your goals more efficiently. The practical steps and real-life examples here offer actionable strategies to improve your time management skills. Embrace these principles and let Stoic wisdom guide your time, ensuring every moment is spent pursuing meaningful and virtuous goals.

LEADERSHIP: STOIC PRINCIPLES FOR LEADING OTHERS

Stoic philosophy offers a profound framework for effective leadership, emphasizing ethical and compassionate principles. In Stoicism, leadership is not about wielding power but guiding others with wisdom and integrity. Marcus Aurelius captured this beautifully when he said, "Waste no more time arguing about what a good man should be. Be one." This quote underscores the Stoic belief that authentic leadership comes from embodying virtues and leading by example.

To lead effectively with Stoic principles, start by demonstrating the virtues of wisdom, courage, justice, and moderation. Leading by example means consistently acting in ways that reflect these virtues. For instance, in decision-making, prioritize fairness and transparency. When faced with a challenging situation, demonstrate courage by taking decisive action. Show moderation by balancing assertiveness with empathy. By embodying these virtues, you set a standard for your team. A practical strategy is establishing core values that guide your leadership. Communicate these values to your team and ensure your actions consistently reflect them.

Another crucial aspect of Stoic leadership is a supportive and ethical work environment. Create a culture where ethical behavior is the norm and team members feel valued and supported. Actively listen to your team's concerns and encourage open communication. This builds trust and promotes a sense of belonging and mutual respect. Implement policies that promote fairness and equity, such as transparent decision-making processes and equal opportunities for growth and development. Creating an environment prioritizing ethical behavior and support empowers your team to thrive and contribute meaningfully.

Empathy and compassion play crucial roles in Stoic leadership. Understanding and supporting your team members fosters a positive work environment and strengthens relationships. Practice active listening to show that you value their perspectives and experiences. When a team member faces challenges, offer support and encouragement. This could involve providing resources, offering guidance, or simply being present to listen. Compassionate leadership consists of recognizing each team member's humanity and acting to uplift and empower them. For example, when a team member struggles with a personal issue, show empathy by offering flexibility and understanding. This helps them navigate their challenges and builds loyalty and trust.

A compelling story of compassionate leadership can be found in the example of a manager who faced a period of low team morale. They recognized the impact on productivity and well-being and turned to Stoic principles for guidance. They began by actively listening to their team's concerns and demonstrating empathy. They implemented changes that addressed these concerns, such as flexible work hours and opportunities for professional development. They significantly improved team morale and productivity by fostering a supportive environment and leading with compassion. This story illustrates how Stoic leadership principles can transform a team and create a positive, thriving work environment.

Exercise: Reflecting on Leadership Practices and Aligning Them with Stoic Values

To enhance your leadership practices, reflect on your actions and decisions. Ask yourself questions like, "How do my actions reflect Stoic virtues?" and "What can I do to better support my team?" Write down your reflections and identify areas for improvement. This self-awareness helps you align your leadership with Stoic principles and fosters continuous growth.

Stoic leadership is about guiding others with wisdom, integrity, empathy, and compassion. You can create a positive and effective leadership style by leading by example, fostering a supportive and ethical work environment, and practicing kindness and compassion. These practical steps and real-life examples offer actionable strategies to enhance leadership skills. Embrace these principles and let Stoic wisdom guide your approach to leading others.

PUBLIC SPEAKING: OVERCOMING FEAR WITH STOIC TECHNIQUES

Public speaking is a common fear that can paralyze even the most confident individuals. Stoic philosophy offers practical solutions to manage and reduce this fear. Epictetus once said, "Men are disturbed not by things, but by the views which they take of them." This insight emphasizes the power of rational thinking in overcoming fear. When you approach public speaking through the lens of Stoicism, you focus on what you can control—your thoughts, preparation, and mindset. This shift in perspective helps you manage the anxiety that may pop up when speaking in front of an audience.

One of the first steps in overcoming public speaking anxiety is thorough preparation and practice. Begin by familiarizing yourself with your material. The more you know your speech, the more confident you will feel. Break your speech into sections and practice each part until you feel comfortable. This method helps you internalize the content and reduces the likelihood of forgetting key points.

Also, record yourself or practice in front of a mirror, which lets you observe your body language and make necessary adjustments. Another effective technique is to practice in front of a small, supportive audience. This simulates the experience of speaking to a larger group and helps build your confidence.

Managing physical symptoms of anxiety is also crucial. You can calm your nervous system with deep breathing and progressive muscle relaxation. Before stepping on stage, take a few deep breaths. Inhale through your nose. Exhale through your mouth. This simple act can reduce your heart rate and help you feel more centered. Progressive muscle relaxation is tensing and relaxing each muscle group, beginning from your toes and working your way up. This practice reduces physical tension and promotes a sense of calm.

Visualization and mindfulness are powerful tools in Stoic practice that can enhance your public speaking skills. Positive visualization involves imagining yourself delivering a successful speech. Close your eyes and picture yourself on stage, speaking confidently and engaging your audience. Visualize the positive reactions and applause from the crowd. This mental exercise creates a sense of familiarity and reduces anxiety. Mindfulness, on the other hand, helps you stay present. During your speech, focus on your breathing and your words. If your mind starts to wander or anxiety creeps in, gently bring your focus back to the present moment. This practice keeps you grounded and prevents your thoughts from spiraling into negative territory.

Consider the story of a professional who overcame their fear of public speaking using Stoic principles. Initially, they experienced intense anxiety before every presentation. By adopting Stoic techniques, they transformed their approach. They began by thoroughly preparing their material and practicing in front of a mirror. They also visualized their success and practiced mindfulness to stay present during their speeches. Over time, their confidence grew, and they became a compelling and engaging speaker. Their journey illustrates the effectiveness of Stoic techniques in overcoming public speaking anxiety.

Exercise: Practicing Speeches in Front of a Mirror or Small Audience

To build confidence in public speaking, try practicing your speeches in front of a mirror. Observe your body language and adjust as needed. Once comfortable, practice in front of a small, supportive audience. This simulates the experience of speaking to a larger group and helps you build confidence.

By integrating these Stoic techniques into your public speaking practice, you can manage and reduce your anxiety. Preparation, visualization, and mindfulness empower you to approach public speaking with confidence and clarity. The practical steps and real-life examples here offer actionable strategies to enhance public speaking skills. Embrace these principles, and let Stoic wisdom guide you in overcoming your fear of public speaking.

BUILDING CONFIDENCE: STOIC EXERCISES FOR SELF-ASSURANCE

Self-confidence is a cornerstone of Stoic philosophy, promoting self-assurance and inner strength. Seneca once remarked, "A man's worth is no greater than the worth of his ambitions." This quote highlights the importance of self-belief in Stoic practice. When you believe in your capabilities, you are likelier to set ambitious goals and go after them with determination. According to the Stoics, confidence stems from understanding your strengths and accepting your limitations. This balanced view fosters a realistic and resilient self-image, enabling you to face challenges with poise and assurance.

To build self-confidence, start with self-reflection and positive self-talk. Reflect on your past achievements and the strengths that contributed to them. Acknowledge your accomplishments, no matter how small, and remind yourself of these successes regularly. Positive self-talk involves replacing negative thoughts with empowering affirmations. For instance, if you think, "I cannot do this," reframe it to, "I have the skills and determination to succeed." This shift in mindset reinforces your self-belief and gradually builds confidence. Another effective technique is setting small, achievable goals. Accomplishing these goals provides a sense of progress and strengthens your ability to succeed. For example, if you need more confidence about speaking up in meetings, start by contributing a small comment or question. Gradually, as your confidence grows, you can take on more significant speaking roles.

Self-awareness and self-acceptance are crucial for building confidence. Understanding yourself—your strengths, weaknesses, and values—provides a solid foundation for self-assurance. Techniques for increasing self-awareness include mindfulness practices and reflective journaling. Take time each day to reflect on your experiences and emotions. Ask yourself questions like, "What did I do well today?" and "What can I improve?" This practice enhances your self-understanding and helps you identify areas for growth. Self-acceptance, on the other hand, involves embracing yourself as you are. Recognize that everyone has flaws and that these do not diminish your worth—practice self-compassion. Be kind and understanding to yourself as you would to a friend. This balanced view fosters a realistic and resilient self-image, enabling you to face challenges with poise and assurance.

Consider the story of an individual who built confidence through Stoic exercises. This person struggled with self-doubt and often felt inadequate professionally and personally. They began by practicing reflective journaling, focusing on their strengths and achievements. Each evening, they wrote about something they did well that day, no matter how small. Over time, this exercise helped them see their value and capabilities. They also practiced positive self-talk, replacing negative thoughts with affirmations like, "I am capable and worthy." Setting and achieving small goals further reinforced their confidence. For instance, they started by volunteering to lead small projects at work, gradually taking on more significant responsibilities as their confidence grew. Through these Stoic practices, they transformed their self-image and became confident and self-assured.

Exercise: Reflective Journaling on Personal Strengths and Achievements

To enhance self-confidence, try a reflective journaling exercise. Each evening, write about a personal strength or achievement from the day. Focus on what you did well and how it contributed to your success. This practice helps reinforce your self-belief and build a positive self-image.

Building confidence through Stoic exercises involves self-reflection, positive self-talk, self-awareness, and self-acceptance. By understanding and embracing your strengths and achievements, you can develop a resilient self-image and confidently face challenges. The practical steps and real-life examples here offer actionable strategies to enhance self-confidence. Embrace these principles and let Stoic wisdom guide you in building a robust and self-assured self.

8

CREATING A STOIC LIFESTYLE

S everal years ago, I was grappling with the chaos of my daily life. Each day felt like a whirlwind of tasks, obligations, and unexpected events. One morning, as I sat quietly with a cup of coffee, I stumbled upon a quote from Marcus Aurelius: "Waste no more time arguing what a good man should be. Be one." This simple, profound statement resonated deeply with me. It made me realize the importance of structuring my day with intention and discipline, embodying the principles of Stoicism in every action. This realization catalyzed me to develop daily routines that have since transformed my life.

DAILY ROUTINES: STRUCTURING YOUR DAY WITH STOIC PRACTICES

Daily routines form the bedrock of Stoic practice, offering a framework to maintain focus and embody Stoic principles consistently. In *Meditations,* Marcus Aurelius emphasized the significance of daily discipline and writing, "Because most of what we say and do is not essential. Ask yourself at every moment, 'Is this necessary?'" This focus on essential actions is a cornerstone of Stoic living. Historical accounts reveal that Stoic philosophers like Seneca and Epictetus adhered to structured routines. These routines concerned productivity and aligning their actions with values and virtues.

Creating a Stoic daily routine begins with setting intentions each morning. Start your day with a moment of meditation or quiet reflection. This practice helps center your mind and set a positive tone for the day. Sit comfortably in a calm space. Close your eyes and focus on your breath. As you breathe deeply, consider what you aim to achieve regarding tasks and personal growth that day. Reflect on virtues like wisdom, courage, and moderation, and set intentions that align with these values. This morning routine is about planning and grounding yourself in Stoic principles.

Evening reflections are equally important in a Stoic daily routine. At the end of each day, review your actions and thoughts. Find a quiet space to sit and reflect on the day's events. Consider what went well and what could have been better. Reflect on your responses to challenges and how well you embodied Stoic virtues. This practice, inspired by Marcus Aurelius's reflections in *Meditations*, helps you learn from your experiences and continuously improve. It fosters self-awareness and personal growth, reinforcing the lessons of the day.

Consistency and discipline are crucial for maintaining effective routines. A consistent routine builds discipline and resilience, essential traits in Stoic philosophy. Maintaining consistency includes setting specific times for your morning and evening practices. Treat these times as nonnegotiable appointments with yourself. Use reminders or alarms if necessary. Overcoming disruptions requires flexibility and forgiveness. Life is unpredictable, and disruptions will occur. When they do, adapt your routine rather than abandon it. If you miss a morning meditation, find a few quiet moments during the day to reflect. The key is maintaining the practice, even if it could be better.

Practical activities can illustrate the effectiveness of these routines. Consider the example of a morning meditation practice. Every morning, I meditate for ten minutes, focusing on my breath and setting intentions for the day. This simple practice has dramatically improved my focus and sense of calm. It prepares me to face the day's challenges with a clear mind and a positive attitude. Another practical exercise is creating a personalized daily schedule. Begin by listing your daily tasks and responsibilities. Allocate specific times for each task, including your morning and evening reflections. Stick to this schedule as closely as possible and adjust if needed for unforeseen events.

Exercise: Creating a Personalized Daily Schedule

Four steps:

1. **Morning Reflection**: Spend ten minutes each morning in meditation or quiet reflection. Focus on your breath and set intentions for the day. Reflect on virtues like wisdom, courage, and moderation.
2. **Daily Tasks**: List your tasks and responsibilities for the day. Prioritize them based on importance and urgency.
3. **Allocate Time**: Assign specific times for each task. Include breaks and time for reflection. Treat these times as appointments with yourself.
4. **Evening Reflection**: Spend ten minutes each evening reviewing your day. Reflect on what went well and what could have been better. Consider your responses to challenges and how well you embodied Stoic virtues.

By structuring your day with these routines, you will enhance your productivity and align your actions with Stoic principles, fostering a life of wisdom, resilience, and inner peace.

THE STOIC DIET: HEALTHY EATING AND MODERATION

Incorporating Stoic principles into your diet can transform how you approach food and nourishment. Musonius Rufus emphasized that our eating habits are fundamental to self-control and balance. He argued that our throats and stomachs are designed for nourishment, not pleasure, and recommended a diet based on simplicity and moderation. This perspective aligns with the broader Stoic commitment to self-discipline and living in harmony with nature. By adopting a Stoic approach to eating, you can cultivate healthier habits that benefit both your body and mind.

First, consider the importance of balance and self-control in your eating habits. Musonius Rufus advised against gluttony and luxurious eating, advocating for simple, natural, and healthy foods. This means focusing on nourishment rather than indulgence. A balanced diet, in the Stoic sense, includes a variety of foods that provide essential nutrients without excess. It is about eating to live, not living to eat. This approach helps you maintain physical health and mental clarity. It lets you focus on what is truly important in life.

Adopting a Stoic diet involves mindful eating and careful meal planning. Mindful eating involves being fully present during meals, savoring each bite, and recognizing hunger and fullness cues. Begin by getting rid of distractions such as phones or televisions while eating. Take small bites, chew slowly, and appreciate the flavors and textures of your food. This practice not only enhances your eating experience but also helps prevent overeating. Planning balanced meals involves incorporating a variety of whole foods, like fruits, vegetables, whole grains, nuts, and lean proteins. Avoid processed foods and excessive sugars, as they can impair both physical health and mental focus.

The benefits of a Stoic diet are manifold. Physically, eating according to Stoic principles can lead to improved health and energy levels. A rich, whole-food diet nourishes your body with the needed nutrients for optimal function, reducing the risk of chronic diseases. Mentally, a balanced diet enhances clarity and focus. When your body is well-nourished, your mind is sharper, and you can think more clearly. This mental clarity supports better decision-making and emotional regulation, which are critical aspects of Stoic living.

One example of a balanced, Stoic-inspired meal plan might include a breakfast of oatmeal topped with fresh berries and nuts, a lunch of a quinoa and vegetable salad with a light vinaigrette, and a grilled fish dinner with steamed vegetables and a side of brown rice. Snacks could include fresh fruit, yogurt, or a handful of almonds. These meals are simple, nutritious, and satisfying, aligning with Musonius Rufus's dietary recommendations. Practicing moderation in food choices means being mindful of portion sizes and avoiding extremes. It is about finding a balance to support your health without overindulgence.

Tips for Practicing Moderation in Food Choices

1. **Portion Control**: Serve smaller portions to avoid returning for seconds. Use smaller plates to help visually control serving sizes.
2. **Listen to Your Body**: Heed your body's hunger and fullness cues. Eat when you are hungry. Then, stop when you are satisfied, not when you are stuffed.
3. **Choose Whole Foods**: Focus on foods close to their natural state. Your diet should include fresh vegetables, fruits, whole grains, and lean proteins.

4. **Limit Processed Foods**: Reduce processed foods containing high amounts of unhealthy fats, salt, and sugar. These foods can lead to overeating and poor health outcomes.

5. **Enjoy Treats in Moderation**: Allow occasional treats, but keep them infrequent and in small portions. This prevents feelings of deprivation while maintaining overall dietary balance.

By embracing these Stoic dietary principles, you can foster a healthier relationship with food. This approach nourishes your body and aligns with the Stoic values of balance, self-control, and mindful living, contributing to physical well-being and mental clarity.

PHYSICAL EXERCISE: BUILDING STRENGTH AND DISCIPLINE

Physical exercise is significant in Stoic philosophy, aligning seamlessly with the principles of strength and discipline. Epictetus often emphasized the importance of physical training. He famously said, "No man is free who is not master of himself." This quote highlights the Stoic belief that control over one's body is as crucial as control over one's mind. Historical accounts reveal that Stoics like Epictetus and Musonius Rufus viewed physical exercise as a means to maintain health and cultivate self-discipline and resilience. They believed that enduring physical discomfort in training mirrored the mental toughness required to face life's challenges.

Incorporating exercise into your daily life can start with setting clear fitness goals. Start by figuring out what you want to achieve, whether building strength, improving endurance, or enhancing flexibility. After you have your goals, break them down into smaller, manageable steps. For example, to complete a marathon, begin with short distances and gradually increase them. This approach makes the goal more attainable and keeps you motivated. Creating a balanced workout plan is equally essential. Ensure your routine includes cardiovascular exercises, strength training, and flexibility workouts. This balance helps you build overall fitness and prevents burnout.

Discipline and resilience are at the heart of physical training. Regular exercise builds mental toughness, teaching you to push through discomfort and stay committed. Techniques for maintaining exercise consistency include setting a fixed time for workouts and treating it as nonnegotiable. Much like your morning meditation or evening reflection, make exercise a part of your daily routine. Overcoming physical and mental barriers requires a resilient mindset. When faced with obstacles like fatigue or lack of motivation, remember the long-term benefits and your initial goals. Visualization can be a powerful tool; envision yourself achieving your goals and the sense of accomplishment it will bring.

Consider practical activities to illustrate the Stoic approach to physical fitness. A daily workout routine might start with a morning run or a yoga session to invigorate your body and mind. Follow it with strength training exercises, such as push-ups, squats, and planks, which require minimal equipment and can be done anywhere. End with stretching exercises to improve flexibility and prevent injuries. This routine, inspired by Stoic principles, builds physical strength and mental resilience. Reflecting on the benefits of physical training can further reinforce your commitment. Spend a few minutes after each workout to jot down how you feel. Note improvements in your strength, endurance, and overall well-being. This reflection helps you stay motivated and recognize the progress you have made.

Exercise: Reflecting on the Benefits of Physical Training

Steps:

1. **Post-Workout Reflection**: Find a quiet space to sit and reflect after completing your workout.
2. **Journal Entry**: Write about the physical sensations you experienced during the workout. Did you feel stronger, more energized, or more flexible?
3. **Mental and Emotional Benefits**: Reflect on how the exercise impacted your mood and mental state. Did you feel more focused, less stressed, or more resilient?
4. **Progress Tracking**: Note any improvements or milestones achieved. Have you increased your running distance, lifted heavier weights, or held a plank longer?

By consistently reflecting on these aspects, you reinforce the positive outcomes of physical training, making it easier to remain committed to your fitness goals. The Stoic approach to exercise is not about achieving perfection but about continuous improvement and resilience. As Epictetus said, "No great thing is created suddenly." This principle applies to physical fitness as much as it does to any other aspect of life.

COMMUNITY AND RELATIONSHIPS: APPLYING STOIC PRINCIPLES SOCIALLY

Community and relationships lie at the heart of Stoic philosophy. Hierocles, a Stoic philosopher, introduced the concept of the circle of concern, which illustrates the importance of expanding our empathy and compassion. He visualized relationships as concentric circles, starting from the self and extending outward to include family, friends, fellow citizens, and eventually all of humanity. This model encourages us to draw people from the outer circles into our inner circles, fostering a sense of interconnectedness and mutual support. Empathy and compassion are vital in this process because they allow us to deeply understand and care for others.

Applying Stoic principles in social interactions begins with practicing empathy and understanding. One effective technique is active listening. When engaging with others, focus entirely on what they say without interrupting or planning your response. This displays respect and helps you better understand their perspective. Another method is to put yourself in their shoes. Imagine how you would feel in their situation and respond with compassion and kindness. These practices strengthen relationships and align with the Stoic virtues of justice and wisdom.

Resolving conflicts with Stoic calmness involves maintaining composure and focusing on rational solutions. When disagreements arise, take a moment to breathe deeply and calm your mind. Approach the situation with a focus on facts rather than emotions. Use "I" statements to express your feelings and not blame the other person, like, "I feel concerned when meetings start late because it affects my schedule." This approach fosters constructive dialogue and helps resolve conflicts amicably. The goal is to seek understanding and find common ground, reflecting the Stoic commitment to fairness and harmony.

Strong community ties offer numerous benefits, contributing to personal growth and resilience. A supportive community gives a sense of belonging and mutual support, which is essential for navigating life's challenges. Engaging in community service is an excellent way to embody Stoic principles. Volunteering for local charities, organizing community clean-up events, or mentoring young people exemplify actionable Stoic values. These activities benefit others and enrich your life, fostering a sense of purpose and fulfillment.

The benefits of mutual support and shared values in a community are profound. You feel understood and validated when you are part of a community that shares your values. This support network can offer guidance, encouragement, and practical help during difficult times. For instance, being part of a Stoic study group or community can provide a space to discuss Stoic teachings, share experiences, and support each other's growth. These interactions strengthen your commitment to Stoic principles and enhance your personal development.

Consider a practical example of a community project inspired by Stoic values. Imagine organizing a neighborhood garden where residents gather to plant and maintain a communal space. This project promotes cooperation, environmental stewardship, and a sense of shared responsibility. It also provides a venue for fostering relationships and practicing Stoic virtues like patience, perseverance, and gratitude. Such initiatives create a stronger, more connected community.

Exercise: Reflecting on Personal Relationships and Areas for Improvement

Take some time to reflect on your relationships. Think about your interactions with family, friends, colleagues, and neighbors. Are there areas where you could practice more empathy and understanding? Identify specific actions to improve these relationships. Write down your reflections and make a plan to implement these changes. This exercise helps you apply Stoic principles in your social life, enhancing your relationships and building a stronger sense of community.

Integrating these Stoic practices into social interactions improves relationships and contributes to a more compassionate and connected community. Empathy, understanding, and mutual support align with the Stoic commitment to living a virtuous and meaningful life.

LIFELONG LEARNING: CONTINUING YOUR STOIC PATH

Lifelong learning is a cornerstone of Stoic philosophy. Seneca often spoke about the value of ongoing education. He famously said, "As long as you live, keep learning how to live." This quote underscores the importance of continuous self-improvement. In the historical context of Stoicism, education was not just about accumulating knowledge. It was also about cultivating wisdom and virtue. Stoic philosophers believed that learning should be an unending pursuit to understand the world and improve oneself.

Engaging in lifelong learning involves setting clear learning goals. Start by identifying areas you want to explore or skills you wish to develop. These goals should be aligned with your values, specific, and measurable. For instance, to deepen your understanding of Stoic philosophy, set a goal to read one Stoic text each month. Accessing diverse educational resources is crucial. Utilize books, online courses, podcasts, and lectures to expand your knowledge. Libraries, educational platforms like Coursera or Khan Academy, and podcasts on Stoic philosophy can be invaluable tools in this process. The key is to remain steadfastly committed and consistent in your learning efforts.

Curiosity and open-mindedness play significant roles in lifelong learning. Maintaining a curious mind means constantly asking questions and seeking answers. It involves being open to new ideas and perspectives, even those that challenge your beliefs. Techniques for cultivating curiosity include reading widely, engaging in discussions, and exploring topics outside your comfort zone. Methods for expanding knowledge and perspectives involve seeking out diverse viewpoints and experiences. Traveling, meeting new people, and participating in cultural activities can all contribute to a broader understanding of the world. This openness enriches your knowledge and fosters empathy and compassion, aligning with Stoic virtues.

Consider the example of a self-directed learning project to illustrate effective lifelong learning practices. Imagine you have a keen interest in ancient philosophy. Start by creating a reading list that includes works by Plato, Aristotle, and Stoic philosophers like Epictetus and Marcus Aurelius. Set aside dedicated time each week for reading and reflection. Take notes, and consider joining a study group to discuss your insights. This project deepens your understanding of philosophy and enhances your analytical and critical thinking skills. It is a practical demonstration of how continuous learning can be structured and flexible, allowing you to explore your interests deeply.

Exercise: Creating a Personal Learning Plan

1. **Identify Learning Goals**: Write down specific areas you want to learn about or skills you wish to develop. Ensure these goals are clear and achievable.
2. **Access Resources**: List the books, courses, podcasts, and other resources you will use. Be diverse in your choices to get a well-rounded perspective.
3. **Set a Schedule**: Allocate specific times each week for learning activities. Treat this time as a priority, much like your daily routines.
4. **Reflect** and Adjust: Review your progress regularly. Reflect on what you have learned and adjust your plan as needed.

Engaging in lifelong learning through these methods aligns with Stoic principles and fosters a more prosperous, more fulfilling life. You continuously grow and evolve by setting clear goals, accessing diverse resources, and maintaining curiosity. This relentless pursuit of knowledge and wisdom is a testament to the Stoic commitment to self-improvement and virtue.

BUILDING A STOIC SUPPORT NETWORK: FINDING LIKE-MINDED INDIVIDUALS

Connecting with like-minded individuals can profoundly enhance your Stoic practice. Epictetus emphasized the importance of companionship, stating, "Associate with those who will make a better man of you." This underscores the value of mutual support in Stoic practice. A network of Stoic practitioners provides encouragement, shared learning, and accountability. In this interconnected age, finding such a network is easier than ever.

Start by identifying like-minded individuals. Join forums or social media groups online about Stoicism. Platforms like Reddit, Facebook, and specialized forums offer vibrant communities where you can connect with others who share your interest in Stoic philosophy. Local meetups and Stoic events are also excellent opportunities. Websites like Meetup.com often list gatherings where you can meet fellow Stoics. Initiate conversations. Be open to learning from others by asking questions, and sharing your experiences, and

Fostering supportive relationships within this network involves active engagement. Regularly contribute to discussions, offer support and encouragement, and share valuable resources. Building a supportive network works both ways. Offer your insights and be receptive to feedback. Over time, these interactions build trust and camaraderie. Consider starting a Stoic study group. Invite a few like-minded individuals to meet in person or virtually regularly to discuss Stoic texts and reflect on their application in daily life. This creates a structured environment for shared learning and growth.

The benefits of a Stoic support network are immense. Having a group of Stoic practitioners provides a sense of belonging and mutual support. When you face challenges, your network can offer encouragement and practical advice based on Stoic principles. Shared learning within the group enhances everyone's understanding and application of Stoicism. For instance, a member might share a personal story of how they applied the dichotomy of control in a difficult situation, offering insights and inspiration to others.

Support networks also provide accountability. When you commit to practicing Stoic principles, having a group to check in with helps you stay on track. Sharing your goals and progress with the group creates a sense of responsibility. If you need more consistency in your Stoic practices, your network can offer encouragement and practical tips to help you stay committed. This mutual accountability strengthens everyone's resolve to live according to Stoic virtues.

An example of a Stoic study group illustrates these benefits. Imagine a small group that meets weekly to discuss a chapter from Marcus Aurelius's *Meditations*. Each member shares their reflections, challenges, and insights. The group offers diverse perspectives and practical advice, enriching everyone's understanding of the text. Over time, members develop strong bonds, supporting each other in their Stoic practices and personal growth.

Exercise: Reflecting on the Value of Supportive Relationships

Take a moment to reflect on the supportive relationships in your life. Think about how these relationships have influenced your personal growth and resilience. Write down the names of individuals who have supported you and describe specific instances where their support made a difference. Reflect on how you can foster and strengthen these relationships further. This exercise highlights the importance of a supportive network and encourages you to nurture these connections actively.

Building a Stoic support network enhances your practice and enriches your life with meaningful connections. By actively seeking and fostering supportive relationships, you create a strong base for continuous growth and resilience, aligning with the Stoic commitment to living a virtuous and fulfilling life.

This chapter explored how to structure your day with Stoic practices, adopt a healthy and moderate diet, build strength and discipline through physical exercise, enhance social interactions and community involvement, engage in lifelong learning, and find like-minded individuals for mutual support. These practices, rooted in Stoic principles, offer a comprehensive approach to living a balanced, resilient, and fulfilling life. Next, we delve into the practical application of these principles in navigating modern life's complexities, providing actionable strategies for integrating Stoicism into your daily routine.

CONCLUSION

As we reach the end of our journey through the advanced techniques of Stoic philosophy, let's reflect on the key components that can transform your life. We have delved into the depths of Stoic principles and explored how these ancient teachings can be applied to modern-day challenges.

At the core of Stoicism lies its advanced philosophy. We have explored virtue ethics, emphasizing the importance of developing moral character and living by nature. The concept of the dichotomy of control teaches you to focus on what you can control—your thoughts and actions—while accepting what is beyond your control. This powerful mindset shift can significantly reduce stress and anxiety. The Stoic view of fate, encapsulated in the idea of *amor fati,* encourages you to embrace life's challenges with acceptance and resilience.

Building emotional resilience is a cornerstone of Stoic practice. Techniques like cognitive reframing allow you to change your perspective on challenging situations, turning obstacles into opportunities for growth. *Premeditatio malorum,* contemplating potential misfortunes, prepares you mentally for adversity. This foresight enables you to face difficulties with a composed and resilient mindset.

Meditation and reflection are integral to internalizing Stoic teachings. Morning meditation establishes a positive tone for the day, aligning your mind with Stoic principles. Evening reflection helps you review your actions and thoughts, fostering self-awareness and personal growth. Journaling, a daily Stoic practice, allows you to track your progress and cultivate emotional resilience. Visualization techniques, like negative visualization, help you appreciate what you have and prepare for future challenges.

In applying Stoicism to modern life, you have learned strategies for navigating social media, managing workplace stress, handling life transitions, and building emotional intelligence. These practical applications demonstrate the timeless relevance of Stoic principles, helping you navigate today's complexities with wisdom and resilience.

Insights from Stoic philosophers like Marcus Aurelius, Epictetus, Seneca, Musonius Rufus, and Hierocles offer valuable lessons. Marcus Aurelius's *Meditations* teaches the importance of self-reflection and humility in leadership. Epictetus's *The Enchiridion* emphasizes personal responsibility and the dichotomy of control. Seneca's *Letters from a Stoic* provides wisdom on mental preparation and inner peace. Musonius Rufus highlights the importance of virtue in daily life, while Hierocles's circle of concern stresses empathy and community.

Cultivating virtues and overcoming adversity are essential aspects of Stoic practice. Wisdom, justice, courage, and moderation guide your actions, helping you navigate life's challenges with integrity and strength. Resilience in adversity builds mental toughness, enabling you to learn from failures and grow stronger.

Aligning your actions with Stoic principles can lead to personal growth and professional success. Setting goals that reflect your values and virtues leads to purposeful living. Rational decision-making, effective time management, and ethical leadership are critical to Stoic success. Overcoming public speaking anxiety and building confidence through Stoic exercises enhance your professional capabilities.

Creating a Stoic lifestyle involves structuring your day with Stoic practices, adopting a healthy diet, incorporating physical exercise, and building strong community ties. Lifelong learning and finding like-minded individuals for support are crucial for continuous personal growth. These elements create a balanced, resilient, and fulfilling life.

As you insert these practices into your daily routine, you will find that Stoicism offers a practical and robust framework for living with wisdom, strength, and inner peace. Remember, the journey of Stoic practice is ongoing. Continuously reflect on your actions, learn from experiences, and strive to embody Stoic virtues in every aspect of your life.

In closing, I encourage you to act. Start with small, manageable steps. Practice morning meditation, engage in mindful eating, or join a Stoic community. These actions will set you on a path of personal growth and resilience. Embrace life's challenges and opportunities, knowing you have the tools to navigate them with a Stoic mindset.

Reflect on this quote from Marcus Aurelius, which we began with: "You have power over your mind—not outside events. Realize this, and you will find strength." Let this wisdom guide you as you continue your journey. Embrace Stoic principles, cultivate virtues, and strive for a life of wisdom, resilience, and inner peace.

As I wrote this book, I aimed to empower you to navigate life's challenges with courage and wisdom. I hope the insights and practices shared here inspire a lifelong journey of self-reliance and personal growth. Thank you for embarking on this path with me. May you continue to gain wisdom, strength, and peace.

FURTHER READING

The Daily Stoic, Ryan Holiday

The Enchiridion, Epictetus

The Handbook of Virtue Ethics, Stan van Hooft

"How Stoicism Could Help You Build Resilience," Donald J. Robinson, Psychology Today, https://www.psychologytoday.com/us/blog/the-psychology-stoicism/202208/how-stoicism-could-help-you-build-resilience

How to Be a Stoic, Massimo Pigliucci

Letters from a Stoic, Seneca

"Musonius Rufus," William O. Stephens, The Internet Encyclopedia of Philosophy, https://iep.utm.edu/musonius/

The Obstacle Is the Way, Ryan Holiday

"Social Media Use and Its Connection to Mental Health: A Systematic Review," Fazida Karim, et al., *Cureus,* https://www.ncbi.nlm.nih.gov/pmc/articles/PMC7364393/

"The Western origins of mindfulness therapy in ancient Rome," Andrea E. Cavanna, et al., *Neurological Sciences,* https://www.ncbi.nlm.nih.gov/pmc/articles/PMC10175387/

Printed in Great Britain
by Amazon

58562064R00077

BEING CARLOS ALCARAZ

BEING CARLOS ALCARAZ

THE MAN BEHIND THE SMILE

MARK HODGKINSON

First published in Great Britain in 2025 by Cassell, an imprint of
Octopus Publishing Group Ltd
Carmelite House
50 Victoria Embankment
London EC4Y 0DZ
www.octopusbooks.co.uk

An Hachette UK Company
www.hachette.co.uk

The authorized representative in the EEA is Hachette Ireland, 8 Castlecourt Centre,
Dublin 15, D15 XTP3, Ireland (email: info@hbgi.ie)

Distributed in the US by Hachette Book Group
1290 Avenue of the Americas, 4th and 5th Floors
New York, NY 10104

Distributed in Canada by Canadian Manda Group
664 Annette St., Toronto, Ontario, Canada M6S 2C8

Hardback ISBN 978-1-78840-623-9
Trade paperback ISBN 978-1-78840-624-6
eISBN 978-1-78840-626-0

A CIP catalogue record for this book is available from the British Library.

Printed and bound in Great Britain.

1 3 5 7 9 10 8 6 4 2

Publisher: Trevor Davies
Project Editor: Rimsha Falak
Copy Editor: Monica Hope
Creative Director: Mel Four
Designer: Clare Sivell
Production Managers: Nic Jones & Lucy Carter
Picture Research Manager: Jennifer Veall

For Dad.

FOREWORD
BY GARBIÑE MUGURUZA

Former world number one,
Wimbledon champion and Roland-Garros champion.

It's funny, because when you talk to Carlos off the court he comes across as a bit shy.

I've had the chance to do a few photoshoots with him and attend the same galas; and when I was still playing, we would often cross paths in the hallways or at lunch during tournaments. We've spoken many times. Maybe he's a little reserved in certain settings, but that shyness disappears the moment he steps onto the court. He commands the centre stage with confidence, almost as if he's telling the crowd: 'Look at me – I'm here and I'm ready to give my best.' On the court, Carlos exudes self-assurance. His body language shifts, reflecting his belief in his game, his mindset and everything he does.

One of the most striking things about Carlos is his smile. If you're familiar with professional tennis, you'll know that's not the norm. Most players maintain a serious demeanour. Roger Federer was composed and stoic, Rafael Nadal was intensely focused and Novak Djokovic, while expressive and entertaining, still radiates intensity. Many players adopt a poker face, not wanting to reveal too much. They don't want to show too many of their emotions. Better not to give anything away. Some even convey the weight of competition, as if to say, 'I love this, but it's also demanding.' Then there's Carlos – this young, energetic player who hits with power, executes daring drop shots and does it all with a smile. Watching him, you can't help but think, 'Wow, he really loves this game.'

Carlos thrives in the spotlight. He loves playing in front of and even engaging with a crowd. There's no doubt he feels the pressure, but he carries it with remarkable ease. It often seems like he plays on instinct, almost unconsciously. Even in tense moments, he finds a way to smile – he's just that kind of player. He's fun.

When I watch Carlos play, I can't help but compare his energy to that of a playful puppy – full of enthusiasm, curiosity and joy. There's still an innocence about him, a natural authenticity that hasn't been shaped or hardened by the professional sports industry. He hasn't become robotic in his approach and hopefully he never will. His presence is refreshing for tennis; he radiates positivity, reminding us that competition can be both fierce and joyful. That's something fans truly appreciate.

What makes Carlos so special is his ability to blend traditional Spanish tennis elements – topspin, quick movement and resilience – with an aggressive, dynamic approach. He's creative, bold and fearless, integrating drop shots and powerful winners into his game. He's taken the strong foundations of Spanish tennis and evolved them into something even more assertive and exciting.

Carlos is already an icon in Spain. His popularity has surpassed even Rafa's at the same age, thanks in part to the excitement and awareness Rafa himself brought to the sport. With Rafa stopping in 2024, joining

Roger in retirement, and Novak nearing the latter stages of his career, Carlos has stepped into the spotlight at just the right moment. He has both the game and the charisma to take the lead in the next era of tennis.

In Spain, his rise has been extraordinary. Many people had wondered who could possibly fill Rafa's shoes. Yet while the comparisons are natural, Carlos is forging his own path. It's easy to say, 'He's the next Nadal,' but Carlos is his own player, with his own style and personality. He has undoubtedly felt the weight of those comparisons but his team has managed expectations well, allowing him to develop in his own way. Rafa was known for his relentless consistency and unwavering focus. Carlos brings something different – a joyful, expressive and bold approach that resonates with fans worldwide.

Because it's not just Spain that loves him. Carlos wins people over everywhere he plays. He has energy and authenticity, always staying true to who he is. On and off the court, he remains humble, with no unnecessary drama or controversy. He's a fantastic role model for young players. As a Spaniard myself, I feel proud that the new face of tennis hails from Spain, celebrating victories with a passionate, '*Vamos!*'

Right now, Carlos is the guy. He's young, successful and full of life. He has already achieved so much – winning Grand Slam titles, reaching world number one – and yet he remains down-to-earth. He still makes light-hearted, funny remarks; and when he speaks in Spanish there's an endearing warmth to him. He's relatable, making the dream of tennis success feel attainable for young players.

If there's one thing you could never say about Carlos, it's that he's snobbish. His background, his accent, his personality, they all reflect his humble roots in the south of Spain. He has put Murcia on the map – it's one of the Mediterranean provinces in Spain with great beaches and warm people known for their easy-going nature, and Carlos embodies that spirit. His family seem grounded, too, and with a clear idea of their role. It's remarkable that such a phenomenal talent emerged from Murcia, rather than Madrid or Barcelona, where there are often greater opportunities in sports. It just goes to show that talent and determination can come from anywhere.

To see a star of his calibre remain humble and grounded is rare – not only in tennis, but in any sport or field. Being around Carlos is a pleasure because he carries himself with such authenticity and humility. Who knows what the future holds? He may evolve as a player, as tends to happen, but I hope he always stays true to the person he is today. His personality, his attitude and his love for the game make him not just a great player, but a fantastic ambassador for tennis.

Coarse, some say of the Murcian accent, possibly a little unkindly. Maybe even comic, others suggest. Entire sentences seem to be constructed only with vowels, according to Emilio Sánchez, a grandee of Spanish tennis. When Carlos Alcaraz speaks Spanish, it's with an accent. While it's not the thickest of Murcian accents, you can hear his provincial roots in his interviews. He's not trying to sound as though he grew up in some chichi Madrid neighbourhood. Lola Jiménez Rivas, Alcaraz's English teacher at his senior school, says she can even detect her old pupil's accent when he is speaking English. For some, Alcaraz's voice is part of his appeal; there's an authenticity and an informality with him that you don't often get with other tennis players.

His entire life, from tennis-obsessed boy to tennis-obsessed teenager to tennis-obsessed man, Carlos Alcaraz Garfia has lived in El Palmar, a village just a few miles to the south of Murcia, a city in sun-bleached south-east Spain in a region of the same name (nationally, it's a middling city). El Palmar is a place of orange trees, palm trees and noticeably purer, fresher air than the city, along with low-rise apartment blocks and other modest housing. There's a large hospital, of a size you might not expect to find in a village, and the population is around 20,000 – which, as Alcaraz has reflected, is about the same number of people who were inside the Arthur Ashe Stadium when he won the 2022 US Open, his first Grand Slam title.

A long way from the borough of Queens in New York City – both geographically and spiritually – El Palmar is a quiet, unpretentious spot in a region of Spain that, with its almost year-round sunshine and fertile fields for growing fruit, vegetables and flowers, is known as 'Europe's Orchard'. (Turns out these are also excellent conditions for growing a tennis player.)

If the villagers tell you Alcaraz is the best possible ambassador for this part of Spain, they really mean it; his official partnership with the Murcia tourism body has included commercials that showed him diving off a boat, kayaking and playing some beach tennis. 'Carlos has truly put Murcia on the map for so many people who might not have known much about it before,' says Paula Badosa, a Spanish tennis player who has been as high as number two in the women's singles rankings. 'Now, when folks hear "Murcia", they immediately think of him – his incredible talent, his vibrant spirit and his inspiring story. There's so much pride in that. It's heartwarming to see an entire region come together in support of Carlos, and how his achievements have brought more visibility and recognition to Murcia, not just in Spain, but all around the globe.'

Alcaraz's voice, with his local accent, might just be a stronger advert for Murcia than any footage of him splashing around in the water. 'Carlitos's accent is quite Murcian,' says Alfredo Sarria, a close friend of the Alcaraz family, who has known Carlos since he was three years old. 'Let's say the Spanish spoken in the provinces furthest from Madrid sounds different. When Carlitos speaks, people like that he doesn't try to hide his origins. He's proud of those roots. Carlitos sounds closer [to spectators, to television viewers or anyone on social media] because he uses language and has a way of speaking that is very familiar to the fans who listen to him. He's not as formal as other players.'

In keeping with this more relaxed approach, which seems to be typical of people in El Palmar and around Murcia, Carlos prefers not to be called Carlos. Sounds too serious, he says. For years, people have been calling him Carlitos, which he likes as it's friendlier and more personal; and when he is talking to himself, such as during matches, or when he is giving himself an off-court talk in front of the bathroom mirror, he's Charlie. He's the global star, massive around the world, who's regularly called the diminutive form of his name: Carlitos. That's mostly how people address him in El Palmar, where everyone pretty much knows everyone else, or at the very least knows of them and follows them on Instagram.

You can tell El Palmar isn't a moneyed village, the locals say, by looking at the apartment blocks and houses. 'This isn't a rich area and it isn't a poor area. It's normal. It's in the middle,' says Alcaraz's primary-school English teacher, Laura Caballero. 'It's a humble area. People work.' Alcaraz's mother, for instance, used to have a job at the IKEA store in Murcia. Alcaraz doesn't come from money. But while the family didn't have many luxuries when he was growing up, and his upbringing wasn't as comfortable as Rafa Nadal's was in Majorca, Alcaraz has said they didn't lack anything either.

For a while, including when he won his first Grand Slam titles, Alcaraz's family lived above a kebab shop. No more. They haven't yet moved – at the time of writing, they're still building a large family home outside the village – but the kebab shop has gone, replaced by a sushi restaurant. There's also a brow bar beneath their home, as well as a couple of hints that the youngest-ever men's world number one and the highest-earning tennis player grew up on this street and still lives there with his parents and brothers. Although Carlos has a small, three-room apartment in El Palmar, he prefers to sleep at the family home, on a small bed in a small room packed with his trophies, his sneaker collection and what looks like IKEA furniture (sometimes he trains at home, in the apartment's outside space). But if you weren't looking closely you could easily miss the tennis-related street art: a small mural of a racquet near the entrance to their apartment building and another of a tennis ball on a court. Murals aside, it's a sporty street, with a tennis court where Alcaraz went to hit some balls with his father for the first time in years when testing a forearm injury in the spring of 2024, along with a small outdoor gym, a tiny running track and a space that doubles as a basketball court and a mini football pitch. There's a large park at one end of the road and a café at the other, and from there it's a short walk to Alcaraz's old primary school.

Most days after lessons, one of his primary-school teachers says, Carlos the schoolboy would go to Real Sociedad Club de Campo Murcia. The country club. But not the kind of country club you might now be picturing, where the super-wealthy indulge in their leisure pursuits. It's not a country club with that sort of demographic and polish. It's earthier than that.

*

Tennis is in my blood, Carlos Alcaraz says. Oddly, there are also pigeons in his back story. Real Sociedad Club de Campo Murcia – where he learned the sport, and where he often still trains today – hasn't always been a country club. Situated on the edge of El Palmar, it used to be a clay-pigeon shooting range, which is why it's still sometimes known as 'Tiro de Pichón' or 'Pigeon Strike'. If that's your thing, you can still shoot at the club today, though there are only a handful of members who have a licence to do so and the guns come out only on Sundays. Until a few years ago, you would have seen a lot of horses there, as the club was one of the largest equestrian facilities in the area; but they are all gone now and it is tennis that dominates, with clay and hard courts and a giant practice wall. Built on several levels, the club has plenty of other facilities, including basketball and football pitches as well as a gym and a pool where in the summer children cool down after tennis.

'My second home,' Alcaraz says of the club, somewhere he thinks of as 'the start of everything'. That's where, at three years old, Carlos first played tennis, using a racquet that was bigger than him and that he didn't have the strength or large enough hands to hold properly. It was also at the club that he made many of the friends he is still close to today.

There's a family story about Carlos hiding his father's car keys for several days that tells you plenty about how much he loved to play tennis and how he reacted when he was prevented from going to the country club. This episode began with Carlos misbehaving – nothing terrible, just 'some typical child's prank', according to Alfredo Sarria, who is so close with Alcaraz's father that he thinks of him as a brother. As a punishment, Alcaraz's dad said his son wasn't allowed to go to tennis training. Carlos's response was to take his dad's car keys and hide them in a bin. 'Not being able to go to tennis training was what hurt Carlitos the most – [hiding the keys] was his revenge,' says Sarria. Alcaraz's father searched for the keys for days on end, until eventually Carlos confessed. 'The anecdote about the keys helps us understand how tennis has always been the most important thing for Carlos,' Sarria says.

Alcaraz couldn't get enough. Some children are forced by their parents to play tennis. While Alcaraz was born into a tennis family, he never needed convincing to spend more time on court or at the practice wall (the practice partner that is always free to play and never misses). The opposite was true. Carlos would sometimes cry if he had to leave the country club. Some evenings, it would get to after 9pm and Alcaraz's father, tired after a long day's work, would be keen to go home but Carlos, still rallying against the wall at that time of night, would plead with him: 'Play with me, here on the wall.' Alcaraz's dad would agree they could stay for another 20 minutes, but then that 20 minutes would be up, and then perhaps another half an hour would go by, with Carlos still hitting the ball against the wall, and that would be enough. Alcaraz's father would say: 'This can't go on; dinner's ready and we have to go home.' Carlos would then start crying again, his father told *The New York Times*. Getting Alcaraz to leave the club without tears or complaints was almost impossible.

As Alcaraz's love for tennis grew, so did his ability. The first time Kiko Navarro watched Alcaraz playing tennis, the boy was just four years old and was rallying with his father. Kiko, who would later coach Carlos, was astounded by the child's technique. Around that age, it was also clear to Alcaraz's father that his son had natural ability. Carlos had excellent coordination and could quickly pick up the technical details without having them explained to him – he learned through watching. Alcaraz's father was realizing, he has said, that there was 'something special' about his son, and that he should help his boy to develop those tennis skills (later in the book, we will be looking at how Carlos became such a creative force). From the age of five or six, Carlos built his life around tennis, in the sense that that was his focus every day – he would much rather spend hours on court, or hitting the ball against the practice wall, than, say, going to the cinema or doing anything else.

Visit the country club today and you're almost certain to run into a Carlos Alcaraz, whether that's the son, the father (who has the same name) or a cardboard cutout of the son. Some days, you'll see all three. Drive or walk up the hill from El Palmar and the first thing you notice when arriving at the club is the giant design celebrating Carlitos's US Open victory and his rise to world number one. Inside the clubhouse, there's a cardboard Alcaraz – which was created by one of his sponsors – near the bar. You might bump into the player himself during the off-season or between tournaments.

The other Carlos Alcaraz – the father – is the director of a tennis academy at the club, which he founded in 1993. Originally called Murcia Escuela de Tenis – the Murcia Tennis School – it's now the Carlos Alcaraz Academy so it's named after both father and son (for some time, Alcaraz's dad had been cautious about using the family name in this way). The Carlos Alcaraz Academy runs camps around the world, including in the United States, Mexico and Australia, where children and adults are taught using the same methods that helped Carlos to become the world number one and to 'enjoy the game with a smile'. It's very much a family operation, as Carlos's older brother Álvaro is one of the coaches, while one of his younger brothers, Jaime, trains there and Carlos, when he has the time, is becoming more involved. But with the father often travelling with Carlos, he delegates to the rest of the team, including Sarria, the academy's technical director and general manager, who is regarded as the dad's right-hand man (as illustrated by a photograph showing Carlos holding the US Open trophy in 2022 with his dad on one side and Sarria on the other).

When the father isn't on the tennis tour with Carlos, he's at the club, where one member describes him as being 'super low-key'. Everyone says the same thing: there's nothing flashy or showy about any of the Alcaraz family. 'They just blend in with everyone else at the club. They're just normal people and that's what's so great about them,' the member says. 'They're not walking around the club saying, "We've got a Grand Slam champion in our family, look at us." There's none of that. They're lovely people. They've got a nice way about them. I couldn't say a bad word about them.'

Alcaraz's great-uncle – not called Carlos Alcaraz – is the club president and a central figure in its history. Hanging by the courts are signs with large red lettering asking for *silencio*; this is somewhere where players take their training and matches seriously, as they should do. But, as you might expect from the country club that produced Alcaraz, there's a happy, joyful atmosphere around the place.

The country club is reasonably priced, members say. A family pays a joining fee of around 2,000 euros and after that it's around 50 euros a month, with an additional cost of a euro to play tennis for an hour and another euro if you use the court lights. Membership numbers increased because of the Covid pandemic – tennis was among the first sports that was allowed again when the restrictions eased, which attracted families to the country club – and after Alcaraz's emergence they kept moving upwards.

Officially, Alcaraz's father hasn't coached his son since he was very young. Unofficially, he has. The dad has been a greater influence on Carlitos's tennis career than the family might choose to let on. You might say that for many years Alcaraz's father coached his son indirectly – passing on information through others – while overseeing his child's training programme. And maybe the most important lesson that Alcaraz's father taught his son wasn't how to hit a forehand or the disguise needed for a drop shot, or anything technical, but something intangible and also fundamental to who Carlos is as a player. It was his dad, after all, who showed Alcaraz to play tennis, the athlete has said, 'with passion and with love'.

'If you know Carlitos and his family, as I do, you will understand his father was always his coach until Carlitos started training with Juan Carlos Ferrero at the age of 15,' says Sarria. 'All of the coaches that Carlitos had were contracted by his father, and it was always his dad who was guiding his career. Always, always. I've seen that. Before Juan Carlos, Carlitos's father was his coach. But the father is never going to tell you this.'

Speak to Alcaraz's father for just ten minutes, Sarria says, and you will come to appreciate he knows more about tennis than anyone else in the sport. Alcaraz says his dad's whole life has been about tennis. Like many other Spaniards around his age, Alcaraz's father had been inspired by the example of Manuel Santana, Spain's first Grand Slam men's singles champion in the 1960s, who did so much to end the perception in the country that only aristocrats could play tennis. In his own modest playing career, Alcaraz's father peaked at number 963 in the world rankings in 1990, and was in the top 40 in Spain, but there's every reason to think he would have risen higher if he had had more financial support (in a later chapter we will be exploring how expensive is to become a tennis player and the piece of good fortune that helped Carlitos to go on to become a multiple Grand Slam champion). Alcaraz's grandfather, also called Carlos Alcaraz and an influential member of the country club, has said his son's forehand was as good as his grandson's (but maybe, he observed, his son's backhand wasn't at the same level as his grandson's). After he stopped playing, Alcaraz's father went on to run his tennis academy in El Palmar.

Alcaraz's father decided against working closely with his son because – with his deep knowledge of tennis – he had seen how some families had been damaged by parents coaching their children. Alcaraz had observed how Sergi Bruguera – a Spaniard who was coached by his father, Lluis, and who won Roland-Garros twice in the 1990s – hadn't always had the easiest or smoothest relationship with his dad. Sergi and Lluis were 'constantly clashing', Alcaraz's father once told *The Times*; and he hoped to get along with his own son, which is why he didn't want to coach him. How could Alcaraz's father have coached Carlos and made it clear to his son when he was talking to him as his coach and when he was speaking to him as his father? Perhaps, Alcaraz's father has mused, he could have put a cap on when he was speaking as a coach and then removed it to go back to being just dad. But, as Alcaraz's dad realized, his son probably wouldn't have fully understood what was going on with a hat. It could have got confusing and messy.

By coaching Carlitos indirectly, Alcaraz's father was doing what he could to avoid the possibility of losing his son. 'Carlitos's father understood what he needed to do if he was going to have a good relationship with his son,' Sarria says. 'He had seen in other families – how if you coach your son, you can lose your son. If you are the coach, you sometimes have to tell your player things they might not like to hear, and that's hard if you're the father. When you're trying to be both a father and a coach, you can have problems; and Carlitos's father understood that. He didn't want to directly coach his son – he put coaches between him and his son.'

Carlos, for his part, is pleased that his father, while involved in his tennis education, didn't try to be a coach as well as a dad. 'That helped me a lot because a lot of fathers don't know how to be a father and a tennis coach,' Alcaraz said on the *Louis Vuitton* podcast. 'When you're at home, you're talking about tennis. If I'm at home and my father spoke too much about tennis, my mother would blow up, she would explode. That's something my father did pretty well.' When he was eight or nine years old, about the only time Carlos would ever get on court with his father was on Sunday evenings, when his coaches wouldn't have been working, and he would say to his dad: 'Let's go to the club and hit some balls for an hour, an hour and a half.'

Carlos Santos, who started coaching Alcaraz when he was five years old and continued until he was 12, called him 'Tarzan': he felt as though the boy was as at home on the tennis court as Tarzan was in the jungle. So at ease on the court, in fact, that sometimes, between points or training drills, Alcaraz would make small mounds out of the clay granules (almost like the tennis equivalent of making sandcastles on the beach). As a young boy, Alcaraz wasn't always the most organized; Santos has recalled how he wasn't always ready to step on court, with his bag and his racquet often not in the same place. Alcaraz didn't always eat properly, according to Santos, who has said that the young Carlos would need others to help him peel an apple or a pear and for a time wouldn't try a banana. But when it was time to play, Alcaraz was engaged. 'Carlos was a very active child who was always very motivated to play,' Santos says. When playing against his peers, or even against older children, Alcaraz didn't ever look nervous when others were watching.

Baseball bats, GoPro cameras and Alcaraz's bedroom mirror were key to his tennis education. To teach Alcaraz how to hit a backhand correctly, Santos would sometimes take the tennis racquet away from the boy and give him a baseball bat. They would walk on to the football pitches at the country club and Alcaraz would hit backhands with a bat. Santos would often bring a GoPro camera to the practice court – and then they would watch the footage back together – as he felt it was important to teach a young Alcaraz about the importance of movement and court positioning. Santos would give Alcaraz homework – he asked him to stand in front of the bedroom mirror and to swish his racquet at the air while studying his reflection, as that would help him to improve his game. 'I would often tell him to practise in front of the mirror. Carlos learned a lot visually,' Santos says of Alcaraz, who had only to watch something twice before figuring out how to do it himself. 'By the time he was just six or seven years old, his technique was perfect.'

Alcaraz's father – with personal experience of how tennis dreams sometimes don't amount to much – didn't get ahead of himself. One of the most dangerous moments for a promising young tennis player is when their parents, carried away by how well they are doing as a child, start to believe they are destined for greatness. That wasn't a concern here. No doubt, Carlos was showing plenty of promise. But, according to Alcaraz's doctor Juanjo López, Alcaraz's father wasn't thinking his son was destined to be the world number one (maybe pause here to consider how Novak Djokovic's father Srdjan used to tell people in Belgrade how his young son was going to be the greatest of all time, and years later he would be proved correct – so that approach can also work). Carlos's dad was aware of how far his son had to go to make something of his tennis. There was something else that Alcaraz's father wasn't doing. While Alcaraz's dad has said in his son's Netflix documentary how he has been living his dream through Carlos, it doesn't appear as though he has been letting that shape his son's career; his advice and guidance are always based on what is best for Carlos.

When Alcaraz was eight or nine – which was when some around the boy first thought there was a possibility he might have a future as a professional tennis player – Alcaraz's father asked Navarro to coach his son. That partnership would continue until Alcaraz was 17 years old (when he was between 15 and 17 years old, Alcaraz worked with both Navarro and Juan Carlos Ferrero). Alcaraz senior had previously coached Navarro himself, so he knew Navarro had strong technique and he liked the way he thought about tennis. Alcaraz's father would still be involved in his son's tennis. 'Carlitos's father didn't want to train. His father considered that wouldn't be good for his son. He wanted to be the father and not the coach,' Kiko says. 'His father said all his opinions to me. His father and I talked a lot.'

Any other father, Navarro says, would have made wrong decisions with a child as talented as Carlitos. Alcaraz has been fortunate to have the father he does, Navarro says. Navarro considers Alcaraz's father to be the most important figure in Alcaraz's career (Sarria, meanwhile, says Alcaraz Senior was the most important person in this story before Carlos turned 15, which was when he started working with Juan Carlos Ferrero). Over the years, Navarro says, Alcaraz's father has made the right decisions for the benefit of his son: 'It's lucky he is an expert, and he knew to step aside at the right moment.'

Carlos would walk around the club with a racquet in one hand, a sandwich in the other and a smile on his face. Only once during his childhood did he lose some of his desire to play tennis and that was when he was told that he would no longer be training with his lifelong friend and rival Pedro Cobacho. They had known each other since Pedro was three years old and Alcaraz was two; and not so long after that had been put together in the same group at the country club. A few years later, they sometimes shared a hotel room if they were staying overnight when travelling to a junior tournament. Having Pedro around had always been fun; it had also been a source of motivation for Alcaraz, who wanted to beat his friend.

Then came the upsetting news that Alcaraz wouldn't be training with Pedro any longer. If Alcaraz wasn't going to be together with Pedro, tennis wouldn't be quite the same. Would it be as fun if Pedro wasn't there with him on court? Alcaraz couldn't understand why he could no longer practise with his best friend and his biggest rival. His motivation dipped, and that was a challenging period for his family and those around him who could see how talented the boy was. They explained to Alcaraz that this was for his own good, as Pedro hadn't developed as a tennis player at the same rate that he had. Carlos had simply become too strong for Pedro, who would sometimes struggle to return or even reach his friend's shots. Their tennis lives, which had been enmeshed for years, separated at that point. But there is still a tennis connection, as Pedro is now one of the coaches for the Carlos Alcaraz Academy. They're also still friends: when Alcaraz is back in El Palmar for a few days they will usually go out for dinner or hang out together.

When Carlos was 12 years old, he went to Roland-Garros with Santos to play in a junior tournament. While he was in Paris, he told a journalist on camera that his dream was to win Roland-Garros and Wimbledon – a video of that interview pops up on social media every so often. They sat on the grass by the Eiffel Tower and watched some of the matches (from the adult tournament) on a big screen. Some things were lost in translation on that trip – Carlos thought he was ordering a cheesecake and got a cheese board, which he passed to his coach to eat instead. But other things were becoming even clearer: this was what he wanted from his life.

Some say there are only two seasons in this part of Spain – summer and winter. It's hot pretty much all year and then suddenly it's winter, but even then it's usually still warm enough to train outside in T-shirt and shorts. Winter quickly passes; soon enough it feels as though it's summer again. The climate makes it an ideal base for a tennis player; you can train there all year round. Before heading to the Australian Open, Alcaraz does his pre-season training in El Palmar and at his coach Juan Carlos Ferrero's academy in Villena near Alicante, which is just over an hour away. He travels enough during the year; there's no need to get on another plane for warm-weather training. Look down the hill at the views of El Palmar and, beyond that, Murcia; it's not hard to see the appeal of Real Sociedad Club de Campo Murcia.

'This is Carlitos's club,' says family friend Alfredo Sarria, sitting in the clubhouse, 'and he wants to be here.' For now, there aren't any indoor courts at the club, so the Ferrero Tennis Academy is the closest place Alcaraz can prepare for indoor events on the ATP Tour. But that could change, according to Sarria, as Alcaraz is willing to fund the construction of some indoor courts at Real Sociedad Club de Campo Murcia. When Carlitos is at the country club, another member says, 'he's just one of the boys', happy to train in the gym alongside everyone else. Alcaraz doesn't expect or receive any star treatment there; though one member says that if it has been raining, people will dry Alcaraz's practice court before he arrives for training.

*

Nick Kyrgios was looking for a tattoo artist in Los Angeles; the Australian wanted someone to create a Pokémon design that would cover his entire back. Carlos Alcaraz messaged him with a recommendation and a personal introduction: 'Yeah, go to Ganga, he's my friend.'

One of the most important connections that Alcaraz made in El Palmar is Joaquin Ganga, who is one of the world's leading tattoo artists and also grew up in the village. Ganga has been an influential figure in Alcaraz's life because of their friendship and because he has been the one to decorate the athlete's skin with a strawberry, the Eiffel Tower and other designs to celebrate his greatest moments in tennis.

Around ten years older than Alcaraz, Ganga developed his creativity through graffitiing bits of El Palmar. With the small amount of money he earned from painting the front of a fruit shop in the village, he bought his first, basic tattoo kit and started practising on his friends. Today he charges around US $100,000 (£75,000) for a day's work and has studios in LA and Murcia, with a celebrity clientele of rappers, actors and athletes. Ganga tattooed the Olympic rings on basketball player LeBron James; he inked an Air Jordan shoe on the side of musician Chris Brown's face and he tattooed Post Malone while the singer was anaesthetized, as part of what he calls his 'No Pain by Ganga' method. Drake, a rapper, was the first of Ganga's big-name clients and, in a demonstration of their friendship, tattooed the tattoo artist. James has done the same, tattooing his crown logo on the inside of Ganga's wrist. How 'insane', Kyrgios thought after Ganga had finished the Pokémon back tattoo, that a tennis prodigy and one of the world's most celebrated tattoo artists both come from the same village.

Bonded by their shared background in El Palmar, Ganga has done all of Alcaraz's body art, including the tattoos to mark his Grand Slam success. When you win a Grand Slam, you're given a replica of the trophy to take home with you. Alcaraz has kept his replica US Open cup in his bedroom, and put the others in the living room of the family apartment – but he wanted something more than a trophy: to immortalize his victories on his skin. While Alcaraz's parents weren't that keen on their son getting tattoos, they didn't try to stop him, suggesting only that he didn't have them in prominent places. 'Like all parents, they would prefer that Carlos didn't get tattoos, but they only suggest that if he wants to get them, that they be discreet,' says Sarria. Other friends say Alcaraz's parents don't care that much about the tattoos because they're small and seeing them brings back happy memories of the important tournaments he won.

Maybe it helps that Alcaraz has assured his parents he will only get Grand Slam tattoos after winning a major for the first time and not after every victory. As his mother and father had suggested, he has chosen reasonably discreet designs and locations on his body; he certainly hasn't had any tattoos on his face, as some of Ganga's other clients have had done. The date that Alcaraz won the 2022 US Open title is inked on Alcaraz's arm. Sunday 11 September 2022 was also when he won the ranking points that took him to number one for the first time. He once told Martina Navratilova that he was fortunate to have achieved two dreams on the same day, with one benefit being that he needed only one tattoo to mark them both. There's also a strawberry and the date of his 2023 Wimbledon title above his ankle, and an Eiffel Tower design and the date on his leg to celebrate winning the 2024 Roland-Garros title. Alcaraz is at ease with Ganga; he was happy to be filmed pretending to tattoo Ganga on his wrist next to LeBron James's crown logo, and then posted that on social media.

Perhaps the most meaningful of all Alcaraz's tattoos is the one on the inside of his left wrist, with the letters 'CCC' standing for *cabeza, corazón, cojones*. Head, heart, balls.

It was his grandfather, who taught him that those are the three things you need to succeed on court – although, as the grandfather later conceded, he hadn't imagined that those words would be repeated so often and would take on such meaning. His grandfather – who didn't start playing tennis until he was 30 years old, and even then only recreationally – hadn't anticipated that his grandson would take the phrase so seriously. He also hadn't anticipated that Carlos would be quite so successful. Alcaraz's grandfather always thought Carlos was very clever, with an exceptional mind, so that was the head covered; and he observed that the heart came naturally with his grandson. As for the balls, Alcaraz's grandfather sometimes used the slang *huevos*, or 'eggs'. He said to a young Carlos that you should use those in a positive way, to win matches, rather than to complain.

Snigger if you wish, but if you visit El Palmar and speak to the villagers – including a café owner who has sold small round pastries in celebration of the Alcaraz *cojones* – it's clear how much the words mean to Carlos. Why else would he have had that tattoo done? And why else would Nike, his clothing and footwear sponsor, have given him some personalized shoes decorated with the words *cabeza, corazón, cojones* along with gold images of a brain, a heart and some tennis balls? For a sneakerhead like Alcaraz – a collector who seeks out rare shoes, such as a Nike pair created by the late fashion designer Virgil Abloh – being presented with those shoes was a thrill (somehow he manages with the limited shoe storage space in his room).

'Carlitos is always trying to put that advice into practice,' says Sarria. 'His grandfather gave him that advice when he was young – he was trying to teach Carlitos that when you play you need *cojones*, but also you need to use your brain, which is the head, and you also need motivation to do what you're doing, that's the heart. Without those three things, it's impossible to be as good as you want to be. Carlitos loves and admires his grandfather. Carlitos's grandfather's teachings remain engraved in him.'

Often, if a match isn't going his way, if it feels as though he's going through a rough moment, Alcaraz will think about what his grandfather told him; and that gives him the inspiration he needs to push himself even further. A grandson should listen and take advice from his grandfather, says Alcaraz's former coach Kiko Navarro, and that's what Alcaraz has done. 'Carlitos appreciates and loves his grandfather very much. The advice from his grandfather about head, heart and balls [impacted him a lot] so when things aren't going well for Carlitos, he will always remember those words from his grandfather,' says Navarro. 'Carlitos tries to give everything in every match. It's important to play tennis with your head and of course to leave everything on the court; and Carlitos knows that and does that.'

Brain, heart and balls – plus kings, queens and pawns. The life lessons from Alcaraz's grandfather also included introducing Carlitos to chess (long before *The Queen's Gambit* made chess fashionable). If Alcaraz ever won one of their chess matches, his grandfather would reward him with a bag of sweets. Alcaraz grew to love chess and still plays as much as he can when he is on tour, as well as at least once in public in Murcia's Plaza de Las Flores against an older gentleman from the local chess club. Alcaraz's grandfather thought that chess would help Carlos to organize his mind. Alcaraz can see the similarities between the chess board and the tennis court – the need to concentrate at all times, knowing that a moment's lapse can cost you victory, and to always be thinking strategically, trying to understand what your opponent is plotting while planning moves that will make him uncomfortable. Chess makes Alcaraz's mind sharper and quicker. Alcaraz's grandfather has been collecting a scrapbook of articles about Carlitos. He has also been happy getting up very early in the morning to watch his grandson, as he doesn't have work in the morning.

Alcaraz's grandparents have shaped how he looks at the world along with what he packs when travelling to tournaments – the racquet bag that he takes on court contains cards depicting la Virgen de la Fuensanta, the patron saint of Murcia, that his grandmother gave him.

2

A former Mister Murcia, a past winner of a local beauty pageant, was able to reassure Carlos Alcaraz's family. To address their concerns that Carlitos, for all his talents, might not have a future in tennis. When Alcaraz was eight years old, and showing real promise on the court, there was some doubt whether the boy would grow to be tall enough to become a professional tennis player. His father isn't the biggest man, after all, and as an athlete your future is shaped, to a large degree, by the genes your parents have passed on.

As a tennis player, you can have the most kaleidoscopic game – with all the hot shots you might want – but you won't amount to very much if you're short. Endless creativity on a tennis court has its limitations if you don't have the height. Alcaraz's father and his then coach Kiko Navarro took Carlos to see former beauty-pageant winner Juanjo López, who by then was a doctor (while he wasn't scared to look in the mirror, he knew he was 'no Brad Pitt', López wrote in his self-help book, *Hábitos para ser el Número 1*, and for some time afterwards kept quiet about being a former Mister Murcia out of embarrassment and because of the chance others might be prejudiced against him). An X-ray was taken of Alcaraz's wrist. By studying the bones in the boy's wrist, and factoring in the father's height, López was able to estimate how tall Carlos would be as a man.

'The issue of Carlitos's height worried us a little as his father is not very tall, although his mother is,' Navarro recalls. Navarro knew, as did everyone around Alcaraz, how 'height is very important in tennis today', particularly when serving. López, an enthusiastic amateur tennis player who was a member of the country club in El Palmar, provided some comfort. Everyone felt a little calmer, Navarro recalls, when López said the most optimistic projection was that Alcaraz would grow to be 1.82 metres (just under 6ft) tall. That didn't alleviate all concern, though. If he grew to that height, that wouldn't be bad, some around Alcaraz thought, but would it be tall enough for him to hold his own against taller opponents on the professional circuit?

López's estimate was very close to what eventually became Alcaraz's full height: he grew to be one centimetre taller than the doctor had predicted. According to Navarro, Alcaraz's father would have liked his son to have been a little taller – though at 1.83 metres (6ft), his child is only just shorter than Rafa Nadal and Roger Federer (both 1.85 metres/just under 6ft 1in) and not much smaller than Novak Djokovic (1.88 metres/6ft 2in). Alcaraz also has relatively long arms, giving him the leverage to hit the ball hard. Several Grand Slam titles later and the player's height is still a talking point. While John McEnroe described Alcaraz as the greatest talent he has seen in the last 20 years, and considers him a pleasure to watch, he worries that big, imposing opponents with fast, high-bouncing serves 'are going to drive him absolutely nuts'.

The first time that López examined the eight-year-old Alcaraz, he looked at the boy's spine and biomechanics and discovered that the child had Sever's disease, which was causing pain in his heel. For a few years after that, López saw Alcaraz occasionally – he would watch him training sometimes or would assess him if he was injured or had some pain. Navarro would also update López on how Alcaraz was doing. In his early teenage years, Alcaraz would have Osgood-Schlatter disease, with inflammation and growing pains around the knee, but that wasn't a huge concern, López felt, as it is common in adolescents.

As Alcaraz got older, and the demands on his body increased, there was a greater need to have López around; and in recent years the doctor has accompanied Carlos to the most important tournaments. These days, you might see López's name and medical services advertised in Murcia; and Alcaraz wrote the foreword for the doctor's book, which he described as 'an easy read' that would improve many people's lives.

López considers himself a friend as well as a team member. He takes a portable ultrasound machine on tour with him to help him diagnose what's wrong with Carlos and advise on whether the athlete should be playing through pain. He's also there, he feels, to offer support during the rough times; and perhaps to offer some perspective that 'this is a sport where you can win or lose, that's it, it's not a war or a disease'. The team shouldn't allow any 'media dramas' or comments on social media to affect the mood around Alcaraz. What's needed, López writes in his book, is to help Alcaraz to disconnect from the pressure by laughing, or through hugs or playful taps on the back, which you will see Alcaraz's team doing a lot. Part of López's role, he believes, is having fun on the tennis tour. It's not just that life is short, López thinks – it's that the team's laughing and joking will allow Alcaraz to raise his level: 'Carlitos's magic depends a lot on his humour and mood.'

Often, when Alcaraz has a day between matches – not quite a rest day, as he will still need to practise and look after his body – the team will do an activity together. That might mean going for a stroll somewhere green, when they will chat and Alcaraz can relax his muscles. They're big on 'Vitamin N', meaning nature, in Team Carlos. Going somewhere green and exposing Carlos to nature helps to improve his gut health, according to his nutritionist Alex Ruiz Galdón, while also helping to regulate cortisol, the stress hormone. Or the team activity might be a round of golf, some light shopping or playing a board game together. To set a good example to Alcaraz – as he does with his own children – López reads and doesn't spend too much time on his phone. He's punctual. He gets up early when he has to. He's showing good values while – and it seems as though this is important – not losing the fun. López and Alcaraz have come a long way since the childhood concerns about Alcaraz's height.

*

When he was at primary school, Carlos Alcaraz didn't have time to watch cartoons. His packed tennis schedule didn't allow for that. He would miss his classmates' birthday parties. Some weeks, he didn't even have a chance to go to the park with his friends. He was often absent from lessons. Carlos was ten years old when his teacher Loli Moreno, who could see her pupil wasn't living the normal life of a schoolboy, asked him whether he was happy with his choices: 'Aren't you paying a high price for your tennis, all this work and so much sacrifice? Is it worth it?'

One great disadvantage of 'being in that world', Moreno says of tennis, was that this young child was often 'alone' and away from his family as he would travel to tournaments with a coach, rather than with his father or mother. 'Carlos was missing a lot of things a child should be doing, normal childhood things,' Moreno says. Was this what Carlos wanted? Moreno wanted to check: 'Do you wish to continue doing this?' Alcaraz had no doubts. He was clear with his teacher: 'Yes, it's worth it.'

Being Carlos Alcaraz has, for about as long as he can remember, meant aspiring to greatness. For a child, Alcaraz was clear and consistent about what he wanted to be when he grew up. If anyone asked him, the answer came quickly: 'A tennis player.' And not just any tennis player, but the best. Alcaraz, who as a child had a duvet cover with a design showing the map of the world, had global ambitions: he was going to be the best tennis player on the planet, the number one. He could see it was possible for a Spaniard to rise that high. Only a very select few men from around the world have reached the top of the rankings – at the time of writing, under 30 men have done so – but even before Alcaraz, Spanish names featured strongly, with Carlos Moyá, Juan Carlos Ferrero and Rafa Nadal.

If he was at school in late May and early June, Alcaraz would run home after lessons to watch Roland-Garros on television, where, almost inevitably, he would see Nadal advancing towards yet another title in Paris. The first match that Alcaraz can remember watching was a twisty, five-set classic between Nadal and Novak Djokovic in the 2013 semi-finals, when the Spaniard came from a break down in the fifth set. Alcaraz, who had just turned ten, was enthralled. An idea had formed in Alcaraz's head, that he was going to add his name to the list of Spanish men's singles champions at Roland-Garros, joining the likes of Moyá, Albert Costa, Ferrero and Nadal. That was Alcaraz's vision. While many young people's dreams and ambitions can shift and fade and develop as they move through childhood and then into the teenage years, Alcaraz's remained the same. Psychologist Josefina Cutillas worked with Alcaraz for eight years and, as she once told *El País*, she thought having clear goals was one of his strengths: Alcaraz's success didn't happen by chance but because he knew exactly what he wanted.

Just as significantly, Cutillas has observed, Alcaraz was aware, from when he was young, what it would take for him to achieve his ambitions. That the sacrifice could be constant. That he couldn't have a regular childhood if he was going to become the number one. Win a Grand Slam at 19 years old and become the youngest number one in the history of men's tennis, and people will call you an overnight success. But a moment like that comes after years of toiling when no one is watching. As a boy, Alcaraz could see that he had a lot of years of work ahead of him.

In an age of instant gratification, when it can seem as though many young people expect things to happen immediately, Cutillas thought it was interesting how Alcaraz was willing to think about the long term. He was willing to make those sacrifices if doing so meant that the rewards would be even greater when he was older. Alcaraz would gladly not watch cartoons as a boy if that meant he could lift trophies as a man. Cutillas doesn't remember anyone ever having to tell Alcaraz that he needed to train, as he would always be ready to go. There were no wobbles, no moments when Alcaraz's motivation was flagging and (returning to that question from his teacher) he wondered whether it was worth it. As a child, Alcaraz didn't choose the easy path, a mindset he has continued into his early twenties. In childhood, Alcaraz figured out something that comes to others only much later in life: there is no secret to success; and you will only get where you want to be by working hard.

Clear vision and an astonishing work ethic for a child; that was the abnormal part. In some other respects he was very normal – like many kids, Alcaraz was occasionally naughty, throwing paper planes in class, Moreno says. Dedicated and methodical about his tennis outside school, Alcaraz was 'a mess' in the classroom, according to Moreno, who says he would often forget his books, his pencil case or something else that was needed for that day's lessons. But, with his smiley nature, he would usually get away with launching paper planes or not having the right textbook. 'Carlos did everything with a smile. He always had a smile, even when he was being told off. He was a very kind boy and a very happy boy,' says Moreno.

When Carlos was going to be away on tennis trips, Moreno would give him some homework; but he usually didn't do it. When he was in school, though, despite being disorganized, he tried to make the most of the time in the classroom and more often than not picked up topics quickly. 'Carlitos was a fast learner. That was true of everything at school, inside and outside the classroom. I used to explain something to him and even if he wasn't always there for that topic – because he was away for tournaments – he absorbed that information.'

Sometimes Alcaraz ended up doing his schoolwork at a tournament. Like the occasion he played in a junior tournament in Paris and was interviewed by a journalist. Moreno had been teaching the children in her class how to do an interview and had said to Alcaraz that he should practise interviewing someone. But it ended up the other way around – with Alcaraz telling the journalist that he wished to win Roland-Garros and Wimbledon when he was older. Alcaraz's father sent Moreno a video of the interview as well as a message: 'Is this interview OK?' Moreno replied: 'Yes, OK, ten out of ten for Carlitos.'

It was when Alcaraz was around ten or eleven years old that his teachers picked up on how serious their pupil had got about his tennis. Not that he was very chatty about it. When Alcaraz returned to El Palmar after tournaments, he wouldn't say much about how the trips had gone and didn't want to take his trophies into the classroom for show-and-tells. 'Carlos wasn't shy but he also wasn't talkative about his tennis: he didn't want to show off. He was modest about his tennis,' Moreno says. 'I said to Carlos that he should bring his trophies into school but he didn't want to. He was embarrassed. He loves winning but he didn't want any attention on himself. If you didn't ask Carlos about his tennis, he wouldn't say anything. I once asked him about one of his trips in front of the whole class as I wanted him to share the experience to motivate them. But he would only share some general information about what he had done and didn't go into much detail.'

Everything else in Alcaraz's life was organized around his tennis. Even the dates of a school trip. It's traditional in Spain for children to go to Madrid to celebrate finishing primary school; Alcaraz's teachers found a time to go that wouldn't clash with the tournaments he was playing. But even then, the teachers recall, Alcaraz's father had to travel to Madrid to fetch his son and take him to his next event.

Alcaraz's teachers were sure that he would go on to be famous. They just didn't know *how* famous. After Alcaraz won another junior tournament, Moreno said to him: 'I want to take a picture with you because you're going to be famous in the future.' That made Alcaraz laugh. Moreno took a picture of the two of them together. And she was right about his fame. Unfortunately for Moreno, she lost that photo, which is a shame, but she smiles about it now.

Alcaraz was popular at school. There was no jealousy among Carlos's classmates, some of whom he is still friends with today. The only time Alcaraz was happy and proud to celebrate a victory in front of his class was when he'd won something as part of a team. When the children were selecting teams, he was always everyone's first choice, whether they were playing football, basketball or any other sport. They knew that the team with Carlitos would surely be the winning team. Alcaraz was a competitive cross-country runner and he picked up badminton very quickly, even winning a tournament within a year of playing the sport for the first time, although there was the time he got in trouble for breaking one of the racquets by hitting a stone with it. When Alcaraz returned to the school for the first time since he achieved stardom, he spoke with his old sports teacher Carlos Bocanegra about playing him at badminton when he had some time.

Every day in class, Alcaraz's old teachers are grateful that his success has stopped them having to listen to the horrific screech of the pupils moving their chairs on the floor. The chairs in Alcaraz's old classroom, and in almost all the other rooms, have used tennis balls on the end of their metal legs, which means that children can move them silently. Those tennis balls were a present from Carlos and his family, who donated 1,800 of them. 'Now when the kids move their chairs around, they don't make a big noise and disturb the whole class,' says Alcaraz's old English teacher Laura Caballero.

Outside, painted on the side of the school, is another reminder that Alcaraz went there – a mural of him based on a photograph of when he was around 11 years old. When Alcaraz returned to the school to have a look at the mural, Moreno took the opportunity to speak to her former pupil about why he no longer followed her son on Instagram: 'Carlitos, you used to follow my son and now you don't.' Alcaraz smiled at his old teacher. That night, Moreno's son noticed Alcaraz was following him again. Moreno has been open with Alcaraz about what she thinks of the outfits his sponsor Nike have selected for him, once telling him: 'I don't like the T-shirts that you wear on court because I don't like the colours. I don't like the browns and the reds. Change to blues and purples, which looks cute with your skin. Pink is also your colour.' Alcaraz told his teacher he didn't choose his own T-shirts. Moreno insisted Alcaraz must pick out some different colours in the future. For his next event, he wore pink.

*

It might have been the most troubling victory of Carlos Alcaraz's life. Carlos was 14 years old when he beat his older brother Álvaro for the first time and he wasn't very comfortable with it. Carlos probably could have defeated his brother – who is three years his senior – before then. But he had held back in their matches as he had thought it would be painful for Álvaro, who had ambitions of his own to be a tennis player, to lose to his younger brother. Carlos's competitive instincts conflicted with his desire not to hurt Álvaro.

Carlos and Álvaro are more than brothers: they are best friends (despite the age gap, they have many friends in common). For several years, they shared a room in the family apartment, with Álvaro taking the top bunk and Carlos below him. As children, Álvaro thought, they were a bit like Zipi and Zape, the naughty Spanish comic-book characters. The Alcaraz brothers once threw popcorn at their grandfather as he tried to watch television; unsurprisingly, that made him cross. No one has a better understanding of Alcaraz's character than Álvaro, who has noted that Carlos can be stubborn, which, depending on the situation, can be good or bad. If Carlos thinks he's right it can be difficult to change his mind. Carlos is also a generous and understanding guy, according to Álvaro.

Like any children who love tennis, the Alcaraz brothers would ask players for autographs when they went as spectators to professional tournaments. These days, when they're at events, Álvaro, who never made it as a player himself, watches as his younger brother signs his name or poses for photographs. But Álvaro is no bystander in elite tennis; he has a key role in his brother's life, on a practical and psychological level. While Álvaro made just US $342 (£257) in his career, he's possibly one of the most influential figures in tennis. One of Álvaro's most important tasks – together with keeping his younger brother smiling and happy – is hitting with Carlos before he plays a match, including before a Grand Slam final.

Hitting with Álvaro before a major final helps to reduce Alcaraz's nerves, as it reminds him of all those times they played together as boys in El Palmar. 'Being on court with Álvaro is very relaxing for Carlitos before a big match because he feels as though they're almost still playing at home, just like they have done hundreds of times before,' says Alcaraz's friend Antonio López.

'Carlitos loves training with his brother – it relaxes his brain,' says Alfredo Sarria. 'Álvaro is the person who trains with Carlitos at most tournaments. Álvaro doesn't have the physical and psychological preparation to be a professional tennis player but he has a good [enough] level to do the things that Carlitos needs before a match. When Carlitos trains with Álvaro, he feels as though he's ready for the important matches. That's what he prefers. Álvaro has prepared Carlitos for Grand Slam finals, such as the 2024 Wimbledon final, when Carlitos gave his best level. It's important for Carlitos to have his father and his older brother with him when he is travelling.'

Tennis can be a lonely sport, Alcaraz says. In a typical year, he might spend 200 days away from home. Having his family with him – often his father and Álvaro – helps to take his mind off tennis, even if that is just for an hour or two. 'It's good for Carlos to have his family with him at tournaments so he can have conversations about something other than tennis,' says Sarria. 'Carlos needs to speak about other things in life. That stops him from thinking about tennis 24 hours a day, which wouldn't be good for him.' Alcaraz appreciates he's fortunate to have a home away from home on the road, as many players wouldn't be able to afford the travel costs of always having family members with them.

These days, Álvaro's role at tournaments is also to help Carlos to feel calm and relaxed, to ensure there are good vibes, which is particularly important the night before a Grand Slam final. On the eve of the 2022 US Open final, Carlos and Álvaro, who were sharing a hotel room in New York City, watched *300*, a film about 300 Spartans fighting thousands of Persians. Others might suggest that the movie, starring Gerard Butler, is silly, but Alcaraz and his older brother found it to be motivational viewing before he played Casper Ruud. The night before the 2023 Wimbledon final, Carlos and Álvaro thought about watching another film but, in the end, they played Parchís, a board game, after dinner in the rental house.

Between matches, the Alcaraz brothers will also play cards and have the conversations that Carlos wouldn't have with his coach or manager. 'Carlitos needs support and he gets that from Álvaro. His brother is the best support in the world,' says Antonio López. 'Álvaro is usually travelling with Carlitos to tournaments. Álvaro talks every minute with Carlitos. I imagine that when Álvaro isn't at a tournament, they will still be speaking every day for sure. Carlitos is talking to his older brother about all the things he needs in life and not just about tennis. As Álvaro is older, he knows a bit more about life. Carlitos looks up to his older brother. Carlitos sees Álvaro as a role model, as a guide to the kind of person he wants to be in the future. Like Carlitos, Álvaro is a really good person.'

Sometimes Álvaro feels the need to assert his authority as the older brother, as he jokingly reminded Carlos in a video that was played at the athlete's 21st birthday party: 'No matter how famous you are, you'll always be my little bro and I'll smack you if I need to.'

There's a happy mood in Alcaraz's team, says his podiatrist Carles Ruiz. But, according to Ruiz, it's the warmth of Alcaraz's family that has a bigger effect on how Carlos is when he is away from home competing: 'The most important thing is the ambience in the family. Some of his family travel with him to tournaments and that makes a big difference. When you are young, you need your friends and family with you.'

Álvaro knows the importance of smiling and joking around his brother, as that helps to bring some balance to his life. 'Álvaro tries to be funny all the time with Carlitos, to smile and make jokes,' says López. 'If Álvaro doesn't have a smile on his face at a tournament, Carlitos will be asking him: "What's happening?"'

*

Carlos Alcaraz's behaviour wasn't perfect as a junior. His coach of many years, Kiko Navarro, remembers being furious with Alcaraz after the boy didn't give his best effort in a match; they had a difficult conversation on the train afterwards, with Navarro telling Alcaraz in the strongest terms how upset he was. 'Carlitos played a bad match due to a lack of motivation, a lack of the right attitude, a lack of desire to win, and that made me very angry and I told him that,' Navarro says. They hadn't travelled all that way, and Navarro hadn't dedicated all that time and effort, just for Alcaraz to perform like that. Navarro was clear with Alcaraz that he expected him to give everything on the court. Neither would forget that conversation and Navarro never had the need to speak to Alcaraz like that again.

As that train ride showed, when it was necessary, Navarro could be strict with Alcaraz. Accompanying Alcaraz to tournaments wasn't always easy as Navarro played different roles: sometimes he was acting as the coach and other times he was behaving more like a friend or an older brother to Carlos. 'I have had a very good relationship with Carlitos,' says Navarro, who could be gentle with Alcaraz in some moments and stern in others, a combination he felt worked well for the teenager. Like all children, Navarro says, Alcaraz loved mobile phones, but the coach tried to control how much time the teenager spent on his. As an aspiring athlete, you didn't want to be staying up late looking at your phone when you could have been resting or sleeping. When they had some time to kill while waiting for a flight at the airport, or when travelling by car or train, Navarro suggested Alcaraz read a book or chat instead.

It was Alcaraz's father, coaching his son indirectly as always, who ensured his son was always pushed on the practice court; Carlitos wasn't ever allowed to coast. Only training hard at a high intensity would help him in matches as he would be used to bringing that focus and energy whenever he was on court. 'All the coaches around Carlitos followed the instructions that his father had given them,' says Sarria. 'Carlitos's father put special attention on the intensity of every one of Carlitos's training sessions. He wanted Carlitos to understand that he had to train very hard every day if he wanted to arrive at a professional career.'

Alcaraz's father will accompany his son to most tournaments during the year. 'There are a lot of things that happen around Carlitos. His father feels as though he has to be there with Carlitos to make some decisions as that helps his son to focus his brain on tennis and not on other matters,' Sarria says. 'The goal of every tournament is for Carlitos to be at his best in every match. In tennis, the manager and the coach sometimes have to make decisions that aren't [necessarily] the best for the player. Sometimes Carlitos needs to have a member of his family there to advise him whether it's a good idea to do something or not.'

When Alcaraz's father is at tournaments, he often does his own thing. 'He tries not to be close to the team,' says Sarria. Tennis parents can sometimes be more interested in the bright lights than their children are. But that's not the case with Alcaraz's father. The team around Alcaraz appreciate that his father has been the one who has helped to set the direction and the tone of his son's career, and it sounds as though every big decision is either approved by him or suggested by him in the first place. But – and this is key – Alcaraz's father has been doing that discreetly and respectfully and without interfering in the day-to-day business of his son's tennis. Alcaraz's dad is usually there at tournaments or he's around at the country club when his son is training between events. And yet he's somehow also slightly removed from it all. The team talk about Alcaraz's dad giving them the space they need to do their jobs.

For Alcaraz's father, doing his own thing at tournaments might mean watching matches that don't involve Carlos or observing how other players train, which might give him some ideas or inspiration for coaching at his academy or something he can pass on to his son.

At the 2023 Wimbledon Championships, someone thought they had seen Alcaraz senior with his phone out, videoing one of Novak Djokovic's training sessions at the All England Club's Aorangi Park practice courts, which led to stories that he had been spying on his son's rival. According to someone close to the family, any suggestion that Alcaraz's father had been involved in espionage at Wimbledon was wrong: 'this was a fabrication' designed to 'destabilize'. Alcaraz thought it was possible it could have been his father filming Djokovic. But that didn't mean that his dad had been spying on the man he would play – and beat – in that summer's final. There were already so many videos on social-media platforms of Djokovic playing matches and practising that Alcaraz hardly needed another one to understand the Serb's game. It might not have even been Alcaraz's father; the man who was supposedly seen filming the session could have been a Spanish journalist.

If it was Alcaraz's father who was recording Djokovic train, that's just indicative of the fact that he's a tennis enthusiast. Throughout the tournament, Alcaraz senior had been arriving at the courts early in the morning and spending the entire day watching players practise and compete before being one of the last to leave in the evening. If Carlos is in love with tennis, it's because he has learned to be from his father, who still adores the sport after all these years – despite his dreams of being a professional player himself not going as far as he'd wanted.

Alcaraz's father takes a close interest in his son's practice sessions. If he notices something that no one else has picked up on, he will have a conversation with Ferrero or Carlos's manager, Albert Molina. 'If Carlos's father notices that there's a problem and that people aren't coming up with solutions day by day, he will say something to the team. He won't do that after just one day but after a period of a few days,' says Sarria. 'Sometimes it's important for the father to tell the team that he knows about tennis and that he doesn't like something and that it's a problem. He will say that he has seen something for a few days and has waited before telling them but that they should be careful about this. Sometimes, as a coach or as a manager, when you are close to a player for many years it's impossible for you to see things and themes that another person from outside the court can see.'

Watching Carlos play can make Alcaraz's mother, Virginia, so nervous and anxious she can't even sit down. She has to get up and walk around. As Virginia once disclosed, she 'really struggles' when her son is on court. There have been times when she has had to stop watching. Virginia has joked that this might even help her son – she once said that Carlos has on occasion been losing a match while she was watching but then started to play better when she stopped. Sometimes Alcaraz's mother, who is originally from Seville, is there in person, sitting in Carlos's box in Centre Court at Wimbledon or some other big event, and if it's very tense, and it's all getting a bit too much, you might see one of her other sons reach over and affectionately rub her on the shoulder. A touch that says: 'We're going to get through this.' In the same way, Alcaraz's father doesn't always find his son's matches easy viewing: on occasion he has said to Carlos it feels as though he's going to have a heart attack.

There are no parenting secrets to how Alcaraz's mother and father have raised Carlos and his brothers. 'Like most parents, they have tried to educate their children well,' says Sarria. You hear a lot about Alcaraz's father but his mother has been just as influential in shaping him as an athlete and a person. 'She is a wonderful person as well as demanding with her children,' Sarria says.

Travelling the world playing the tennis, and getting to see new cities and places, is a good life for Alcaraz but, being so close to his family, he would rather be at home in El Palmar than anywhere else. One of the joys of being at home is that Alcaraz can enjoy his mother's cooking

('There's no food in the world like my mother's, let me tell you,' he said in his Netflix documentary in 2025). She does a great paella, Alcaraz thinks. He also adores the Andalusian food she prepares, including a soup and mix of meats. But really what he wants is just to be with his parents and brothers. Psychologist Josefina Cutillas once heard the player say that being with his family gave him the calm he needed 'amid a whirlwind of emotions'. While Alcaraz would like his mother to travel to more tournaments, he understands that's not possible as she is at home in El Palmar looking after his two younger brothers, Sergio and Jaime. 'Carlitos wants his mother to travel more because he loves her. Carlitos wants his mother to be with him. But she needs to be at home, even if there are a lot of people around the family who can help sometimes,' says Sarria, whose son is best friends with Jaime.

It alarms and worries Alcaraz when the media and others speak about Jaime, who has been showing some promise on the tennis court, as 'the next Carlos'. As we will see later in the book, being spoken about as a 'Mini Rafa' wasn't helpful during Alcaraz's own development, so he knows what it's like and how damaging it can be to be thought of as the next someone else when you're trying to make your own way. 'Sometimes the media can be a bit harsh,' Alcaraz told Molusco TV. Alcaraz has felt the need, he has said, to 'step in' and say that people shouldn't be putting such high expectations on a child. When Alcaraz is at home, he can offer some guidance – including telling Jaime how to avoid some of the mistakes he made himself – but he doesn't want Jaime to be looking at him as Carlos Alcaraz the tennis player. He would much rather Jaime saw him for what he is: an older brother who wants the best for him.

*

Carlos Alcaraz's rise has changed El Palmar. It looks different now, with an enormous mural of him as you drive into the village (in addition to the one on the wall of his old primary school and the artwork on the outside of the country club). There's also a new vibe. When Alcaraz is playing in a Grand Slam final, the villagers put up a giant screen, get the chairs out and everyone's invited to watch the match together. 'Carlos's success has lifted the mood of the village,' says Laura Caballero. 'When he is playing in the final of a big competition, and everyone is watching in front of the big screen, we're so proud of him and you can feel that emotion.'

Alcaraz also seems to have transformed El Palmar in a way that has done much to improve the quality of life there: since he became a Grand Slam champion, the village has been cleaner, according to Lola Jiménez Rivas, his English teacher at the Marqués de los Vélez senior school, which is close to his family's home. 'Carlos has put El Palmar on the map. A lot of people come to the village asking for Carlos. They want to know more about the origins of Carlos Alcaraz – they go to the neighbourhood where his family's apartment is, and they visit where he went to school, and they go to see the mural on the edge of the village,' Lola says. 'Maybe it's because of that interest in Carlos that the village now has a better appearance. It looks cleaner than before. It seems to me as though the village has been tidied up.'

3

Carlos Alcaraz's first sponsorship contract – signed when he was only
eight years old, and without which he might not have become the player
he is today – was just a single sheet of paper.

Legal documents involving tennis players and brands aren't usually
this short and simple. This one was light on clauses and complexity
because Alfonso López Rueda, the president of Postres Reina – a dessert,
yoghurt and cake company based in Murcia – hardly wanted anything
in return from Carlos. The contract stated how much money Alfonso
would contribute that year towards the costs of Carlos's coaching, travel
and all-round tennis development. When Carlos was playing, he would
be expected to wear a Postres Reina patch on his kit. But, Alfonso says,
there was 'little else' in the document.

Alcaraz adores Postres Reina's custard-cream dessert with a cookie
on top. Of all their desserts, that's his favourite. But that's not why he
feels deep, lasting gratitude towards Alfonso and his dessert company.
Sponsoring Alcaraz was warm-hearted philanthropy rather than a

cold, calculated marketing move, especially in the early years when the tennis player had almost no profile. How much exposure was the company really going to get from a boy playing junior events? Given the large sums involved – a six-figure total, in euros, over the years – this deal made no financial sense for Postres Reina. But that didn't matter. All Alfonso cared about – because he loves tennis and because he felt the company should be doing more to support young people near to its factories – was contributing money that would allow Carlos to continue playing tennis. 'I wanted to help the kid and his family,' Alfonso says.

It was, financially speaking, a seven-year sugar high for Alcaraz and his parents. In some ways, the contract was irrelevant. Alfonso didn't ever stick to what was written on that piece of paper. Or to any of the other contracts he signed with Alcaraz until the Murcian was 15 years old. Alfonso regarded the number in that document as the minimum amount he would be transferring to the Alcaraz family that season. In this loose and seemingly ever more generous arrangement, Alcaraz's parents would tell Alfonso how much they needed for Carlos and Alfonso would happily send the funds. Whatever Alcaraz needed, Alfonso would pay for it. When, for instance, a ten-year-old Alcaraz wished to travel to Croatia, for what would be his first tournament outside Spain, Alfonso funded the trip as he could see it would be a significant step in the boy's development. On his return, Alcaraz was certain of what he wanted from his future: to become a professional tennis player.

Junior tennis gets increasingly expensive as you get older – especially when you start competing around Europe as well as in your own country. It felt as though the costs jumped from one year to the next, but Alfonso and Postres Reina were totally fine with that. So maybe they gave Alcaraz around 25,000 euros in the first year, approximately 35,000 euros in the second season and in the region of 50,000 euros for year three, and up from there. Most weeks, it seemed, there would be a bank transfer. It's telling that, because of their generosity, Postres Reina can't easily estimate how much money they gave to Alcaraz over the seven years.

Money, or the lack of it, is often the biggest barrier to becoming a professional tennis player. Alcaraz's father knows that about as well as anyone. After showing some promise as a 14-year-old, he was invited to train at the Bruguera Tennis Academy in Barcelona, which was founded by Lluis Bruguera, father of two-time Roland-Garros champion, Sergi. But the monthly fee for attending the academy, around 80,000 pesetas, was more than Alcaraz's (Carlitos's) grandfather was then earning each month: 60,000 pesetas. Even when the academy offered them a scholarship with a 50 per cent discount on the fees, it was financially 'impossible', according to Alcaraz's grandfather. For much of his career, the grandfather worked as a draftsman but then, after losing his job, worked in construction and later opened a real-estate agency. He did what he could to provide for his family – as did Alcaraz's grandmother, who ran a bookshop in El Palmar. But there wasn't enough money to pay a tennis academy's fees.

Alcaraz's grandfather has also recalled how his son had been competitive against the likes of Sergi Bruguera and Àlex Corretja, who would go on to play in two Roland-Garros finals. Alcaraz's father could possibly have become a professional. Looking back, he has wondered whether that was the moment he should have left Murcia, but without the money what were his options? Alcaraz's father, who recalls growing up in a working-class neighbourhood, was 19 or 20 years old when he realized his tennis dream was over.

Limited resources had also been a problem for Kiko Navarro, Alcaraz's coach at the time, when he had wanted to become a professional player himself. Kiko was adamant that Alcaraz wouldn't also be held back by a shortage of money. 'I know how in this sport you need money when you are young – both Carlos's father and I couldn't try to become tennis players because of a lack of it and that is why I was clear that I didn't want that to also happen to Carlitos,' Navarro says. With the cash from Alfonso and Postres Reina, Alcaraz wouldn't be constrained by his family's modest circumstances.

Alcaraz might not have appreciated this at the time, because he was young and his focus would have been on playing the game rather than on money, but he was very fortunate to have had Alfonso. Most tennis players aren't that lucky. Around 70 per cent of the players at the Grand Slam tournaments, including some of the most celebrated names, have been reliant on funding from wealthy businessmen and women who will then want a return on that investment if the athletes make it (breaking into the top 50 in the singles rankings is usually what counts as making it in these arrangements). Contrast with Alfonso, who didn't want anything apart from a patch on a T-shirt and the knowledge that he was helping.

Some desperate juniors and parents have ended up in bad situations through these funding arrangements, according to Max Eisenbud, who is head of tennis clients at the International Management Group (IMG) agency that represents Alcaraz (though they weren't involved when Alfonso first started funding Alcaraz or for four years after that). A few players find themselves giving as much as 20 per cent of their prize money to their investors for the rest of their career, Eisenbud said in a frank conversation on Andy Roddick's *Served* podcast. This goes way beyond paying the money back plus interest; in the worst cases, players could end up handing their investors significantly more than they received on the way up. Trying to unwind these agreements with lawyers doesn't tend to be straightforward or pleasant.

Alcaraz, though, managed to swerve all that stress and angst and debt, thanks to Alfonso.

Here was some astonishing, life-changing luck for Carlos. It just so happened that Alfonso was playing tennis several times a week at the country club in El Palmar. His doubles partner was Alcaraz's great-uncle, Tomás. However, according to José Manuel Lag, the managing director of Postres Reina, Alcaraz's great-uncle wasn't the one who initially said something to Alfonso about Carlos needing some financial support, as he hadn't wanted to put his tennis partner in an awkward position. Kiko was also giving lessons to Alfonso's son, Manuel, at the time.

Kiko would tell Alfonso about all the great things that Alcaraz was doing, including how he was beating boys several years older than him. Persuading Alfonso to help Carlos was very easy, Navarro recalls: 'Alfonso was and is a very good friend of mine; he loves tennis and he loves to help people.'

(Carlos Santos, Alcaraz's first coach, has written in his book *Alcaraz: La Forja de un Campeón*, published in 2025, that he stopped coaching Carlitos as he wasn't happy about sharing the role with another coach, Kiko, whose influence had grown after helping to secure sponsorship money for the boy and his family. Santos wanted more commitment from the family, in the form of a long contract, and Alcaraz's father declined to give him that. Santos's relationship with Alcaraz's father has cooled since the book was published.)

When Alfonso watched Alcaraz training, he could see the boy was gifted and was putting all his time and energy into going after his tennis dream. Alfonso's generosity extended to helping out Kiko, according to Lag. If Kiko had been with Alcaraz all week, he wouldn't have had the time to coach anyone else and so wouldn't have made any money. Alfonso ensured Kiko was compensated for the days he had spent with Carlos.

The arrangement between Postres Reina and Alcaraz was so loose, according to Lag, that 'the contract wasn't really a contract'. Alfonso didn't, for instance, ask for a clause in the contract that could have possibly ensured that Postres Reina would be part of Alcaraz's story, and portfolio of sponsors, for years to come. If the moment ever came that larger, wealthier companies wanted to sponsor Alcaraz, Alfonso would gladly step aside, knowing that he had given the young player the opportunity to progress to a point where those types of brands were interested in being associated with the athlete.

Would Carlos have been a teenage Grand Slam champion and become the youngest world number one in the history of men's tennis without the money from Postres Reina? Alfonso can't give a definitive answer to that: 'We'll never know, but what's clear is that Carlos had all he needed. He's an extraordinary person with enormous talent and a capacity for sacrifice, and he would surely have gone far.'

Navarro says we can never know how Alcaraz's career would have played out without the backing of a dessert and yoghurt philanthropist. Alcaraz would have been on a different trajectory. But Navarro believes that, even without that money, Alcaraz would still have become a professional tennis player. He believes Alcaraz's father would have found another sponsor and that Alcaraz is so gifted he would surely have reached the top anyway. But would they have found a sponsor as generous and as undemanding as Postres Reina, who let Carlos rise so fast? Extremely unlikely.

When Alcaraz was 14 or 15 years old, his manager Albert Molina was looking for a new clothing deal for his player. According to Lag, Adidas indicated it would be possible for Alcaraz to play in a T-shirt with a Postres Reina logo on the front while the teenager's then clothing sponsor, Lotto, initially said no to a patch before changing their minds. The highest offer, Lag says, was from Nike and they wanted Alcaraz's outfits to be clean, without any logos apart from their own Swoosh. That was the moment that Alfonso and Postres Reina, after all those years of astonishingly generous support, stepped away. 'We couldn't afford to support Carlos anymore,' Lag says. Alfonso still occasionally sees Alcaraz at the country club, he still plays doubles with Alcaraz's great-uncle and Postres Reina sponsors the academy that Alcaraz's father runs. They have also supported the Ferrero Tennis Academy.

At Postres Reina, there's pride in what Alcaraz has gone on to accomplish. They're very happy for him. Maybe in the future, Lag says, Alfonso and Postres Reina will resume their commercial relationship with Alcaraz, but that's simply not possible right now.

Alcaraz and his family are enormously thankful for the help they received during the years when it was needed the most. That's why Carlos's father still invites Alfonso to attend Grand Slams and other tournaments. 'Carlos's father knows perfectly well that without financial help it's hard to grow up to become a tennis player,' says Lag. 'I think Carlos's parents will be grateful forever to Alfonso for how he helped the family.' Each summer, Alcaraz and his family would spend a day at Alfonso's house by the beach in La Manga del Mar Menor. This gave Alcaraz the opportunity to show Alfonso some of the trophies he had won. In the summer of 2022, Carlos sat next to Alfonso at lunch, updating him on how his tennis was progressing, not knowing that, within weeks, he would be a Grand Slam champion.

*

Carlos Alcaraz was ten years old when Babolat, a French brand that was supplying Rafa Nadal with his racquets, started giving him free products. Alcaraz had already been playing with Babolat racquets so that suited him just fine. And so began a partnership that developed into the longest-standing commercial arrangement of his life (he has played with Babolat throughout his career and is contracted to them until at least 2030, by which time he will be 27 years old). The brand had scouted ten-year-old Alcaraz at the Babolat Cup, a junior tournament in Spain. They liked how he played tennis; even then his game was more fun and creative than the way others went about it. But it wasn't just how he hit the ball that was so interesting. Babolat loved how Alcaraz smiled and brought positive energy to the court.

'When Carlos was ten years old, we saw huge talent and not only in terms of tennis performance but also in terms of charisma,' says

Jean-Christophe Verborg, global sports marketing director at Babolat. 'It was the way he behaved on court. He was smiling and enjoying himself. He had the technical talent and loads of charisma. Even when he was ten years old, you could really feel that character in him. But when you sign a ten-year-old, you never know what's going to happen.'

A brand that is two years older than Wimbledon – Babolat started in 1875 and celebrated their 150-year anniversary in 2025 – is going to be capable of taking a long view on a player.

Some in the tennis industry had been saying that Babolat had got lucky with Nadal. What would happen after Rafa? Convincing more established players to join Babolat was a challenge. Verborg and his team were looking for the star players of the future, for the athletes who would elevate the brand after Nadal. 'Is it normal to sign a ten-year-old? But that's what we had to do. It's complicated because you have to let the young players develop without too much pressure of money and results. But the positive thing about signing them when they are young is that you really build a story. They get to know Babolat and we invest time, money and product. That creates a strong relationship,' Verborg says.

In Alcaraz, Babolat had a young player who could 'wow' a tennis crowd. When Alcaraz was 13 years old, he won the Babolat Cup – and the prize was an improved contract. Wanting to secure a player they regarded as a special talent, Babolat moved Alcaraz from their Spanish roster to their international team. 'Sometimes you have a player with a wow effect,' Verborg says. 'We thought, "OK, we have one of those and we have to keep him."'

Signing a child is different to agreeing terms with an established player. Just as they had done with Nadal, the team at Babolat got to know Alcaraz's parents. 'They're lovely people,' says Verborg. When he is around Carlos and his family, Verborg feels 'the respect and the education'. Babolat thinks of itself as a big brand with a small family. Family is a word that keeps coming up in the Alcaraz story. There's his biological family, of course. Carlos is very close to them. There's Babolat and, as we will see in a later chapter, there's the family feel of the Ferrero Tennis Academy. When Babolat sponsors a child under the age of 18, the parents must also sign the contract with the company and, in Verborg's experience, the father and mother often don't tell their son or daughter what is being paid. The parents believe that keeping that information from their child will allow the young player to continue enjoying their tennis, rather than exposing them too early to money and outside pressures.

*

In Spain, you finish primary school at 12 years old. That was also the age at which Carlos Alcaraz's parents agreed he should work with an agent, the very same one he has today. Even in tennis – a sport where you must commit very early to trying to become a professional, and where you can become a global star as a teenager – it's rare to have an agent before you even hit your teens. When Albert Molina from IMG told Alcaraz's father that his son was gifted and said he would like to manage him, was it any wonder that Carlos's dad wasn't sure, that he initially had his doubts about whether it was necessary? Even after Molina had persuaded Alcaraz's father it was in Carlos's interests for the boy to be managed by IMG, his dad still thought it was possibly a touch premature to have an agent at that age.

'Getting an agent at 12, that's not normal,' says Garbiñe Muguruza. The Spaniard won two Grand Slam titles, at Roland-Garros and Wimbledon, and was the women's world number one, but recalls having to go find an agent early in her career because 'they didn't come looking for me'. On the *Served* podcast, Max Eisenbud told Andy Roddick how managing an 11-year-old, as he did with Maria Sharapova, is 'such an outlier, such a rare thing – it's hard to explain because it's just not normal'. IMG aren't generally looking to sign tennis players in their pre-teens; they would rather sign athletes when they are older – around 15 or 16 years old – as by then they are a little more mature. But sometimes you get players who stand out from the rest – Maria Sharapova because of her drive and intensity and Alcaraz because of his fun and creative tennis – and then it's just different.

If you end up winning a Slam as a teenager, there's a good chance you would have had several years of guidance to get there, according to Eisenbud, which would have started when you were 11 or 12 years old. But that doesn't make it normal. A tiny number of players win a major as a teenager, especially in the men's game.

Babolat's Jean-Christophe Verborg says that if you go to some junior tournaments, you will see a few agents there. 'Everyone is trying to have the huge talent from the beginning,' Verborg says. 'The game is that everyone – the agents and the brands – is trying to sign a player before everyone else. They're trying to sign a player with high potential as soon as possible. That's maybe not the dark side of life of the job but when you sign a young player – and here I am also speaking as a father – let them enjoy life and tennis. You're looking to find the right balance. With Carlos, I think things have been done properly, step by step.'

There's no guarantee that someone who plays well at 12, who appears to be ahead of their peers, will go on to become a professional player. Muguruza says you generally can't tell much from watching a player when they're that young. 'You normally can't see anything at 12. If you see anything, you're seeing discipline or a kid who concentrates well, who seems serious and professional. But you can't tell much more than that. Probably when you start to notice potential is at 14 or 15. You can see that a player has the talent and that he competes nicely and has good technique. But 12 years old is too young. So many things can happen between 12 and possibly becoming a professional. But management companies sometimes like to take a bet on a player, as they did with Carlos, because that's part of their strategy and they're not investing that much.'

The 'Carlos Project', they would call it inside IMG. Molina first heard of Alcaraz when the boy was 11 years old. The following year, Molina was interested enough in Alcaraz's future that he travelled to several cities in Spain to watch him playing on the Rafa Nadal Tour, a junior circuit. Alcaraz wasn't like other players his age, thought Molina, who observed that the boy, while skinny, could hit every shot in tennis and loved to play drop shots and to finish points at the net.

Molina started to build a relationship with Carlos's father. But at first Alcaraz didn't understand why Molina was taking such a close interest in him; what was this all about? If Alcaraz's father was uncertain about his son signing with an agent, he eventually came around to the idea, by which time Molina had been watching Alcaraz for around eight months. While Alcaraz's father knew his way around the tennis world, as a player and then as a coach and a director of an academy, Molina impressed on him that it would be useful to have someone outside the family to help them guide Carlitos's career. This wouldn't just be about going out and getting contracts but putting the right support structure in place to allow Alcaraz to develop. While Carlitos's tennis life would have seemed reasonably straightforward when he was 12, if he was going to be successful it was necessarily going to become a lot more complicated.

Not normal. That phrase again. Molina knew it wasn't normal to be working with a 12-year-old boy. But he was determined: he has said he 'really pressured' IMG to sign Alcaraz. In his role at IMG, Molina had worked with the likes of David Ferrer, the 2013 Roland-Garros finalist, who was known for his work ethic, perhaps shaped in some way by the Spaniard's experience of his coach locking him in a small room for several hours as a punishment for not wanting to practise one day. Another client was Nicolàs Almagro, who never went beyond the quarter-finals at the Grand Slams. Both Ferrer and Almagro were elite players who got very close to the top of the sport; but, for all their efforts, they weren't the kind of players thought of as generational talents or who brought many new fans to the sport. Molina saw something in Alcaraz. He thought that, with the support of IMG, Alcaraz could potentially become the best player in the world.

By the age of 12, Alcaraz was already a couple of seasons into his partnership with Babolat. In those early years, Alcaraz also had a clothing sponsor in Lotto. That arrangement lasted until 2019, at which point he switched to Nike, who are known for being more supportive of young players than many other clothing companies (and which means they are in a good position when those juniors break through as seniors – Alcaraz would be wearing Nike when he won his first major titles and all subsequent Grand Slams).

For the first seven years that IMG represented Alcaraz, the agency 'didn't make a penny off him and I think we're going to be OK about it,' according to Eisenbud. Seven years would be from when Carlos was 12 years old until he was 19, which was the age he went stratospheric. To help Alcaraz's family during those expensive early years – when you probably need around US $100,000 (£75,000) a season – IMG waived their commission on the endorsement contracts they had brought in, which they tend to with their young players. IMG didn't need the money.

Around this time, Alcaraz was for a short while that very rare thing: a celebrity schoolboy. Whenever he could, which wasn't very often because of his tennis schedule, he attended the Marqués de los Vélez senior school in El Palmar. Inside the classroom, Alcaraz was a normal child, according to his teacher Lola Jiménez Rivas, but outside the school gates he was already standing out for what he was doing with a tennis racquet: 'At the time, Carlos was already becoming famous in the area for his tennis. He was popular. He appeared very frequently in the newspapers.'

When Lola's more recent pupils have discovered that she once taught Alcaraz, they have been curious to know more: 'Was Carlos well behaved at school? Was he a good student?' Lola has replied that Alcaraz was a calm, kind and polite boy who didn't get into any trouble with the teachers. And while he missed lots of lessons, and his grades weren't spectacular, he still managed to pass: 'Carlos got his certificate when he was 16. But he was already devoted to becoming a tennis player.' Lola can see now that it all worked out for him. As we will explore in a later chapter, by the time he was 21 years old, he was already the highest-earning tennis player in the world, making more than US $750,000 (£564,000) a week.

4

Think of this as the ultimate tennis retreat, a place of dust and sweat and homemade olive oil. It's so wholesome at the Ferrero Tennis Academy – the campus in the Spanish countryside where Carlos Alcaraz went from being a skinny boy to a man who self-identified as a bull – that they make their own oil from the olives grown there. Every year, Juan Carlos Ferrero feels as though the olives and the oil they produce taste a little different. But he is always pleasantly surprised, as are many others at the academy, by how delicious they are.

If you wish to understand Ferrero, you must appreciate why being somewhere rural and semi-remote – close to the city of Villena but surrounded by farmland, and where you're getting long views rather than distractions – is where Alcaraz's coach is happiest. This has been Ferrero's home for more than 30 years. Since arriving at the academy aged 14 – when it had a different name – he has never lived anywhere else, and he says he has no plans to ever relocate: 'The academy will always be my home and I'll have my house here.' Ferrero's wife, Eva, is from Elche, a city around half an hour's drive from the academy, and they go there 'a lot' as a family, he says, and perhaps in the future they will buy a house there, too, if that's what's best for their children. But he's never going to break his ties with this spot, somewhere he feels able to decompress, or coach with full focus, depending on what's needed. 'Working in high-performance sports, you need to make a lot of effort in order to rest properly, to be able to disconnect as well as to be truly focused when it's time,' Ferrero says. 'Living at the academy means being far away from certain distractions and that helps with this.'

Off grid, on your game: the countryside suits Ferrero's personality more than any city. Ferrero's wife is so chatty, he has said, and so willing to strike up a conversation with anyone, that she would possibly even talk to a tree. They balance each other out, he thinks, as he's much more introverted and it can take a while for people to get to know him.

Ferrero is also quite different to Alcaraz. 'Carlitos and Juan Carlos, they're opposites,' says Antonio Martínez Cascales, the founder of the academy and a hugely influential figure in Spanish tennis who has coached two world number ones in Ferrero and Alcaraz. 'Carlos is an extrovert – he's friends with everyone. Juan Carlos is more introverted or shy. Reserved, you might say. He doesn't want to open up to people he doesn't know. He doesn't like doing interviews with the media. What Juan Carlos likes is being at the academy – the location, in the countryside, is brilliant for him as here he's surrounded by people he's familiar with. When Juan Carlos is talking to people he knows, he always seems to have the right words for them.' (As Cascales acknowledges, Ferrero and Alcaraz are also similar in many ways:

ambitious, competitive, hard-working and humble, along with being willing to listen.)

The nearest bar or nightclub is several miles away, which keeps the young players focused on what they're there to do: become better athletes. And, anyway, the young tennis players can't just leave the academy whenever they please – they're not allowed to simply order a taxi. There are only three taxi companies in and around Villena and the staff at the academy, including Cascales, have contacts at each one. If a player tries to sneak out without permission, Toni, as many people call him, would hear about it (there are no secrets in the Spanish countryside). And, with the academy situated where it is, walking isn't an option either.

'Here we are very strict about players going out of the academy. Every time a player wants to go out, we call a taxi for them,' says Cascales. 'The players can never call a taxi themselves and because Villena is a small place, there are just three taxi companies so we know them all. The players can go out on Saturdays and Sundays, but it's very controlled. There would be more temptations for a young player who is living in the centre of a city or very near a big town, but living there at the academy, in the countryside, they don't have the same distractions.'

When Alcaraz returns to the academy these days to train with Ferrero, he can, of course, leave whenever he pleases. But in the years when he was boarding full time here, he had the same restrictions on his movements that all the other young players did; there were no special exemptions or privileges because he was working so closely with Ferrero. Maybe the car journey to some life outside the academy isn't actually that far but – and Alcaraz thought this when living here – it somehow feels longer, making the location seem even more remote.

Cascales's views on taxis, swerving temptations and a multitude of other subjects are of some significance to Alcaraz's story. Toni coached Ferrero from ten years old all the way to being a Grand Slam champion and ranked number one in the world. That means he helped to create the man, in Ferrero, who in turn helped to create Alcaraz, making Cascales – who has been working in tennis for around 50 years – a kind of grandfather figure here. Many of the central characters at the academy talk about each other as if they are family. Cascales regards Ferrero as being almost like his son. Ferrero considers Cascales to be 'like a second father': 'He taught me so much, not just in tennis. We are really close. He lives at the academy too and is the godfather of my eldest. I learned a lot from him. In coaching, I would say I learned from him to always be looking at what is better for the player. Maybe you'll get it wrong but at least you'll know the reason was correct.'

In this tennis family, Alcaraz thinks of Ferrero as his second father, while Ferrero views Alcaraz as his 'fourth kid', in addition to his three biological children. Cascales has also been directly involved in Alcaraz's development, as a second coach. When Ferrero has needed a break, Cascales has accompanied Alcaraz to tournaments – and he has evidently done a fine job, as in the summer of 2024 he was recognized as the coach of the month on the ATP Tour (if this sounds a bit like a burger chain's employee of the month, it's more meaningful than that).

It's Ferrero's name on the academy now, but it was initially Cascales's idea to build this place – which was originally known as the Equelite

Academy – and when he's not travelling, that's where you'll find him. This piece of land has shaped Ferrero since the mid-1990s – first as a boy, then as a teenager trying to make his way in tennis, and also as a man, during his playing career and subsequently as a coach. When ten-year-old Ferrero started training with Cascales, it was at a club near Villena. In 1994, when Ferrero was 14 years old, Cascales bought the land and property where the academy is today. Why, Cascales thought, should the promising players from the area have to leave to train in Barcelona and other distant cities? Cascales wanted somewhere that the players could stay overnight, avoiding the hassle of going home every night – and Ferrero made it his base.

This was a start-up in the middle of nowhere. In the beginning, there was next to nothing on the land that Cascales had purchased; he had bought some wheatfields that came with a little, red house, and he would create the academy around that property, which would need rebuilding. On that farmland, Ferrero and the other children helped Cascales with the construction of the clay courts, including moving the building materials around with forklift trucks and unloading them where needed (they say you have to learn how to suffer to play well on the surface, but could Ferrero be the only Roland-Garros champion who in his youth helped to build a clay court?). It was a rustic, basic existence; there were times when they didn't have running water and would have to carry jugs of water from nearby to fill up their bottles for practice. When Cascales turned on the two electric heaters in the small house, the lights would go out as they didn't have enough power. For warmth, the players sat close to a large fireplace. If Cascales ever wanted to punish his young athletes, he would send them out into the cold to collect dried grapevines, twigs and anything else they could throw on the fire.

In those early years, when the academy was reachable only via a dirt track, there was trouble when it rained; you sometimes couldn't get your car through the mud, and visitors would have no choice to stay overnight. Accommodation was also basic. For a while, Ferrero slept on the top bunk while Cascales was on the bottom bunk and they also shared that room with a dog called Alaska, the academy's mascot. There were moments when it was far from certain that the academy had a future. But somehow it kept going. On Friday nights, everyone would gather around the television to watch a horror film together. Those were happy times for Ferrero. The players had a name for their academy: 'La Casa'. Home.

As a player, Ferrero was often known as 'El Mosquito' on account of his speed and slender build and, presumably, his ability to 'bite' his opponents. It wasn't a nickname he liked very much, if at all, but what could he do about that? He was sometimes also known as 'Chavalito', meaning 'Little Kid' or 'Little Fella'.

Ferrero also didn't care for being a celebrity. The first time he felt famous, after winning the Davis Cup with Spain in 2000 when he was 20 years old, he didn't leave the house for almost two weeks 'because it was truly unbearable, with a flood of people, photos and autographs – I couldn't stand it, it overwhelmed me, it stressed me out,' he told *El Mundo*. Ferrero has recalled being very introverted and craving solitude. Consider that this was before the age of smartphones and social media, which would later make Alcaraz's experience of new fame all the more intense and impossible to escape (these days, going into your house and closing the door behind you doesn't make it all stop, as it did for Ferrero). In time, Ferrero came to accept that there was a part of his life that he'd previously thought was just his but that he would have to share with others. Slowly, he became used to the idea of being a public figure, but he never sought the spotlight; he wanted peace and quiet – and there was plenty of that in the countryside near Villena, as there still is today.

Cascales and Ferrero have so many memories as they walk around the academy. Over the years, Cascales did what he could to upgrade the academy as well as Ferrero's tennis. As Ferrero's profile grew, it became easier for the academy to borrow money to expand and improve their facilities. Just a month after Alcaraz was born, Ferrero won a very one-sided final against unseeded Dutchman Martin Verkerk to take the 2003 Roland-Garros title. That same season, Ferrero also reached the US Open final. He didn't bring his best level against Andy Roddick, and lost that match, but he had already done enough to become only the second Spaniard in the modern era (the first being Carlos Moyá) to hold the number-one ranking. He was 23 years old at the time – so by no means the youngest number one – and would spend eight weeks in total at the top.

Ferrero could possibly have achieved more in his own playing career. Rafa Nadal has told Ferrero on a few occasions that he could have won Roland-Garros three or four times. Ferrero tends to agree. While he reached the 2002 final, he wasn't at his physical best (having twisted his ankle in practice earlier at the tournament) and lost to fellow Spaniard Albert Costa. After landing that first title in Paris in 2003, he had some terrible luck with chickenpox and injuries and was never able to get back to his peak – and would never again go beyond the third round at a Grand Slam that suited his game. Three times during his career, Ferrero was part of the Spanish team that won 'La Ensaladera', which is the affectionate nickname that the Spanish have for the salad-bowl-shaped Davis Cup. When Ferrero retired aged 32 in 2012, he wasn't facing the emptiness that is a problem for so many ex-athletes as he already had an academy to focus on. In that moment, and for a while afterwards, there were no thoughts about going back on tour as a full-time coach. He took padel seriously for a while. But mostly Ferrero put his energy into the academy.

As you might expect, Ferrero's accommodation has improved over the years. After those early days of sharing a room, he moved to a house in the grounds and eventually built a new, larger property for himself and his family, where they continue to live. 'Ferrero smells amazing,' Andrea Petkovic, a German player turned broadcaster, podcaster and writer, noted at the 2025 Australian Open. Back home in Spain, with a house inside the academy, Ferrero can, he has said, 'smell tennis' every day.

In this age of TikTok, Ferrero knows young players can still be distracted in the countryside: 'Nowadays, with phones and all the technology, the location matters less.' But you shouldn't enrol at the Ferrero Tennis Academy imagining you're going to be spending hours every day scrolling on your phone. To stop players from becoming 'addicted' to their phones, before going on court or to the gym they must lock their devices inside clear, plastic boxes mounted to a wall. There's no temptation to take your phone from your bag during practice and have a peek. 'When Juan Carlos came to the academy for the first time, which was more than 30 years ago, we used to have one of those payphones that you had to feed with coins,' Cascales says. 'That was the only connection with the outside world. And when the coins ran out, the call dropped out. Now we have a big problem with phones because players can always be connected. It's dangerous because they are almost addicted to their mobile phones. We had this idea to put these boxes there to avoid distractions when they are on court or in the gym. Obviously, the players have times during the day when they can look at their phones. They can use their phones between two and three in the afternoons and also at night, but apart from that they are training or they have school and it's impossible.'

At the academy, Alcaraz would have been reminded that too much screen time can be destructive for a young player's tennis career. 'It's a big problem for players to be on their phones the whole time. Only players who reach the top 100 will leave tennis financially comfortable and it's so difficult to reach that level. Being on your phone a lot can be a distraction,' Cascales says. 'We try to keep them busy – watching matches on the TV, for example, or doing some mental work as part of a special programme. But that's not enough. When a player is on court, they are improving their techniques; but off the court it's so important to train your brain. It's important to keep focused and motivated – young players have to be committed on and off the court. They can't be on their phones too much.'

The Ferrero Tennis Academy is an industrious place, with a large screen displaying the plan for the day, showing when and where players are training and when they have sessions with a physiotherapist, a psychologist or a nutritionist. But if it suits Ferrero, what about Alcaraz? Home-grown olive oil; tranquillity, farmland all around you. Is this the kind of environment you imagined helped to create Alcaraz, one of the sport's great showmen and entertainers?

Put a bunch of teenagers together at a tennis academy and there's a chance a few of them are going to be partying hard or almost going feral – Andre Agassi went to a facility in Florida that he thought 'slowly turned us into animals', to the point it felt like '*Lord of the Flies* with forehands' – but the Ferrero Tennis Academy isn't like that. For Alcaraz, this was an academy where he could feel, as he once said to *The New York Times* in a mix of English and Spanish, 'really *tranquilo*'. In the calm of the countryside, and with a quiet mind, Alcaraz spent his days, as all the other players did, on 'tennis, tennis and more tennis'. Here's what they say about Ferrero's academy: it's somewhere you go to sweat under the Spanish sun.

After retirement, Ferrero had been living a secluded life and enjoying moments to himself and his family. At that point, there was only one way he would go back to being talked about in the media almost every day – and that was by coaching a player who would be contending for Grand Slam titles. And that's what would happen, though his fame would be different second time around: in public, Ferrero would no longer just be Ferrero, who was once the best in the world at what he did, but Alcaraz's coach. A former champion with a large ego would have struggled with that concept. But it would prove absolutely fine by Ferrero. In recent years, there have been all number of 'superstar coaches', with former champions returning to elite tennis to advise players. Nadal had one of those in Moyá, a past Roland-Garros champion and world number one, while Roger Federer has worked with Stefan Edberg and Novak Djokovic has employed Boris Becker,

Agassi and, most improbably of all, Andy Murray, just months after he retired as a player.

All those partnerships started when the younger players were already established at the top of the game and were looking for the insights or nuanced strategy that might give them an edge. It was different with Ferrero, who started working with Alcaraz when he was raw and 15 years old. Ferrero is a former Grand Slam champion and world number one who is about as far as you get from being a celebrity coach – he was there from the early years and he doesn't like being feted, gawped at and talked about.

As Ferrero's standing in tennis has risen again, so has his price tag. Chris Lewit, an American coach with a strong interest in Spanish tennis, says a friend contemplated paying US $2,000 (£1,500) for an hour's private lesson with Ferrero – which was the price he was quoted – but, in the end, decided against it. Lewit had the impression that the price wasn't high because Ferrero is money-minded but because setting the cost at that level stops him from being constantly asked to do private lessons. Undisturbed, Ferrero gets to quietly go about his day.

*

Going back to his childhood, Juan Carlos Ferrero has always had a ferocious work ethic. When Antonio Cascales was coaching Ferrero, there were days when they would spend four hours on court together – four intense hours – and that wasn't enough for Ferrero: he wanted even more tennis. Ferrero wished to continue, to keep on doing what he could to improve. 'Juan Carlos has always been committed to his tennis,' Cascales says. 'I remember Juan Carlos was a perfectionist. Everything had to be perfect. Everything had to be the way he wanted it to be.'

The only time Ferrero's love of tennis dimmed was after his mother died. 'Juan Carlos's mother passed away when he was 16 years old and he decided to stop playing tennis. He lost all of his motivation because of the death of his mother. I helped him, and so did others, including his father, to get back on track,' Cascales says. Cascales was part of the tennis boom in Spain that followed the end of General Franco's dictatorship in the 1970s, when the number of tennis clubs surged as playing the sport became a signifier that you were part of the affluent middle class with money to spend on leisure. But there has never been anything leisurely about Cascales's approach to tennis. Or Ferrero's: 'My strong work ethic comes from working daily on developing good habits.'

In their work together at the academy, Ferrero and Cascales have always felt as though the only way for any player – Carlos Alcaraz included – to realize their potential was by giving everything to their tennis. Humility and good manners are also key; you can't let your ego get in the way of needing to spend more time on court or in the gym. If other facilities feel like tennis fame academies, that's not how it goes in Villena. Ferrero and Cascales don't like to see players getting ahead of themselves. 'At the academy, we believe it's important players recognize there's a long road ahead of them. We don't want to see young players, who are just taking the first steps, thinking they are bigger than they are,' Cascales says. 'The main philosophy at the academy is, as you might imagine, allowing young players to reach professional tournaments. But there's a priority on humility and hard work.'

Cascales wants players to be 'docile'. Not in matches, but in practice. Docile also doesn't mean soft or weak or pathetic. Just coachable. Willing to listen and to learn. 'When they are working together, it is truly helpful for the player to believe in his coach and to do what they command,' says Iñaki Etxegia, chief executive of the Ferrero Tennis Academy. 'If the player is asking why they should do certain things or they are avoiding doing some of what the coaches have asked of them, that's not good. The player shouldn't be docile while competing but they should be when they are working to improve.'

Coaches at the Ferrero Tennis Academy want the children who train there to be good humans as well as great athletes. When deciding whether he wished to work with Alcaraz or not, Ferrero evaluated much more than pure tennis talent. He wanted to be sure that Alcaraz, despite his early success in junior tennis, wasn't becoming overly confident, as other young players sometimes do. 'Juan Carlos knew Carlitos had been winning a lot of tournaments in Spain and around the world, but he could see that Carlitos wasn't showing off,' Cascales says. 'Carlitos was still acting normally. He was the same. Seeing how Carlitos was staying grounded, that was one of the factors that helped Juan Carlos to make that decision.' (When Alcaraz was older, he was perhaps more emotionally volatile, Ferrero has recalled, with the teenager sometimes a little 'cocky' after his victories.)

After Alcaraz joined the academy, all the indications were that his parents had done a good job raising him. There was a natural warmth, friendliness and humility about Alcaraz as he played football, cards and other games, or just chatted, with his fellow players, the coaches and the maintenance staff (though perhaps he was a little shy with Ferrero in the beginning, as he got over the shock of being coached by a former Grand Slam champion). At the end of every session, Alcaraz would say thank you to his coaches – a small act that means a great deal to those around him. 'Saying thank you shows Carlos is humble,' says Cascales, 'and that he values the work the team are doing.' (Several Grand Slam titles later and Alcaraz continues to say thank you to his coaches at the end of every practice, according to Cascales.)

Alcaraz's collaboration with Ferrero had started with a bold pitch from Alcaraz's agent, Albert Molina. Would Ferrero be interested in working with a junior who had yet to make any impact on the wider sport? Ferrero had recently split with Alexander Zverev, a German in the world's top ten. Ferrero wasn't without offers. Several established players wanted to hire him, including Dominic Thiem and Simona Halep. Going with any of them would have been a safer and easier option for Ferrero, though also potentially less satisfying. What Molina was proposing was something riskier but potentially more rewarding. Molina was offering Ferrero 'a project'. That intrigued Ferrero.

Cascales had guided Ferrero from a low level all the way to the very top of the sport. Could Ferrero now do the same with Alcaraz, who had all the shots but sometimes got into a muddle about which one to play, and who needed to learn how to focus on every point? And who also needed guidance about all sorts of other things, such as knowing how to rest, eat and recover and the importance of sacrifice and being on time. Ferrero thought about it and he liked the idea. Of course, there was no guarantee that Alcaraz could become a top player, but Ferrero had the opportunity to shape how Alcaraz thought and trained and competed and that excited him.

Thiem wanted Ferrero for only 15 weeks a year. Cascales thought Ferrero could potentially combine that job with coaching Alcaraz. Wouldn't Alcaraz be useful as an occasional hitting partner for the

Austrian? But Ferrero wasn't interested in splitting his time between two players, as he felt that wouldn't allow him to do his job properly. Only if Ferrero worked full time with Alcaraz could he hope to get the most out of the teenager.

Before Ferrero saw Alcaraz play, he had heard about him – about this boy who was playing such wildly creative tennis. Alcaraz, meanwhile, had been talking to his parents about the former world number one. Just imagine, Alcaraz said to his mother and father, if he won Roland-Garros with Ferrero sitting in his coaching box. The first time Ferrero had seen Alcaraz compete was in 2017, when the under-14 Spanish teams championship was held at his academy. Alcaraz was the stand-out player, winning all his singles and doubles matches to lead Murcia to the title, and after that he started spending time at the academy.

By February 2018, when Alcaraz was 14 years old, it was 'clear' – according to Etxegia – that the academy would be 'helping Carlos'. That month, Ferrero and Cascales went to watch Alcaraz play his first professional match at a Futures tournament – the lowest level of pro tennis – at the Real Murcia Club. Alcaraz defeated Federico Gaio, an Italian ranked 292 in the world, and went on to win his next match as well, taking him into the quarter-finals, where his run ended. He won US $438 (£329) that week and acquired something else even more important: the belief that he would end up being a professional tennis player (Alcaraz's father and family friend Alfredo Sarria were dreaming about the junior winning a professional tournament one day – they couldn't have imagined that just five years later Alcaraz would be a Grand Slam champion). The following month, the academy gave Alcaraz a wild card into a junior tournament that was held there.

'Around that time,' Etxegia says, 'Juan Carlos had decided to take on Carlos personally.'

Ferrero liked Alcaraz's game. With the confidence to come to the net to finish the point off, and his inclination to play inside the court rather than deep behind the baseline, Alcaraz wasn't your typical young Spanish player. Alcaraz was different, Ferrero thought, with a highly dynamic and aggressive game. Alcaraz's tennis was a little uneven at the Futures tournament in Murcia, following one spectacular set of tennis with another that was less than brilliant. But that was to be expected from a 14-year-old. Alcaraz also didn't have the strength and the physicality of his older opponents. But they could work on that.

The eight months that Ferrero spent with Zverev hadn't been at all straightforward – but they had certainly been educational for the Spaniard, teaching him about the kind of player he wanted to work with in the future. Ferrero didn't think Zverev had been as committed to his tennis as he should have been. In Ferrero's view, Zverev was often distracted and unable to focus on tennis. Zverev seemed to always be on his phone, either messaging or on calls, Ferrero observed. The German also 'wasted time on Instagram', Ferrero said on the *3 Iguales* podcast. People would suddenly appear in Zverev's life. When they were supposed to be training for three hours, Zverev was able to perform at a high level for only about half that time, according to Ferrero. When Ferrero addressed this with Zverev, questioning his attitude and also his lateness for sessions, the two of them had 'an argument'.

Zverev had a different take on why their professional relationship broke down, suggesting that Ferrero had been disrespectful to everyone in his team. That was why, Zverev said, he felt he should stop the partnership.

Ultimately, Ferrero said, he and Zverev had different opinions about what it meant to be professional, perhaps because they weren't from the same culture. One thing they agreed on was that it was best not to continue. When Ferrero chose to work with Alcaraz, it helped that the two were both from southern Spain. While they had different personalities, they have the same culture and they understood each other from the outset. As professional tennis is a small community, Ferrero was always going to run into Zverev again in a big moment, adding a subplot to what was happening on court. In 2024, when Alcaraz won Roland-Garros for the first time, he did so by coming from two sets to one down against Zverev in the final.

Coaching Alcaraz would mean a significant pay cut for Ferrero. It wouldn't be possible for Alcaraz to pay Ferrero anything like the money he would have received while he was advising Zverev. For this to work, IMG would pay a portion of Ferrero's salary, with Molina telling *El Partidazo de COPE*: 'We helped with part of it.' Ferrero would have to accept a lower rate, with the prospect of being rewarded in the future if Alcaraz became a top player. It helped, Molina thought, that he had known Ferrero for a long time and that they trusted each other; Ferrero could be sure that Molina, IMG and the Alcaraz family wouldn't let him down and would be true to their word. Had Ferrero coached any of the top players who had been asking him, he could have continued to have lived a life of five-star hotels and occasional rides on private jets, which he had experienced with Zverev. Instead, in the beginning with Alcaraz, they wouldn't always fly between cities; sometimes they would get in the car and road-trip between events. Other coaches would question Ferrero's choice, saying to him: 'What are you doing? You were the world number one. How can you travel with a kid, driving back and forth?'

This was, in so many ways, a significant commitment from Ferrero. 'Juan Carlos made a big personal investment with Carlitos, treating him like he was his son. It's a lot to take on a kid when he's 15 and try to turn him into a big player,' says former top-ten ATP player Emilio Sánchez, an influential figure in Spanish tennis who first saw Alcaraz play in junior events at his own academy outside Barcelona. Sánchez has known Alcaraz for years and Ferrero for even longer. 'Carlitos had big skills then but he was still a kid. Juan Carlos is a big part of Carlitos's fast improvement. Juan Carlos took a diamond and cleaned it up. Carlitos going to Juan Carlos's academy also showed selflessness and humility on the part of Carlitos's father. He's a tennis coach and he was giving his kid to someone else. Judy Murray did the same when she sent her son Andy to me at my academy in Barcelona. She was a coach and she had great vision. Carlitos's father saw they needed a coach with experience to guide their son and Juan Carlos had won a Grand Slam and been the world number one and been through that. But it says a lot about Carlitos's father that he has always been happy to be in the background.'

The reality was that Alcaraz had become too good to stay in El Palmar. There wasn't anyone around who was at a high enough level to train with him; and it was hard to persuade others to travel there to hit with him. Had Alcaraz stayed in his village, he would still have made it to the ATP Tour, but it would have taken him longer to get there and he wouldn't have been the teenage phenomenon that he became. At the academy, Alcaraz would always have a high-quality player to hit with. The likes of David Ferrer, Nicolàs Almagro and Pablo Carreño Busta – all Spaniards who reached the top ten in the ATP rankings and in Ferrer's case the top three – have trained at the academy over the years (when he was new on the ATP Tour, Alcaraz said Carreño Busta was his best friend on the circuit, despite the age gap of more than ten years, the pair having bonded over chess and golf as well as tennis).

Moving to the academy was when tennis stopped being a game for Alcaraz, who until then hadn't appreciated how much work goes into being an athlete. He was given a bed in one of the bungalows or huts on site. Alcaraz's tennis was a little messy, the coaches thought, when he first arrived. For all his promise, his serving technique wasn't brilliant. Ferrero got to work, making a biomechanical adjustment to Alcaraz's serve, and it wasn't always easy.

There were plenty more adjustments that needed to be made. He needed to be fitter, stronger, more astute. It was a big life change for Alcaraz, moving away from his family and friends in El Palmar, and he missed them. There were periods of homesickness. But Alcaraz always knew – this was clear to the people around him – that being at the academy was best for him. Only after joining the academy did tennis become Alcaraz's career, according to family friend Alfredo Sarria. 'Carlitos was winning a lot when he was younger, but it's hard to know whether a 13-year-old will end up being a professional tennis player. There are thousands of people who play tennis very well but being a professional is different. That's why tennis only became a career for Carlitos when he was 15 and not before.'

Years later, by which time he was a Grand Slam champion, Alcaraz would make a short motivational speech to the young players at the academy, telling them how moving there as a boy had helped him to focus on what was important and what he was trying to accomplish: 'I always say that maybe my tennis career so far would not have been possible without the help of everyone, without the help of Juan Carlos, and without having lived here. In the end, that made me focus, made me really concentrate, think about tennis and have a clear goal in my career.'

Another significant change came when Alcaraz turned 16 (not long after he had almost beaten Ferrer, a former Roland-Garros finalist, in a practice match that Ferrer still brings up with Alcaraz today). Until that moment, Alcaraz had divided his time between Villena and El Palmar, where he still had his family and friends. He had been returning home at the weekends and sometimes on Wednesdays when he had a lighter training schedule than other weekdays. But when Alcaraz was 16, Ferrero and Cascales had a conversation with Alcaraz's parents; they wanted him to live and train at the academy full time. As much as Ferrero and Cascales liked Alcaraz's friends, those schoolmates weren't trying to become professional tennis players. Moving to Villena would remove the distraction of friends and parties.

*

Think *Rocky* but in the Spanish countryside, surrounded by olive trees and with the soft thwack-thwack of players hitting tennis balls on nearby courts. Carlos Alcaraz loves watching the training montages from the *Rocky* films. He went through something similar himself at the Ferrero Tennis Academy, going from a gangly 15-year-old, with hardly any muscles at all, to the physical force he is today. Becoming quite possibly the best mover in tennis, and perhaps even the fastest and most electric athlete the sport has ever known. Alcaraz was so slim when he joined the academy that Juan Carlos Ferrero called him 'Little Noodle' (wearing Nadal-style sleeveless shirts was unthinkable then). Alcaraz remembers being 'a super-skinny guy' who didn't have the strength to play as aggressively as he wanted to.

Before joining the academy, Alcaraz had been practising only once a day and hadn't been doing much fitness work. In a significant change to his schedule, he had tennis and fitness in the morning at the academy, and would then train again in the afternoon. In the beginning, the effort required was quite shocking for Alcaraz; and during his first pre-season training block he was almost in tears, one of the fitness coaches at the academy told *Vanity Fair* magazine. But Alcaraz soon got used to it, just as he had become accustomed to everything else that was expected of him, such as keeping his room tidy and looking after his belongings. Physically and mentally, Alcaraz couldn't help but grow up faster than he would have done if he had stayed at home in El Palmar.

Day by day, fitness session by fitness session, a new disciplined and hardened Carlos was emerging. He was putting in the effort and taking care of the details like never before, with Ferrero telling him how much impact it would have on how he played on court. In all his years working in sport, as a podiatrist for tennis players, footballers and other athletes, Carles Ruiz has never known someone with a body like Alcaraz's, with that combination of flexibility and force. 'When I met Carlitos for the first time, I saw there was something different – and not just different to other tennis players but different to other athletes too,' says Ruiz, who first studied Alcaraz when he was 17 years old. 'What I saw in Carlitos I had never seen before with anyone. And it wasn't just one part of his body. But all of him. I could see he had potential in every part of his body.' Alcaraz had 'very good flexibility and force', which Ruiz hadn't previously seen in other tennis players. Alcaraz's flexibility means he can stretch to reach balls that most other players wouldn't even get close to.

After that first biomechanical analysis of Alcaraz, Ruiz compared the young player to a Ferrari. Ruiz thought Alcaraz 'had good genes inside him'. But being genetically blessed was never going to be enough for Alcaraz. 'If you have good genes and sit on the sofa, you're going to have nothing. You have to work and Carlitos did a lot of work,' says Ruiz. 'When I started working with Carlitos, he was skinny, but his body changed a lot with the special training he was doing. If you look at Carlitos, you can see how much work he has been doing, and why he became a better tennis player much earlier than we had all thought.'

Every three months or so, Ruiz has travelled from his clinic in Valencia to Murcia to do a biomechanical analysis of Alcaraz; to discover where the stresses were and how the multiple Grand Slam champion might have been overloading his body. The podiatrist has looked at Carlos's feet, knees and hips. He examined how Alcaraz was functioning. How did the latest measurements of Alcaraz's body compare to the ones Ruiz had taken three months ago? In short, was Alcaraz's body in a better or a worse state than it had been then?

The information that Ruiz has passed on to Alcaraz's physiotherapist, Juanjo Moreno (who considers Alcaraz to be like a son or a little brother), and the rest of the team has been invaluable.

It has helped determine the training that Alcaraz has done before and during tournaments. Ruiz's expertise has also helped Alcaraz to avoid injuries that could have destroyed his season or even threatened his career. 'I need to see Carlitos every three months, as tennis players have a lot of injuries and overload their bodies during the season,' Ruiz says. 'I study how he moves on the court and also on my machines. I can look back at my past measurements to see if he has improved or whether he is getting worse. The foot, knees and hips are changing a lot during the year because there is a lot of stress and other things.'

Ruiz's work with Alcaraz has included making custom insoles by hand. For years, Alcaraz hasn't trained or played a match without those insoles inside his shoes. They have stabilized Alcaraz's feet, helping to protect against ankle sprains and absorbing some of the impact when landing, which is especially important on unforgiving hard courts. The insoles – hidden from public view, and quite possibly covered in perspiration – are a kind of secret weapon. Alcaraz is the quickest tennis player Ruiz has ever seen. The insoles probably make him go even faster (Ruiz can't say for sure, though, because Alcaraz always wears them so there's no easy comparison).

Ruiz's expertise has enabled Alcaraz to travel quickly around the court without putting too much energy and force – and therefore stress – on his body. Part of Ruiz's role has been advising Alcaraz on which shoes to wear; as Alcaraz is contracted to Nike, that has meant suggesting which of their products would be best for his feet and for his performance on court. Taking that further, and helping Alcaraz to have more of an edge over his opponents, Ruiz has been working with Nike to develop a personalized shoe perfectly suited to Alcaraz's feet.

*

The improvement in Carlos Alcaraz's fitness at the Ferrero Tennis Academy was rapid. Just four years after joining, and aged just nineteen, he was as strong, fast and physically resilient as anyone else in tennis. That year, 2022, he won three successive five-set matches to reach the US Open final, including a fourth-round match against Marin Čilić that lasted almost four hours and wasn't completed until gone 2am. It was 5am by the time Alcaraz got into bed (after doing his warm-down, showering, eating, speaking to the media and travelling from the US Open site in Queens back to his hotel in Manhattan). His next match, a quarter-final against Jannik Sinner, was even longer and went on even later – this time, play continued for more than five hours, taking them all the way to 2.50am. Such was Alcaraz's strength that night, he shouted, 'I'm a bull!' in Spanish in the direction of Juan Carlos Ferrero and the rest of his team, inspired by what his coach had written on one of his water bottles: '*Vamos, toro*' – 'Let's go, bull.' Rafa Nadal had always been depicted as the raging bull, and here was another Spanish tennis player who identified with that animal (contrast with Ferrero, who will forever be associated, and not through his choice, with a mosquito). The latest-ever finish in the tournament's history meant Alcaraz didn't get to sleep until after 6am. Then came another five-setter in his semi-final against Frances Tiafoe.

Clearly, recovery after matches is easier when you're only 19 years old. Nonetheless, on top of the exhilarating and entertaining tennis that Alcaraz was playing, that was an astonishing physical feat by the teenager at the US Open. In all, Alcaraz spent 23 hours and 39 minutes on court during that tournament – so almost an entire day, and a record for the US Open or at any of the other Grand Slams – on the way to landing his first major title. No one was calling him 'Little Noodle' then.

You don't get this strong without eating a lot. When Alcaraz appeared at the ATP Finals in Turin one year, the other seven men who had qualified for the season-ending tournament all agreed that it was the Spaniard who loaded his plate with the most food from the hotel's breakfast buffet.

*

When players are new to the Ferrero Tennis Academy – and Carlos Alcaraz wasn't any different – they can be shocked at how long the days are. In addition to their tennis training, they have school for at least three and a half hours a day, going up to five hours on Wednesdays. Monday to Friday, breakfast is followed by morning lessons that start at 8.30am and go on for an hour and a half. Every weekday except Wednesday, after several hours of practice and fitness sessions, the players return to the classroom from 6.30 to 8.30pm. Training is shorter on Wednesdays, allowing for more lessons from 5 to 8.30pm (later comes the most challenging part of the day, according to Antonio Cascales, which is trying to ensure all the teenagers are in bed and asleep by 11 or 11.30pm).

'The grades aren't brilliant but some students are getting As. Bs and Cs are the most common,' says Patricia Tortosa, headteacher at the academy's school. 'We try to teach them that they could be injured tomorrow so they need to have a Plan B and that's their studies. When players first come to the academy, school isn't so important for them; but we try to introduce that idea into their brains. But after two or three months of being here, they realize their studies are very important. They see every day how players are injured and might have to go home for three months or so. It's a reality that they can see.'

It's important, Juan Carlos Ferrero says, that the academy gives the students an education away from the tennis court. 'We work to take care of the person [as well as the tennis player],' Ferrero says when asked about the academy's guiding values and philosophies. 'All students come here looking to be professionals but we need to provide a full education. We try to educate them in values as they're living with us 24 hours a day. The academy tries to keep pretty familiar. We can make errors but we should always be looking to do the best for the kids. Not treating them just like players.'

A year before he became a Grand Slam champion, Alcaraz put the books aside, giving himself more time to spend on his tennis. 'When the players finish their school studies at 18, they decide whether they continue their studies at university or whether they just focus on tennis,' says Tortosa. 'Carlos didn't want to carry on. He decided to stop to focus on his tennis.'

5

Even in normal times, the Ferrero Tennis Academy feels a little cut off from the world. During the global pandemic, it was even more so. As Covid spread around Spain and the rest of the world, Carlos Alcaraz was separated from his family and locked down in the academy for around a month and a half. It was an upsetting experience for him yet also, in some ways, the making of him. The players and the coaching staff who chose to spend lockdown inside the academy were fortunate, Juan Carlos Ferrero says: 'Everybody struggled with the lockdown experience but we were not alone. For sure, it was easier for us than for others as we were able to keep in contact with other people, play sports and so on. We got lucky.'

During that time, Alcaraz couldn't even see his family, not even on his 17th birthday, which he celebrated without his parents and brothers. For a teenager who is as close to his family as Carlos is, that separation was 'hard', according to Antonio Cascales; but of course that period was challenging for everyone, and not just for ambitious young tennis players. 'Lockdown was very difficult for Carlitos,' says Kiko Navarro, who was coaching Alcaraz at the time, in combination with Juan Carlos Ferrero. 'We tried to talk a lot with Carlitos because it wasn't easy for him to be away from home and away from his family for so long. It wasn't a comfortable situation for him.'

Being away from your family, out there on the tennis road or training away from home, is part of being a tennis player but usually not for as long as a month and a half – and not in such extreme and disturbing circumstances. Staff at the academy provided extra psychological support for the teenagers who were struggling without seeing their families. The Spanish players seemed to find the experience harder than the international guests. 'In Spain we are very close to our families and it was difficult for the players not being able to see their parents,' says headteacher Patricia Tortosa. 'Maybe a player's grandmother or aunt had passed away. But they were here inside the academy.'

It was Alcaraz's father who had suggested his son should spend lockdown in the academy, inside the tennis bubble – though of course he couldn't have known how long that period would last and how severe the restrictions would be. In February 2020, a 16-year-old Alcaraz, ranked outside the world's top 400 and wearing a pair of multicoloured shorts that were about as vivid as the tennis he played, had won a match on the ATP Tour for the first time. It was no ordinary day – and night – for Alcaraz, with that first victory coming against a fellow Spaniard, Albert Ramos-Viñolas, in a match on the clay of Rio de Janeiro that lasted for three and a half hours and was completed at 3am.

Unfortunately for Alcaraz, that breakthrough victory came just before tennis – along with much of the rest of the world – was shut down, depriving him of the chance to build some momentum. With the lockdown starting in Spain in the middle of March, Alcaraz wouldn't play another tournament until August that year – a long block of time for a teenager who, with that first ATP match victory in Brazil, would have felt as though he was just getting going.

Just before Spain went into lockdown, Alcaraz had returned from a tournament during which he and Navarro had seen on the television news that a virus was spreading around the world. With heavy restrictions on travel and mixing with people who weren't living with you looking increasingly imminent, Alcaraz's father said to Navarro that Alcaraz should quickly get to the academy. That would be best for Alcaraz, his father thought, as it would allow him to continue working on his game and his physical conditioning. Just a day after taking Alcaraz to the academy, Navarro recalls, everyone was locked up in their houses. Had they dithered, had Alcaraz spent lockdown in El Palmar, that could have had an impact on his tennis education. Alcaraz's father had moved quickly and decisively. Navarro considers this to have been another good decision taken by the dad to help his young son.

The first couple of weeks of being locked down inside the academy were the weirdest. Not knowing who had the virus, they kept their distance from each other, eating their meals on their own on separate tables and not touching or going anywhere near each other.

But a fortnight into lockdown, the 40 or so players and around 10 staff realized they were all healthy and they stopped with the social distancing, though they still couldn't leave or let anyone visit. Some of the younger players didn't understand why they couldn't travel to see their families, or why their parents and siblings couldn't come to see them. 'We weren't living the reality that people were living outside the academy, but it was hard for the players not to be able to see their families,' Tortosa says. 'The players couldn't understand why we couldn't go out. They weren't reading newspapers or choosing to watch the news. We used to put the news on the TV because we wanted them to see the reality of what was happening in the world. We explained to them that people were dying outside the academy and what the situation was. We told them they were lucky to be at the academy.'

To keep the players' spirits up, the staff served themed dinners (such as Mexican night or American night), organized games and online talks from professional players and brought in a projector and covered the windows of the clubhouse with blankets for a cinema club. Staff also devised ways to keep players motivated in training. 'The environment was pretty safe and healthy. The 40 players that stayed were well looked after by the members of staff who had also stayed there during the pandemic,' says Cascales. 'We gave the players all the attention they needed and arranged many activities for them to enjoy the stay and feel good.'

Living and training at the academy is always intense, with a busy schedule of training and schoolwork, but that three-month stretch brought additional challenges. It also meant that Alcaraz would have minimum distractions in his life, allowing him to get even more serious about his tennis. 'Without any doubt, being in the academy helped Carlos as he lived in a professional tennis environment,' says Cascales. 'As a teenager, he was at a complex age and it would have been easy to get distracted. From 16 to 17, Carlos became a young adult.'

It was a different, more focused Carlos who emerged from the academy. 'We saw a change in Carlitos during the pandemic,' says Alfredo Sarria. 'That was a difficult time for Carlitos – at one point, he didn't see his family for months – but it brought about a change in his mentality. We noticed at the end that he was even more focused on his career. We saw that if he had a lot of distractions away from tennis, his brain wasn't so focused on his career. He took some difficult decisions around that time. He broke up with his girlfriend, even though he loved her. He was also spending less time with his friends and with his older brother Álvaro, who is his best friend, and their younger brothers. But you can now say that living at the academy during the pandemic was a good decision for Carlitos. That's when he became more professional. That's when tennis became his life.'

Even before the pandemic, there had been a family feel to the academy. Everyone celebrates everyone else's success there. From modest beginnings – from essentially being just wheatfields – Cascales's creation has become one of the leading academies in the world; and it has done so, according to Patricia Tortosa, without losing its humanity and humility. One of the academy traditions that demonstrates that sense of togetherness is the annual football match between the players and the coaches at Christmas (while Alcaraz doesn't play much football, because of the risk of injury, he has made an exception for that match, breaking off his preparations for the Australian Open to take part, and you might also spot Ferrero on the touchline, shouting instructions into a megaphone).

The academy's family feeling was enhanced by spending lockdown together hitting tennis balls. 'One of the differences between our academy and others is that we are like a big family. We all have that feeling here,' Cascales says. 'This is the only academy where the owners live on site. Juan Carlos has a house here and I also live here. One of the philosophies of the academy is that the coach has a close relationship with the player – that he gets along very well with the player and enhances their game. Living together like one big family during the pandemic, that only made the family feeling even stronger.'

Some have speculated that the pandemic – which meant months without competitive tennis, and with all the restrictions placed on athletes who would usually be moving from one country to another from week to week – slowed Alcaraz's path into the tennis elite. Would he otherwise have won his first Grand Slam and become the youngest world number one before the 2022 US Open? 'If it wasn't for Covid, it's possible that Carlos would have won a first Grand Slam at an even younger age,' says Alcaraz's first coach, Carlos Santos. Likewise, Cascales suggests that the pandemic slowed Alcaraz's development – the Spaniard had been offered wild cards into events that weren't then played (having Ferrero as your coach didn't do Alcaraz any harm when tournament directors were choosing who to give wild cards to). Sarria suggests the reverse could be true, though – that Covid accelerated Alcaraz's rise: 'Being at the academy [during lockdown] could have helped him to arrive at the top even faster.'

In any case, just two and a half years after the pandemic lockdown, Alcaraz would be a Grand Slam champion. And just over a year after that, in October 2023, the centre court at the academy would be named after him. Driving into the academy, you might notice the plaque on a pile of stones marking the occasion when that court officially became 'Pista Carlos Alcaraz'. In each corner of the court are posters celebrating Alcaraz's Grand Slam victories and how he was the youngest-ever number one. It's Ferrero's name on the academy and this is also his home, and there are posters and framed newspaper articles of him hanging inside the clubhouse. But he's more than happy to share wall space, with more posters celebrating Alcaraz's fast rise. Since Alcaraz's success, more players from Spain, Europe and across the world have been interested in training at the academy; and there are plans to build more courts and to extend and upgrade some of the buildings.

Being locked down in the academy doesn't seem to have done Alcaraz much harm.

*

Carlos Alcaraz mustn't be late for a practice session with Juan Carlos Ferrero. Ferrero 'demands punctuality' from Alcaraz, according to Antonio Cascales. Note the verb: how the coach 'demands' rather than 'asks' or 'requests'. If Ferrero and Alcaraz have agreed to train at a certain time, the player must be there on time, 'ready to practise', Cascales says. Ferrero also insists that Alcaraz follows specific routines off the court, such as going to bed early. He doesn't want Alcaraz staying up late, spending hours scrolling on Instagram.

Alcaraz's second father can be a disciplinarian when he needs to be. The warmth of Ferrero and Alcaraz's relationship was clear from Alcaraz's emotional reaction when his coach – who had been in Spain for his father Eduardo's funeral – surprised the teenager by flying to Florida to support him in the final of the 2022 Miami tournament. Alcaraz hadn't expected Ferrero to be there. When Alcaraz saw Ferrero he jumped up from his seat and gave his coach a hug, and then another. Ferrero was touched. They would hug again when Alcaraz beat Casper Ruud in the final, when Ferrero would be in tears.

But Ferrero's affection for Alcaraz doesn't mean he goes easy on him; he's not afraid to challenge his player, to say things that might make him uncomfortable, or to tell him when he's strayed from what is expected of him. Tired today? Doesn't matter; you still have to train with the same intensity as always. 'For sure, Juan Carlos's [strict approach] has helped Carlitos to be more disciplined,' Cascales says, with what sounds very much like approval. While Ferrero is reserved and understated, he can also be direct, which is something that others in Spanish tennis admire about him. 'I like speaking with Ferrero. He's such an easy-going guy. At the same time, he tells you right away about this and that,' says Garbiñe Muguruza. 'There's no bullshit with him.'

When Ferrero is strict with Alcaraz, the player accepts that's how his coach needs to be. 'First of all, Juan Carlos is an unbelievable human being. He loves Carlitos and treats him like a little brother. That's very important,' says Àlex Corretja, a Roland-Garros finalist in 1998 and 2001 and former world number two from Spain. 'But Juan Carlos knows how tough the sport can be and he wants Carlitos to avoid struggling in those situations. I've known Juan Carlos for so long and I can see how hard he has been working with Carlitos over the years. They've already been very successful and I think in the next few years they could still grow together.'

Alcaraz benefits from Ferrero's measured approach. 'It's a good combination because what Juan Carlos brings is the consistency, while knowing that he has a genius that he needs to help express himself as best as he can,' says Corretja. 'For sure, they have had times when Carlitos wants to do one thing and Juan Carlos says, "I think you should do this." But I think they understand each other very well. What Juan Carlos has done with Carlitos has been amazing. He pretty much educated him, starting in the Futures and the Challengers [the lower levels of professional tennis]. He helped him to understand the game and brought him to the ATP Tour. He exploited all the potential that Carlitos has. Juan Carlos is one of the reasons why Carlitos has been so successful so early in his career, why it has happened so quickly.'

You might wonder how that combination of personalities could possibly work. 'Carlos and Juan Carlos, they have different personalities, but they complement each other,' says Emilio Sánchez, himself a former Davis Cup captain who was ranked as high as seven for singles and one for doubles. 'If you have two people who are the same, they're probably going to clash, and that would create more issues. Carlos and Juan Carlos's personalities match perfectly because Juan Carlos gives balance in some ways. They also have the same values of humility and respect.'

Ferrero is friendlier than he might appear. 'Juan Carlos is really friendly – he sometimes looks more serious than he is,' says José Perlas, Ferrero's former coach, who also worked with Carlos Moyá, another Spanish world number one, and himself captained the Spanish Davis Cup team. 'Juan Carlos is really smart. He's an unbelievable professional. He knows exactly what it takes to improve. Juan Carlos has been doing what he has to do. As player and coach, you are friends, travelling around the world and sharing a lot of things. You spend a lot of time together. But if you're the leader of the project, as Juan

Carlos is, you have to organize. Being strict is part of our job as coaches. Carlos accepted that perfectly. He's so happy to have Juan Carlos leading the project.'

Ferrero's strict approach hasn't stifled Alcaraz's creativity. Far from it. There's still room for flair and fun. Cascales has never regretted watching Alcaraz practise at the academy, as every time he has done so – without exception – Carlos has played some wonder shot. Cameras on the practice courts capture Alcaraz's trickery. Recording training sessions is useful for the players at the academy because watching themselves back can often be the best way of assessing their own level of play, as well as their attitude. They turn the cameras on for some of Alcaraz's practices so that Cascales can replay them later if he wasn't there to see Carlos train live: 'One of the most amazing aspects of Carlitos is that he always does something special during training.'

Being a good coach, Ferrero has learned, can be complex: you also have to be a psychologist, a friend and a confidante. You need the player to trust you and to feel comfortable opening up, as Alcaraz has done with Juan Carlos or 'Juanki', as many call him. Alcaraz can trust that Ferrero is speaking from experience. In Alcaraz's words, he has had a coach who's already 'lived it from the inside' (though, of course, Alcaraz has over time ended up doing some things that were beyond his coach's own experience and so were fresh for both of them). Alcaraz can benefit from all the mistakes that Ferrero had made himself as a player. If it looks as though Alcaraz is about to make a wrong choice, Ferrero can step in. 'Juan Carlos was a good player and has lots of knowledge,' says Muguruza. 'Before Carlos makes an error, Juan Carlos can say to him, "Don't do that. I've done that. It sucks. Do this instead."'

That advice extends to guidance on dyeing his hair. Alcaraz has joked with Ferrero that he is going to go blond, as his coach did when he was a player. Ferrero advised against it: 'No way, don't do that.' Alcaraz replied: 'Juan Carlos, you did it when you were my age. What are you talking about?' But Ferrero kept on warning Alcaraz off bleaching his hair: 'Don't do it, it was different.'

Paul Annacone, a coach who has worked with Pete Sampras, Roger Federer and Taylor Fritz, says Ferrero has been the 'model coach' for Alcaraz. 'Having someone like Juan Carlos in your corner throughout your development as a youth is incredible. To then have him by your side as you climb the ranks is even more valuable,' the American says. 'Juan Carlos has been there, understands the pressures, the situations and the work necessary to be confident to execute in the biggest moments. Most importantly, he understands how to manage success and disappointment, which is a huge benefit. The dangerous aspect of the meteoric climb is the word "expectation". If that can be managed and accepted, then the sky is the limit.'

In 2023, the year that Alcaraz won his first Wimbledon title, Ferrero said he was still able to hold his own against his player for around 45 minutes on the court. Only then would Ferrero, who was by this time in his early forties, feel his age – clearly, living at the academy, with easy access to the court and a gym and healthy food, had allowed him to stay in shape. However, he lost some of his conditioning when he damaged his knee playing padel, an injury that required surgery and kept him away from the 2024 Australian Open; and Samuel López, another coach from the academy, accompanied Alcaraz to Melbourne instead (with the time difference, there were some early starts for Ferrero watching from Europe, as some of Alcaraz's matches started around 4am Spanish time). Before the 2025 season, Alcaraz added López to his team; he would accompany Alcaraz to some tournaments when Ferrero wanted to take a break from travelling. López was with Alcaraz in Rotterdam in February 2025, with the player winning his first indoor title on the ATP Tour.

*

There's something Juan Carlos Ferrero got very wrong: how stressful it is being a tennis coach. When Ferrero was playing, he didn't fully appreciate the emotional challenges of watching a match when seated close to the court rather than being out there yourself. He used to say to his coaches: 'Your job is so easy. You just sit there and it's so relaxed.' It was only when Ferrero became a coach himself that he understood the reality. When Ferrero watches Carlos Alcaraz compete, he feels whatever his player is feeling. That means going through the same nerves and tension. All the pressure. As a coach, you're still on edge; there are times when it feels even more fraught because you're not in control. Unlike your player, you're unable to move around and burn off some of that nervous energy.

Before he coached Alcaraz, Ferrero had already inspired one player to win their first Grand Slam title: Maria Sharapova. And he had done that without even trying or knowing about it.

In the spring of 2004, the Russian's agent had arranged for her to train at the academy near Villena in preparation for the European clay-court swing; and while she was there, she developed what she has since called a 'serious crush' on Ferrero. It wasn't just how he looked (which, according to Sharapova, was 'lanky, not too tall, with tousled hair, dark but dyed blond, and warm, mischievous eyes') but his cool, calm air. And the way he handled himself, the way he brushed that hair from his eyes. Sharapova would watch him practise. She would monitor his movements. She would even stand by the closed curtains of her cabin – or *cabaña*, as she called it – peeking out at the window to see if she could spot him. Everyone at the academy was aware that Sharapova, who was then just 16 years old, had become infatuated with Ferrero, who was then in his mid-twenties and had a girlfriend. Sharapova has recalled in her book, *Unstoppable*, that Ferrero was kind and respectful towards her when they spoke, while still letting her know that it wasn't going to happen.

Weeks after joining the academy, by which time Sharapova was 17, Ferrero was telling the media at Wimbledon that she would win that summer's women's singles title. He couldn't have known the effect that those words, spoken 'in that Spanish accent of his', would have on Sharapova. They happened to bump into each other on the stairs, with Ferrero telling Sharapova about his public prediction. As silly as it sounds, she has recalled hanging on to that memory for the rest of the tournament; she had already wanted to win Wimbledon, of course, but now she was motivated to show that Ferrero had been right to back her. When she won the title, beating Serena Williams in the final, she fell to her knees and looked at the sky – the exact same celebration that Ferrero had done when winning Roland-Garros the year before. She hadn't set out to copy him but perhaps had done so unconsciously, as she had been captivated by that image of him on the front page of a newspaper.

It's one thing to be another player's muse. That's not much of a time commitment. It's quite another to be their full-time coach. But Ferrero has been helped by coaching a player of Alcaraz's quality. 'The first reason that their coaching partnership has been working well is because Ferrero was a very good tennis player. He knows about tennis,' says Toni Nadal, Rafa's uncle and former coach. 'The second reason – and the most important one – is that Carlos is a wonderful tennis player. When you work with Carlos, everything is easier. It's easier then to be a good coach.'

When Alcaraz felt as though something had changed or shifted and he was good enough to win a certain category of tournament for the first time – starting with success on the second-tier ATP Challenger Tour and going all the way up to the sport's biggest prizes, the Grand Slams – he would inform Ferrero. 'I'm ready to win,' Alcaraz would say and Ferrero would understand that the player hadn't said those words casually, but really meant what he said. It seemed that Alcaraz has always had a good sense of what he is capable of. Those conversations felt special to the coach, probably because Alcaraz would speak openly and would then usually be holding another trophy not long afterwards.

In August 2020, after all that time in the Ferrero Tennis Academy, Alcaraz re-emerged in the world to play competitive tennis again for the first time in six months – the sport had started up again, albeit with players wearing face masks for post-match media duties and trophy presentations, and the Spaniard felt as though he was ready to win a first ATP Challenger title (the level below the main tour). Playing just his second tournament back, and not ranked high enough to gain an automatic place in the main draw, a 17-year-old Alcaraz came through two qualifying rounds and then five more matches to take the title in Trieste in Italy.

Alcaraz's emergence came at a weird time for tennis, and for the world. In the middle of a pandemic, the qualifying rounds for the 2021 Australian Open were held thousands of miles from Melbourne Park, in Doha in Qatar. Alcaraz won three rounds there and travelled on to Australia. With players having to quarantine on their arrival in the country, he didn't breathe fresh air for a few days. And there's only so much training that can be done in a hotel room, even if players were being creative by taking mattresses off the beds and using them as practice walls, helping to keep some rhythm on their groundstrokes. Despite those unusual circumstances, the 17-year-old won a main-draw match at a major for the first time by beating Dutchman Botic van de Zandschulp. When he went two sets up, Alcaraz had thought that in a regular tournament, with matches played over the best of three sets, he would have already won. But he kept on going, winning in straight sets. Alcaraz's run came to an end in his next match but his trip had, after the initial weirdness, been a success.

Just days after turning 18, Alcaraz qualified for the main draw of the 2021 Roland-Garros tournament, where he went on to become the youngest man to reach the third round since 1992. Wimbledon that year was also significant for Alcaraz, as it was the first time that his ranking was high enough for him to gain direct acceptance into the main draw. No more having to hustle in qualifying. He went out in the second round on the grass.

In those early days at the top of men's tennis, Carlos sometimes couldn't stop himself behaving like a fan around the players he had been watching on television for years. Suddenly, he was among them. Occasionally, Alcaraz would ask them to pose for a picture, even following them to find the right moment. Sharing a locker room and a gym with his idols could be a challenge – he'd try to act naturally when any of them asked him something, but that wasn't always possible when he felt so excited to be there. 'I tried to keep a poker face, but many times I couldn't manage it,' he told Molusco TV. If he played against any of those idols, that would feel surreal. But Alcaraz, who was quickly adjusting to his new reality, had something to tell Ferrero: he felt capable of winning his first ATP Tour title – and that's what he did in Umag in Croatia in the summer of 2021.

The first time Alcaraz played in the US Open's Arthur Ashe Stadium – the largest arena in tennis – was when he faced Stefanos Tsitsipas in the third round of the 2021 tournament. The Greek was astonished by the 18-year-old's ball speed. In all his years playing tennis, Tsitsipas had never seen anyone hit the ball that hard. Tsitsipas, who was the third seed that summer, tried to adjust his game to cope with what was coming from the other side of the net; but it was Alcaraz who won the match in a fifth-set tiebreak. Ferrero had, of course, already known about Alcaraz's power, but he learned something else that day: just how comfortable his player was on that stage and in that atmosphere. Going out into that stadium, as Ferrero knew from his own playing days, 'you feel the bigness of the court'. You're also struck by the noise and the fact that there are people everywhere, Ferrero has observed.

None of these things unsettled Alcaraz. Quite the opposite; he was energized by it all. It looked to Ferrero as though Alcaraz was at home on the court, surrounded by thousands of New Yorkers. Alcaraz was just going for it, Ferrero thought. Alcaraz, who had never beaten a top-five player before, was into the fourth round of a Grand Slam for the first time. Winning his next match made him the youngest quarter-finalist at the US Open since the 1960s, as well as the youngest man to make the last eight at any of the Grand Slams since Michael Chang at Roland-Garros in 1990. Unfortunately, he ended up retiring from that quarter-final, against Canadian Félix Auger-Aliassime, because of injury. But Ferrero had seen enough during the tournament to make him think Alcaraz had it in him to reach the very top of the sport. Something else happened during Alcaraz's run, which would help him a year later: he developed a strong connection with the New York crowd, who loved the energy that he brought to the Arthur Ashe Stadium.

Later that year, Alcaraz won the Next Gen ATP Finals, a tournament for players aged 21 or younger, but it already felt as though he could compete against opponents of all ages.

In early 2022, Alcaraz snaffled his first ATP 500 title in Rio de Janeiro, just as he had told Ferrero he could. There was a telling moment in Brazil. While Alcaraz's team celebrated with beers, he chose a bottle of water, which he took with him to the gym and drank while he warmed down on a bike and spoke to his family on the phone. Iñaki Etxegia of the Ferrero Tennis Academy said that was when he understood that Alcaraz was 'for real'. 'We were all cheering and happy and we made a toast with beers that the organizers had provided us with, but Carlos made it with water. Carlos followed all the usual routines after the match. He was just 18 years old, with the biggest achievement of his career until then, but he kept his focus,' Etxegia says. 'There are many examples of players that make the best achievement of their careers like that and in the next tournament they lose in the first round. I got the feeling that wouldn't happen to Carlos. I was amazed by the ambition that this short moment proved about him.'

There was no letdown after Rio. Alcaraz made the semi-finals of his next singles event, the ATP Masters 1000 tournament at the Indian Wells Tennis Garden in California. Showing how well he knew his own game – and how it compared to the level that others were producing – Alcaraz had told Ferrero he was capable of taking a ATP Masters 1000 trophy and he won the 2022 Miami title. That run in Florida taught Alcaraz plenty about where he was at in his career. Before he won Miami, he had believed he could put together some strong results at the Grand Slams, but he didn't feel as though he was ready to be a major champion. Victory in Miami, at the highest category of tournament except the majors, changed how he saw himself and he said to Ferrero: 'Juan Carlos, I'm ready to win a Grand Slam.' Taking another ATP Masters 1000 title in Madrid – where he defeated Rafa Nadal and Novak Djokovic along the way – would have reinforced how he felt about his game.

While Alcaraz didn't conquer the clay of Roland-Garros that spring, he did make his second Grand Slam quarter-final. He reached the fourth round of Wimbledon that summer, his deepest run to date on London's grass courts. But it wasn't long before Alcaraz demonstrated that he really had been ready to be a major champion. When Alcaraz won the US Open later that year, others were surprised by what a 19-year-old was capable of. His coach wasn't.

6

Maybe some things in Spanish tennis will always be unknown, and even a little mysterious – in all their years together on tour, Rafa Nadal's uncle and former coach, Toni, never thought to ask his nephew why he was obsessed with his water bottles.

Toni wasn't even a little curious about why Rafa used to arrange the bottles so they were all in a line, with the labels or logos all facing in the same direction. Toni says he only ever wanted to talk to his nephew about tennis, and not about subjects he considered unimportant, so he can't now tell you why Rafa did what he did. Even more of a blank in Toni's head is why Carlos Alcaraz – who would prefer it if people didn't compare him to Nadal – has sometimes fussed over his water bottles in a way that looks very familiar. This we do know: Alcaraz carefully arranging and then rearranging his water bottles – as he did at Melbourne Park as he prepared for the 2025 Australian Open – was only going to encourage those who, even now, several Grand Slam titles into Alcaraz's career, like to say he's a 'Mini Rafa'.

Alcaraz doesn't feel as though he's anything like as extreme with his water bottles as Nadal once was; while the Majorcan had to make sure his bottles were perfectly positioned, Alcaraz merely wants to avoid his looking messy, he has said. Alcaraz's old friend Antonio López doesn't think Carlos picked up that habit from Nadal. López has, however, noticed that Alcaraz does something else that was among Nadal's repertoire of habits or superstitions: he tries to avoid stepping on the lines between points.

Like lining up his water bottles, dodging the lines of the court, or playing with the same French racquet brand as Nadal (Babolat) and having the same American clothing and shoe supplier (Nike), Alcaraz going sleeveless at a Grand Slam can provoke a reaction; it sets off all those who think of him as 'Baby Rafa' or the 'Second Nadal' or the 'Next Rafa'. When Alcaraz wore a tank top at the 2021 Roland-Garros – which was the first time Nike had dressed him like that at a major – his navy outfit might have been a tribute to Nadal and to Carlos Moyá, another Spanish Grand Slam champion who used to free his biceps in matches. In years to come, wearing a sleeveless top was more than a style statement or a continuation of a Spanish tennis tradition; it was also an opportunity for Carlos to show the work he had been doing in the gym. Alcaraz still adores playing in a singlet. People can call him the Next Rafa all they want but that's not going to stop him from going sleeveless.

Biting on a trophy Nadal-style, as Alcaraz did after winning a tournament in Madrid in 2022 – having beaten his fellow Spaniard along the way – was hardly going to stop people from saying how much like Rafa he was. But apparently Alcaraz, all giddy after winning the title, had jokingly nibbled on the trophy to play along with a request from a photographer. There's more: Alcaraz's energy before a match can be very Nadalesque. Nadal used to jump up and down when he was at the net for a pre-match coin toss, which perhaps helped him to deal with some of the nervous tension he was feeling. As bouncy as a kangaroo, some said. Alcaraz has been just as jumpy in those pre-match moments (though he hasn't looked quite as nervy as his compatriot once did).

In his younger years, Alcaraz idolized Nadal. He used to wear a T-shirt with Nadal's face on the front. Alcaraz doesn't read many books but he made an exception for Nadal's autobiography. As a boy, Alcaraz played junior events on the Rafa Nadal Tour, and he would put the trophies he won – which were modelled after Nadal's logo, which is shaped like a bull's horns – on a shelf in his bedroom. Alcaraz was a Rafa expert. 'When Carlos was 12 years old, he knew perfectly all of Nadal's records. Such as being the youngest to win certain titles and to achieve things on the ATP Tour. It was incredible,' says Postres Reina's José Manuel Lag.

Alcaraz was 12 years old when he met Nadal for the first time; he was playing in a junior event during the ATP tournament in Madrid and managed to have his photo taken with his idol. In 2018, around the time of his 15th birthday, Alcaraz was invited to spend a couple of days in Barcelona, where he would be involved in a trailer Nadal was filming for a Nintendo Super Mario tennis video game. Alcaraz didn't feature in the final version of the commercial but he wouldn't have seen the trip as wasted, as it meant he was able to spend a little time with Nadal – albeit in an unusual situation, with the Majorcan pretending to battle it out with Mario on court. Something that Alcaraz picked up from Nadal was how to bring the same intensity to every shot and every moment; it didn't matter whether it was the first point or the last, or whether he was facing a human or Mario – Nadal went all out and that was inspiring.

Alcaraz hadn't even won a first match in the main draw of a Grand Slam when people started comparing him with Nadal. Speak to people close to Alcaraz and they will tell you, in fairly strong terms, that he hasn't always appreciated those comparisons. That being talked of as the 'Next Rafa' used to make him uneasy. To the point that Kiko Navarro, who was part of Alcaraz's coaching team until 2020, began shutting down the media's questions about Nadal. He felt there had already been too many of them and that they were adding to the expectation and pressure building around Alcaraz, which wasn't welcome: 'It wasn't comfortable for me or for Carlitos.' Juan Carlos Ferrero also didn't like how people kept linking Alcaraz with Nadal, saying once: 'The comparisons aren't very nice.'

It was just as well, Josefina Cutillas thought, that the boy from El Palmar had a maturity beyond his years and a strong sense of his own identity. While Alcaraz looked up to Nadal, and the Majorcan was reinforcing in the Murcian's mind the importance of working hard, that didn't mean Alcaraz wanted to *be* Nadal. Maybe Alcaraz had said when he was young that he wished to be like Rafa, but he felt differently when he was no longer a child; he still looked up to his idol but he wanted to be his own man. Like Cutillas, Navarro felt as though Alcaraz handled the situation well: 'Rafa was and is an example for Carlitos but Carlitos will make his own path and his own story.'

Comparisons with Nadal were, of course, a compliment. Alcaraz recognized that they indicated he was making good progress. The first time it happened, when he would have been around 16 years old, he thought it was 'cool'. Even so, Alcaraz didn't want to be distracted by that thought and was focused on being himself. And for tennis fans in Spain and around the world to recognize him as such.

There are some things that Nadal did that Alcaraz doesn't do – such as rearranging his underwear so often on court, or generally being so fidgety between points. Alcaraz saw Nadal going through all those routines and didn't copy them. There are other bigger points of difference, too. Where Nadal brought a stern face and warrior-like spirit to the court, Alcaraz brings a smile. While Nadal was a defensive player, Alcaraz is almost always in attack mode. Nadal cared only about winning; Alcaraz would like to put on a show while winning. Nadal is from Majorca; Alcaraz is from the Spanish mainland. Nadal was a lefty; Alcaraz is right-handed. Hardly a mini-me, then.

His old friend Antonio López says Alcaraz's strong mind helped him to ride this out. 'All of us Spaniards grew up watching Rafa Nadal play and he was many people's idol. But Carlitos wants to engrave his own name in the history of tennis,' López says. 'Although some people are saying he is the next Rafa, I don't think Carlitos has found it too difficult to manage. Carlitos has an incredible mentality; and his family and his team are good people and they're not going to give Carlitos the opportunity to start thinking a certain way. Carlitos is always thinking he wants to be himself, Carlitos, and not the next Rafa.'

It's telling that one of the three episodes of Alcaraz's Netflix documentary is called 'I'm not Rafa', and that Nadal openly says being compared to someone else can distort and confuse how you think about yourself and your own game. One way of dealing with the comparisons is thinking how ridiculous they are. 'For people to be saying that Carlos is the next Rafa Nadal, that's absurd. Rafa is unique. No one is going to be like Rafa,' says Àlex Corretja. 'In my eyes, there is no chance that anyone else will do what Rafa did in the tennis world, winning Roland-Garros 14 times. No chance. That's impossible. That's insane. Crazy. What Alcaraz needs to do is to find his way and not to compare himself to anyone else – and especially not Rafa. Carlos has dealt with this situation well because he wants to be Carlos Alcaraz and not the next Rafa Nadal. It's impossible to compare yourself to anyone else in the world; and if the comparison is with Nadal, even less. Everybody's different. You need to ask what can you learn from the others and how can you exploit your own potential.'

Spanish tennis fans should stop with the comparisons. 'We have another Spanish guy who is capable of producing the same amount of desire from people and who has been winning Grand Slams,' says Corretja. 'That's nearly a miracle. We need to be grateful for that.'

It's fortunate that Alcaraz has Juan Carlos Ferrero to help him. 'The expectation, and people comparing Carlos to Rafa, that's not easy to manage. Luckily, Juan Carlos understands perfectly what the situation is and the way to cut those ideas,' says José Perlas, Ferrero's former coach.

Alcaraz is his own man. 'Rafa was unique as a player. His strengths were unique, and so was his behaviour, as well as his mental game,' says Emilio Sánchez. 'Carlos is also unique because of his game and his presence and his aura, and the way he enjoys playing. That has nothing to do with Rafa.'

For some time, though, Alcaraz's parents were worried. As his mother has said, they didn't want their son to end up like 'a worn-out toy'. They had seen what had happened to another young Spanish player called Carlos who had been talked up as the next Rafa. Carlos Boluda-Purkiss is the only boy to have won two titles at Les Petits As, a 14-and-under indoor world championships held in Tarbes in France, with the list of former champions including names such as Nadal and Ferrero, which suggests that it's a strong predictor of future success in men's tennis. Like Alcaraz, Boluda-Purkiss had trained at the Ferrero Tennis Academy and people were expecting great things from him. But being compared to Nadal, and all the other hype and outsized expectations, appear to have been unhelpful for him.

Troubled by others' expectations for him and increasing mental pressure, while also being physically impaired by a wrist injury, Boluda-Purkiss came to hate tennis on some level (though at the same time maybe deep down he still loved it). Boluda-Purkiss's last competitive tennis was in late 2020; he was 27 years old and had never risen higher than 254 in the singles rankings. He eventually wrote an open letter detailing the pressure that he had experienced as a child and how damaging that had been for him.

Some in Spanish tennis consider Boluda-Purkiss's to be a cautionary tale. Alcaraz's former psychologist Josefina Cutillas once suggested, in an interview with *La Opinión de Murcia*, that the player was an example of how a promising talent can be ruined. 'Carlos Boluda-Purkiss was a great boy with bad luck and his conditions were different from those of Carlitos,' says Alfredo Sarria. 'But, of course, the family was worried about the comparisons with Rafa for a long time.'

Everyone around Alcaraz was going to ensure that the same thing – or anything close to it – didn't happen with him too. 'For me, Carlos Boluda-Purkiss – who had won all the tournaments since he was little – is the best example of not knowing how to handle the pressure of being compared to Nadal,' says Antonio López. 'I don't know what Carlos Boluda-Purkiss's family are like but Carlitos's are intelligent and very humble and I think they have always helped Carlitos to keep being down to earth.'

According to Alcaraz's agent Albert Molina, everyone around Carlos had seen what happened with Boluda-Purkiss when the balloon was overinflated. Boluda-Purkiss's story had taught Alcaraz's people how not to approach a young player's career and what could go wrong. To avoid the Alcaraz balloon becoming too big – to stop it from bursting – the team had to stay grounded and to appreciate that there was a long way to the top of the sport. While he didn't have much time outside tennis, Alcaraz was given some space to occasionally live like a normal teenage boy, which would help him to cope with the pressures.

*

The day Carlos Alcaraz became an adult was also the day he took on his childhood idol for the first time. There was cake. There were also so many nerves, heightened by watching Rafa Nadal's warmup routine of sprinting and jumping, that Alcaraz couldn't play his usual tennis, as he has acknowledged: 'Scared shitless would be an understatement.'

On Alcaraz's 18th birthday, when he was ranked 120 in the world, he faced Nadal in an early round of a tournament in Madrid in 2021;

and he was so terrified on the clay of the Caja Mágica or Magic Box facility that he won just three games. Nadal had destroyed him, Alcaraz thought. Alcaraz's birthday was about to become even more surreal, though: moments later, the tournament director, Feliciano López, appeared with a chocolate cake so large he had to carry it out to the court on a wide tray rather than a plate. While the crowd sang 'Feliz Cumpleaños' and a few fans held up a giant banner wishing Alcaraz a happy birthday, the three of them – Alcaraz, Nadal and López – posed in their Covid-era facemasks with the cake, for what today looks like a very strange image and even in the moment didn't quite fit with the match that preceded it. Very briefly, Nadal pulled down his mask to tell Alcaraz, 'Don't eat all of it.' Nadal wished Alcaraz a happy birthday. In all, quite the day.

When they played again, Alcaraz couldn't allow himself to be overwhelmed by the situation – because if he couldn't find a way of coping with moments like that, what possible chance did he have of becoming the best? He wasn't scared; this time he told himself that he would 'go for it', that he would do all he could to defeat Nadal. That match, in the semi-finals of the 2022 hard-court tournament in Indian Wells in the Californian desert, was much more competitive; Nadal won again, but the match went to three sets and took more than three hours. After coming off court, Alcaraz said to Juan Carlos Ferrero: 'I think I'm ready now to beat Rafa.' Nadal was saying that when he looked at Alcaraz, it reminded him of himself as a teenager – an insight that hardly shushed all those who were making comparisons between the two. Nadal was also likening becoming an elite tennis player to making a salad: you need all the right ingredients, such as passion, talent and humility. And Alcaraz seemed to have those.

If ever there was a mini-series that showed Alcaraz's rapid development it was the three matches he played against Nadal. The final part of that trilogy was in the quarter-finals of the Madrid tournament in 2022. Just days earlier, when he was still 18 years old, Alcaraz had broken into the top ten of the world singles rankings, becoming the youngest man in that elite group since – who else? – Nadal.

In the year that had passed since he was crushed by his idol on Spanish clay and in front of the Spanish tennis public, Alcaraz felt as though he had done a lot of growing up and was now able to handle his emotions. After winning the opening set, Alcaraz dropped the second set 6–1, seemingly bothered by an ankle injury. He left the court for a bathroom break, washed his face and gave himself a pep talk: 'OK, Charlie, if you're not going to pull out, think about playing. Don't think on your ankle. Don't think on nothing else. Fight till the very last ball, because you know you are capable of doing it.' Galvanized for the final set, Alcaraz won the match and felt as though the crowd – which included King Felipe VI of Spain – was starting to love him a little more. All excited afterwards, as he processed what he had just done, Alcaraz wrote on the lens of a television camera: '*Qué ha pasado*?' What just happened?

In 2022, López had a gift for Alcaraz that was even more appealing than chocolate cake; he was saying that Alcaraz had a 'brutal charisma' with an engaging way of playing tennis. That generational battle was quite the moment for Alcaraz, and for Spanish tennis; and it would have been understandable if Carlos had played below his best in his next match. But Alcaraz kept on going, defeating Novak Djokovic and then Alexander Zverev to become the youngest champion in the history of the tournament; and then celebrating by doing that Nadal-style nibble on the trophy. When he returned to El Palmar, he stood on the balcony of his family's apartment, showing off the trophy and waving to a large crowd on the street below – which included several drummers, adding to the party atmosphere.

Every time Alcaraz plays at Roland-Garros, he can't escape the mentions of Nadal, who won that Grand Slam an absurd number of times: 14. That chatter would be loudest in 2024 when, after Nadal lost in the opening round on his final appearance in Paris, Alcaraz was trying to win that tournament for the first time. 'At Roland-Garros in 2024, everyone was watching Carlos and saying, "Rafa's gone, now it's your turn, show us something," ' says Garbiñe Muguruza, a former Roland-Garros women's singles champion herself. 'If you're Spanish and you're coming after a great player like Rafa, everyone is going to be expecting you to also win Roland-Garros. Because why not? You really should. We've had this for 20 years – all these wins from Rafa – and now you're not going to win it?'

It's tempting to think that one Spanish tennis superstar has been frequently advising the next. But that hasn't been the reality with Nadal and Alcaraz. Nadal's role in shaping Alcaraz (who, for some time, was nervous when speaking to Rafa off the court) can be overstated. No doubt, they get along; and they have spent a fair amount of time together, including appearing in the Netflix Slam exhibition in Las Vegas in 2024 and playing doubles together at the Olympics that same year, which was 'a dream', Alcaraz said. Alcaraz was sleeping on a narrow, cardboard bed in the Olympic Village, and some nights he felt as though he was going to fall out, but he didn't care; he was consumed by trying to win a doubles medal with Rafa at his idol's last Games. That's what Rafa deserves, Alcaraz was thinking. Together they were known as 'Nadalcaraz', but, in their first tournament as a doubles team, they lost in the quarter-finals, which 'really fucked me up', Alcaraz told Netflix, and which potentially contributed to his defeat to Novak Djokovic in the singles final (though he might have lost anyway as the Serb was energized by the prospect of winning a first gold medal).

Between matches and practice sessions, Alcaraz and Nadal had played the Parchís board game off the court and had some chances to chat. A few months before the Olympics, Andre Agassi had told Alcaraz to be 'smart' and to ask Nadal for advice and to learn in ten minutes what it had taken Rafa ten years or more to understand. And Alcaraz has asked Nadal a few questions, eliciting some useful insights. But it would be going too far to suggest Nadal has been mentoring Alcaraz.

Nadal's uncle and former coach, Toni, says it's a simple matter of geography: 'I'm sure Carlos doesn't need help from Rafael because Carlos has a very good team with Juan Carlos Ferrero. It would have been different if Rafael and Carlos were from the same city, but Rafael hasn't had that kind of relationship with Carlos. Rafael lives in Majorca and Carlos lives in Murcia.'

As Nadal neared the end of his career, he was rightly focused on himself and his own game.

'I'm not so sure that Rafa has been so close to Carlitos. I honestly don't think it was Rafa's job to have been helping Carlitos to become a better player,' Corretja says. 'It's difficult when you're playing on the same tour, when you're playing for the same goals, and then to say, "OK, now I'll try to help you." I don't think that was what Rafa was doing. Rafa was taking care of himself and he had several issues in the last two or three years. That happened as Carlitos was growing up and playing good tennis. Rafa also knew that Carlitos had his own team. I'm not so sure that Rafa played a major role with Carlitos, even if they had some good moments and Rafa passed on some advice that was very valuable.'

The advice that Nadal passed on was 'great', Alcaraz has said, but it was mostly about his personal life and not about tennis. It was a sensitive time for Alcaraz and Nadal, according to Jean-Christophe Verborg at Babolat, who supplied racquets to both players: 'I know Carlos has huge respect for Rafa and Rafa really inspired him. It was sensitive because Carlos was rising and Rafa was still there. That wasn't easy for [either] of them.'

But maybe Nadal didn't have to say too much to his countryman. Maybe Alcaraz learned enough just from observing Nadal on and off the court. 'You can be sure that Carlitos watched Rafa a lot and he learned a lot from him,' says Corretja. 'Anyone who wants to improve in their tennis career, or in their personal behaviour, I think they should watch Rafa play. He's the ultimate professional to watch. He's the perfect athlete to learn from.'

Being the next Spanish star after Nadal hasn't been as challenging for Alcaraz as some have suggested, according to Toni Nadal. 'People shouldn't say it's been hard because we see that it hasn't been. Carlos has won several Grand Slam titles and he has been the number one. Too many times, people talk and say it's hard to come after a player like Rafael. But the truth is that when you're as good as Carlos is, it's not so hard. It's true that people will compare you but the main thing is that Carlos came after Rafael and he reached the top without too many problems. That wasn't too difficult for him,' says Toni.

'When you see that a player close to you has got to number one,' Toni continues, 'you can think, "If he can do it, I can too." Then there's a little chance. But it's not normal that after Rafael was so good, along comes another wonderful number one from Spain. After Djokovic, it would have been difficult if there had been another guy from Serbia as the number one, or after Federer another guy from Switzerland to be number one. But that's what Carlos did. How did this happen? We have many good things in Spain. In Spain we love sport. We also have the weather, which makes it easier to practise tennis most days.'

*

Carlos Alcaraz and his team would sometimes joke among themselves about Roger Federer being such a refined and sophisticated tennis player that even the way he relaxed off the court must have been classy. Someone in the group would ask: 'What would Federer be doing right now?' Perhaps, another voice would say, the Swiss was listening to classical music? Or maybe, someone else would chime in, Federer was reading a book while sitting in front of a lit fire by a window with views of Switzerland's snowy mountains? Every one of the Big Three has influenced Alcaraz on and off the court, not just his fellow Spaniard. While Alcaraz admired and idolized Rafa

Nadal, he felt as though watching Federer play tennis was like looking at a work of art, he once told *Vogue* magazine. There was something beautiful and enchanting about Federer's 'elegant' and 'magnificent' game, Alcaraz thought.

When a 16-year-old Alcaraz travelled to London to play in the junior version of Wimbledon in 2019, he had the opportunity to see for himself what Federer was like as Ferrero organized for the two of them to practise together. They were just about to start when Alcaraz said to Ferrero: 'I won't be able to do it. I'm shaking all over.' Alcaraz was too nervous to say anything to Federer apart from hello. And yet when Alcaraz got on court, he was flawless and didn't miss a ball – yet another occasion when Ferrero felt as though the teenager had something about him. Like Ferrero, Federer thought Alcaraz performed well and that it had been a decent practice (maybe it helped that Federer's practices were notoriously relaxed and that he would often goof around, which Ferrero didn't allow Alcaraz to do much of, if any).

When Ferrero went back to Federer a day or two later and asked whether he would like to hit with Alcaraz again, the Swiss declined. Federer said he would rather practise with Ferrero. That wasn't a slight on Alcaraz; it was just that Ferrero had been Federer's contemporary and he wanted to see how his old friend was hitting the ball (like Alcaraz, Ferrero didn't miss a shot, according to Federer, who thought Alcaraz's coach was in good enough shape, several years after his retirement, to still be competing on the tour). Being politely turned down for a second practice didn't spoil the experience for Alcaraz; he would put a photograph of him and Federer, taken on one of Wimbledon's courts, on the shelf above his bed.

Alcaraz loved how Federer attacked whenever he had a chance, or even a half-chance, blending aggression with colour and creativity. Alcaraz sees some similarities between his tennis and Federer's. One of Federer's former coaches, Paul Annacone, shares that view. 'I see Roger in the way Carlos moves as well as in how he sees the court and the variety of his shot selection,' Annacone says. 'He has so many options because of his skill set – he's truly an artistic player who moves like he is floating.'

People say Alcaraz's timing was perfect, that he emerged at just the right time. But in one way, it really wasn't: he never had the opportunity to play a match against Federer. Just days after Alcaraz announced himself in New York City, winning the 2022 US Open, the Swiss had an emotional retirement party on the other side of the Atlantic at the Laver Cup (a Europe against the rest of the world team competition) in London. From Federer's side, not getting to play against Alcaraz was disappointing.

A couple of years later, Federer and Alcaraz spent some time together at the Laver Cup in Berlin, and at the Shanghai ATP tournament, including a light training session at the practice courts. The grunts from Alcaraz during that practice were an indication of the effort that he was putting in to ensure he gave a good account of himself against his boyhood idol (Federer, who at 43 was more than double Alcaraz's age, was silent). When it seemed as though the session was drawing to a natural end, Federer said: 'You're happy or anything else?' To which Alcaraz replied: 'Happy days.' Federer also offered – and this sounded like a joke – to play a set against Alcaraz.

Even more impactful for Alcaraz was the conversation he had with Federer in Shanghai, in which they discussed Alcaraz's game and his

A mural of Carlos Alcaraz, based on a photograph of the tennis player at 11 years old, on an outside wall of his old primary school in the village of El Palmar.

The chairs in Alcaraz's old classroom at his primary school have used tennis balls on the ends of the metal legs to prevent screeching when children are moving them – the balls were a gift from Alcaraz's family.

'My second home,' Alcaraz says of Real Sociedad Club de Campo de Murcia, the country club where he was introduced to tennis.

From the age of five or six, Carlos built his life around tennis and spent as much time as he could at the club (sometimes crying when he was told to go home).

Alcaraz would walk around the country club with a racquet in one hand, a sandwich in the other and a smile on his face.

Posters in each corner of Pista Carlos Alcaraz at the Ferrero Tennis Academy celebrate Alcaraz's achievements, including becoming the world number one at 19 years old.

Carlos Alcaraz with his father, also called Carlos Alcaraz, after achieving the athlete's childhood dream of winning the Roland-Garros title.

Wearing shorts almost as vibrant as his tennis, Alcaraz was 16 years old when he won a match on the ATP Tour for the first time, at a tournament in Rio de Janeiro.

Alcaraz was 17 years old when he qualified for the 2021 Australian Open and won his first main-draw match at a Grand Slam.

In a big moment for Alcaraz, and for Spanish tennis, he beat Rafa Nadal for the first time at a tournament in Madrid in 2022.

Aged 19, Alcaraz won his first Grand Slam title at the 2022 US Open, with his victory also making him the youngest ever men's world number one.

With his five-set victory over Novak Djokovic in the 2023 final, a 20-year-old Alcaraz won Wimbledon for the first time.

At 21, Alcaraz won the 2024 Roland-Garros title to become the youngest man to win Grand Slams on three surfaces: hard, grass and clay.

With his 2024 Wimbledon victory, Alcaraz completed the Channel Slam – winning majors in Paris and London in the same season.

A silver medallist at his first Olympics, the Paris 2024 Games, Alcaraz poses with gold medallist Novak Djokovic and bronze medallist Lorenzo Musetti.

Carlos has described his coach Juan Carlos Ferrero as his 'second father'.

life away from the court. Alcaraz asked Federer for advice on how to stay motivated over a long career and the Swiss said he had always tried to enjoy himself along the way and to seek out fun at tournaments. Alcaraz had lost in the quarter-finals of the Shanghai tournament, and ordinarily wouldn't have returned to the site, but he stuck around to watch the final between Jannik Sinner and Novak Djokovic as he had the chance to sit next to Federer in the stadium. Alcaraz and Federer were completely at ease in each other's company and there was plenty of laughter that day.

*

'*Qué pasa, Titanito?*'

That's how Novak Djokovic sometimes likes to greet Carlos Alcaraz. What's up, Little Titan? Alcaraz, meanwhile, calls Djokovic a 'beast' or 'Superman'.

Rafa Nadal used to be the favourite tennis player of Stefan Djokovic, Novak's son. But by the spring of 2022, it was Alcaraz. They are almost 16 years apart, and they are rivals, but Alcaraz is friendly with Djokovic. The Serb has been welcoming towards Alcaraz. While Alcaraz defeated Djokovic in two successive Wimbledon finals, in 2023 and again in 2024, you could see from their backstage interactions at the 2025 Australian Open that there is something close to a genuine friendship there (it's hard to have an open and honest friendship with someone who wants the same things you do, Grand Slams, and is going to be doing whatever they can to stop you achieving what you want). From the beginning, Djokovic noted approvingly that Alcaraz was humble and, in the Serb's mind, had good values.

Djokovic admires the energy and intensity Alcaraz brings to the court.

Some of their matches have been played at such a high level that they must have inspired spectators to get into the sport or even pick up a racquet for the first time, Alcaraz has thought. One of the most epic and exhilarating matches of Djokovic's long career, he has said, was against Alcaraz in Cincinnati in 2023. Djokovic was so excited about winning that three-set final – which lasted for almost four hours in the heat, and during which he saved a championship point – that he tore his shirt off, and it felt to him a lot like a Grand Slam match. Just a few weeks later, Djokovic won his 24th Grand Slam title at the US Open, reinforcing his status as the greatest of all time.

If Djokovic gets a lot out of their matches, so does Alcaraz. Always looking to find the joy in competition, Alcaraz has been happy to have had those experiences on court with Djokovic. Their matches have also been an education: Djokovic pushes Alcaraz to his limit, and that's only going to help Alcaraz to improve every aspect of his game. He's learning by watching how Djokovic handles certain situations. Practising together has also been an opportunity for Alcaraz to study his rival, to see up close how he goes about his business. Alcaraz often has Djokovic on his mind. Djokovic has inspired Alcaraz to keep on pushing and working; he wants to be an even better player the next time they face each other.

Alcaraz is supposedly a mixture of the Big Three, the trio he is trying to surpass. Even Djokovic has said that. Alcaraz was just 20 years old and had just beaten Djokovic in the 2023 Wimbledon final when the Serb was saying he had never played someone like the Spaniard before:

'Carlos is a very complete player.' Djokovic could see elements of his own game, as well as some of Roger Federer's and Rafa Nadal's, in Alcaraz. Djokovic could see Alcaraz had 'the Spanish bull mentality' that Nadal had always had, as well as a strong defence like Nadal. Alcaraz's sliding backhands reminded Djokovic of his own. Djokovic thought Alcaraz could defend and adapt like him.

Imagine if the Big Three were all in one body, and that player couldn't stop smiling. You're imagining Carlos Alcaraz, says Mats Wilander, a former teenage Grand Slam champion who won a total of seven majors during his teens and twenties. In the Swede's view, Alcaraz's movement is as good as Djokovic's, he brings the same passion to the court that Nadal did and he has the same craft and grace and feel as Federer. But is Alcaraz actually a hybrid of Nadal, Federer and Djokovic? Or, despite the Big Three's domination of tennis, has he managed to be his own man? In the next chapters, we will take a more detailed look at Alcaraz's game, to appreciate how it's like nothing tennis has seen before – with the smile, the drop shots and the fun and creativity. Being Carlos Alcaraz means being a tennis original.

7

An artist, they call him. And that's without knowing what he once did with some colouring pencils.

Carlos Alcaraz was so young when he started seeing a psychologist – just eight years old – that he would communicate his thoughts, emotions and ambitions through drawing pictures, as well as through talking. With his colouring pencils, Alcaraz was showing what he wanted from his future; he would draw himself holding La Coupe des Mousquetaires, the Musketeers' Cup, after winning the men's singles title at Roland-Garros.

Josefina Cutillas, the psychologist who worked with Alcaraz for eight years, until the player was 16, still has some of that art. Though she would never share the self-portraits without his permission, they are a reminder of the advantages of working with an athlete at such an early age. Talking to a psychologist isn't unusual in tennis. Having one from eight years old is noteworthy. At that age, Cutillas told *La Razón*, Alcaraz wouldn't have had any preconceived notions about winning and losing;

so, given the plasticity of a child's brain, she was able to influence how he thought about his tennis. When they spoke on a Monday, Alcaraz wasn't allowed to tell Cutillas whether he had won or lost his latest match, only how he thought he had played. Giving attention to the result would have reduced Alcaraz's tennis to winning or losing, to being a success or a failure, and Cutillas didn't want that for him.

As much as Alcaraz wished to win Roland-Garros one day, Cutillas was hoping that as a boy, and maybe also deeper into his tennis life, he would be less interested in his results than in whether he was improving and meeting the standards he was setting for himself. Cutillas was helping Alcaraz to continue being intrinsically motivated to play tennis; to enjoy the process of developing his game. Not talking about whether he had won or lost would be good for his motivation and confidence and allow him to take a long-term view of his tennis rather than defining himself by his last result.

Alcaraz is a naturally sunny character. First Cutillas and then another psychologist, Isabel Balaguer, have helped him to continue showing that joy on a tennis court. Despite all the stresses, Alcaraz has managed to stay connected to his playful side. When people say to Alcaraz, 'Thank you for bringing joy to tennis again' – and that happens a lot – he doesn't always know how to respond. He will say something along the lines of: 'OK, thank you, I guess.' While Alcaraz has won multiple Grand Slam titles and been the world number one, he still has the same goal that he has always had: to continue enjoying himself on court. The best way he knows to stop himself feeling the pressure is to feel joyful. It's when Alcaraz is feeling 'dead serious', he has said, that he starts to become more nervous.

When Andrey Rublev, a Russian who has been as high as fifth in the world rankings, looks at Alcaraz on court, it's clear to him that the Spaniard isn't there because of the lifestyle that he can fund by playing elite sport. He's there because he loves tennis. A happy boy drawing pictures of future Grand Slam success grew to become the smiliest champion the sport has ever known, who says things like: 'I'm in love with the game of tennis.'

*

The smiley, sunny, toothy tennis player from a village in southern Spain. Carlitos – little, cheeky Carlos – with a big grin. How Pixar or Disney might imagine a tennis player to look and be: free of cynicism; someone who just keeps on radiating happiness, no matter what. For some, he's a cartoon because this can't be real. Tennis players aren't supposed to smile this much on court, especially after losing a point, but that's what Alcaraz will do if that point was fun to play. Go on YouTube and you will find video compilations with titles like 'Tennis Points That Made Carlos Alcaraz Smile' – and he lost some of those points. He's not just smiling, he's extending his arm over the net to indicate to his opponent that, in a show of respect and admiration for what they had created together, he wants to slap hands (because it's too long to wait until the post-match handshake). The most entertaining points tend to be longer than average, and it can feel as though they have greater psychological value than shorter, less spectacular rallies. Alcaraz, who should be feeling and looking crushed if he loses one of those long points, smiles instead. There's something else that tennis players aren't supposed to do: grin their way through Grand Slam finals.

People in tennis talk: how can a professional player – or any athlete for that matter – possibly be enjoying himself as much as Alcaraz appears to be? Andre Agassi has been asking: how can you smile after losing a point, and be such a happy presence on court, and then dominate tennis? Is that possible?

Alcaraz will even smile before a championship point at Wimbledon, which is about the most intense moment any tennis player will experience on court (or indeed anywhere). Alcaraz was grinning when he reached championship point against Novak Djokovic in a third-set tiebreak in the 2024 final, just minutes after he had had three points for the title when serving at 5–4, 40–0 in that set, only to be broken. Other players would have had a different expression on their faces in that situation – they would have either been super-focused or completely terrified – as they tried to fight off a psychological collapse. Alcaraz, though, smiled away the tension on the way to another Grand Slam title, as perhaps only he can. 'Carlos has a smile on his face. That's very offensive to people like me, who played in kind of a miserable, stressed-out state most of the time,' Andy Roddick, a former US Open champion and world number one, said on his podcast that day. 'But it's fun to watch. Who doesn't love this kid? The game is in great hands.'

Suffering is a key part of Spanish tennis, some say. Coaches suggest every Spanish player should be willing to struggle – to endure all sorts of physical, emotional and psychological pain – for their tennis. Learning the game on clay, where the points are longer and don't come cheaply, feeds into that. It's unusual for a tennis player from any country to smile as much as Alcaraz does on court; it's even more surprising because he comes from a tennis nation with a culture that embraces the hardship.

Nadal almost always looked as though he was suffering on court. Even when Nadal won in straight sets, he had the face of someone who was going through a lot. 'I don't know how many times Rafa smiled during a match in all those years on the circuit, but it can't have been many,' says Emilio Sánchez. 'That's one of the things that makes Carlitos so different to Rafa. Rafa was super-focused on the battle while Carlitos is focused on the enjoyment of the battle. Tennis is a very emotional sport. Carlitos's game is happiness and he's showing his happiness.'

Maybe Nadal was a little smilier in his younger years, Garbiñe Muguruza observes, but tennis players often 'become a bit more serious' as they age and that's what happened with Rafa. Nadal didn't make playing tennis look that much fun (even though it was of course enjoyable to watch). Alcaraz, by contrast, doesn't look like a tennis masochist. He's also willing to suffer for his art, just like every other Spanish tennis player, as he wouldn't have been so successful without that. Alcaraz knows tennis can't just be about playing pretty points. Part of what Alcaraz loves about tennis is the struggle. As he once told his team, there's joy in suffering, in battling for hours on court. But if Alcaraz loves to suffer, that's mostly hidden by his smile, by the white of his teeth and his general razzle-dazzle.

'Happy tennis,' Alcaraz calls his own game. Roger Federer once described the Australian Open as the 'Happy Slam' because everyone always feels good in Melbourne in January at the start of the season; and that's how many now think of it. But that was just one tournament. Alcaraz has taken the idea further, to play his 'happy tennis' around the world; he considers himself a happy person off the court and so that's how he likes to play tennis, with a lot of joy. Is it any surprise that one of his closest friends on tour is Frances Tiafoe, an ebullient American? Alcaraz considers Tiafoe to be the nicest guy on the tour, as well as the funniest and the loudest, and if he was looking for 'a wingman on a night out', he has said, he would also pick the guy he played in the semi-finals of the 2022 US Open. The pair have played some exhibition matches, including in Puerto Rico in 2025. Tiafoe is fun and he's smiley. But he's not nearly as fun or as smiley as Alcaraz is – he doesn't often grin after losing big points, for instance.

There have been smiley tennis players before, of course. It's just that they tended to smile between matches and not during them. There have been other tennis players primarily known for their facial expressions and emotions on court, too, but they have mostly been defined by their rage. Angry young men like John McEnroe. Traditionally, nothing gains you more attention in tennis than rage: tantrums and throwing racquets and insults. But Alcaraz, the antithesis of McEnroe, and the brightest of bright young things, is showing the power of a smile. Every time Alcaraz goes on court, he tries to do something that others wouldn't even attempt: to be happy during matches. 'Carlitos is a very smiley boy,' says his former coach Kiko Navarro. 'That's his personality, the way he is. Off the court, he also smiles a lot, and he has won over the public from all around the world.'

For Alcaraz, everything – from his star power to his tennis mojo – starts with the smile. 'Carlitos smiles all the time on the tennis court,' says his friend Antonio López, who has known Alcaraz since their days on the junior tennis circuit in Spain. 'Obviously, he smiles when he wins points, and that's expected. But when he loses points, he also smiles. When Carlitos walks on to a court, he goes there to enjoy himself. It doesn't matter whether he wins or loses; he's going to enjoy being there.'

When Alcaraz's first coach, Carlos Santos, is watching him play, he need only look at Alcaraz's face to instantly know what is going on inside his head in that moment, and to have a good sense of whether the Murcian is going to win. If Alcaraz is smiling, Santos will be confident Alcaraz is going to have a good day.

Tennis tests your psyche like no other sport. But, remarkably, for the most part Alcaraz keeps smiling. It's crucial, he once told *Vogue* magazine, that he walks out on to court smiling and feeling happy: 'That helps you mentally. For me, it's everything.' Deep into a Grand Slam final, Alcaraz's smile can instantly change the energy on court, allowing him to play his expressive and explosive tennis. 'Carlos has the same face now that he did when he was younger. When I see him playing, I can see what he is thinking,' says Santos. 'As a boy, Carlos was always smiling, always. Carlos plays better tennis when he is smiling, absolutely. If he is smiling on the court, he's going to be more relaxed and enjoying himself. It's important that he enjoys himself. Carlos smiles more than any other tennis player.' As Santos observes, other players don't look happy in the middle of matches but Alcaraz has the rare ability – and this might be his defining feature – to be able to focus and smile.

Smiling allows Alcaraz to deal with the pressure and expectation. 'There's lots of pressure around Carlos. I don't mean from his family and from his team. I mean the situation that he's the focus of everybody in this sport in this world, and it's not easy to manage these things,' says

Ferrero's former coach José Perlas. 'The solution for Carlos is to smile and laugh because when he's smiling and laughing, he's relaxing and it's easier to manage what's happening inside. Rafa was a warrior on court, but everyone feels the pressure and the tension in certain moments and they manage that in different ways. Carlos has found his way and that's been working. That's why Juan Carlos sometimes asks Carlos to smile on court – as then he will relax and get the best out of himself.'

For Alcaraz's opponents, seeing the Spaniard's smile across the net must be crushing.

They know that when Carlos is smiley, he tends to produce his most devastating tennis. 'When we are happy, everything works better. If you're having fun, you take pressure off the moment and everything flows better,' says David Ayuela, who captained Spain's 2018 Junior Davis Cup-winning team, which included Alcaraz. There's no doubt, says Alcaraz's old sports teacher Carlos Bocanegra, that the athlete is more likely to play at a higher level when he looks happy.

Alcaraz's smile is a big reason – possibly even the biggest reason – why he's celebrated around the world. As the actor Steve Carell says, Alcaraz sometimes can't help but smile after losing 'crazy rallies' as he has had fun in those points, which is partly why he 'seems like a kid as he plays – you can feel the childlike nature of the play with him'. If Alcaraz had had the same success but had won all his titles with a stern, serious face, he wouldn't have anything like the same appeal in the sport. Alcaraz doesn't have to force anything with a tennis crowd. The smile mostly comes naturally and so does the adoration of a crowd, wherever he is playing. On court, Josefina Cutillas told *Tennis Majors*, Alcaraz is 'sheer passion and pure positive energy' and puts on 'a magnificent show'.

Authenticity is key to Alcaraz's appeal. Cutillas observed the Murcian athlete is 'transmitting truth, honesty and closeness and he has kept his essence'.

Calling it a million-dollar smile would be to undersell it; it's worth much more than that. The smile is very good for business: IMG's Max Eisenbud told *Sports Illustrated* that, after losing big points in Grand Slam finals, the Spaniard 'has this goofy grin like he is playing with his buddies down at the park'.

That smile endears Alcaraz to his corporate backers and, more widely, to the sports industry. 'Rafa, Novak and Roger, those guys were great but, in my opinion, they were more serious. The new generation is looking for a bit more fun,' says Jean-Christophe Verborg at Babolat, Alcaraz's racquet sponsor. 'Carlos performs the way he does – winning Grand Slams and being the number one – while smiling. You have this feeling that he's enjoying playing tennis. He's showing sport can be about performance and you can miss a shot, and you can lose, but you can still laugh and smile; and that's the essence of sport. This guy drives so many good things and the best values of sport, in my opinion. A lot of people were worried about tennis after the Big Three. But someone like Carlos has brought a kind of fresh image of tennis. It's different. The world has changed.'

*

But what if it's too simplistic to say that Carlos Alcaraz smiles all the time? What if he doesn't smile quite as much as people say he does?

In the weeks leading up to the 2022 US Open, for instance, Juan Carlos Ferrero felt as though Alcaraz had lost some of his joy on court, that he wasn't his usual self and that this was harming his performances.

There was a heaviness about Alcaraz at a tournament in Montreal, where he lost his opening match. For the first time in his career, he felt as though he couldn't handle the pressure and he lost his opening match. His tennis was a little better at his next event, in Cincinnati, where he made the quarter-finals, but he needed to bring the joy back before the US Open began. What changed for Alcaraz, transforming him into a Grand Slam-winning force in New York City? It wasn't a technical tweak to his game, some new strategy or because he was feeling physically stronger; it was because, with the help of Ferrero, as well as the rest of his team and his family, he rediscovered the joy of playing tennis.

Ferrero was urging Alcaraz to follow his instincts and play his natural, aggressive game: to attack any short ball and get to the net whenever he could. It was tactical advice but also something deeper than that, and a way of restoring the essence of Carlos Alcaraz. Ferrero knew that if Alcaraz was on the attack he would go back to enjoying himself again – and that would mean smiles and a higher level of tennis.

An expectation has built up around Alcaraz's smile. If he's not smiling, people will wonder what's wrong. If Carlos isn't smiling and he isn't at his best, people will say that is why he lost. On days when he isn't grinning, his team and family might ask him what's going on.

They noticed that about Carlos in the first few months of 2024; they thought he looked sad at the start of the Indian Wells tournament in March that year. Alcaraz wasn't enjoying himself on court. He didn't feel like himself. Confidence was low. Alcaraz hadn't won a title in almost nine months, since the 2023 Wimbledon Championships. For all his ambitions, and his dreams of making tennis history, Alcaraz cares more about how he feels on the court, and whether he's enjoying himself, than he does about winning titles. Winning in Indian Wells that year was a significant moment because of the mental shift; he had been able, as he described it, to 'overcome a lot of problems in my head' as well as some physical difficulties. He remembered how much he adored tennis. Alcaraz even said he found himself again in the desert.

Alcaraz enters another dimension, and plays his most creative tennis, when the focus is on enjoyment. When his mind wanders and he thinks too much about results, and winning a tournament, he risks losing his joy.

If Alcaraz is feeling down in a match – if it seems as though the smile is fading – he takes a moment to remind himself that being on that court was what he always wanted for himself, that he has dreamed of being on that stage since he was a boy. That reminder can sometimes be enough to change how he is feeling and to bring the smile back. Or he can tell himself that every time he is on court is 'a gift' and tennis is supposed to be fun. 'This is just a game,' Alcaraz sometimes tells himself. 'This is nothing more than a game.'

You can smile or you can scream. If you're Alcaraz, and you're on Centre Court, those are a couple of good options for you. Letting out a giant scream in the middle of a match, as Alcaraz did one year at Wimbledon, can be an effective way of getting rid of some of the nervous tension in his body. After screaming – which is mostly covered up by the sound of the crowd cheering – Alcaraz is more likely to enjoy the occasion, to smile and to manoeuvre and manipulate a tennis ball as only he can.

Sometimes Alcaraz's fans can make him chuckle on court – and for long periods, as happened for almost a whole set in a match he played at the Indian Wells Tennis Garden in 2025. The unlikely reason for his laughter? A group of spectators who had come to the stadium dressed as bees, wearing black and yellow striped tops. In 2024, Alcaraz had been playing a quarter-final in the desert against Alexander Zverev when the match was interrupted by a bee invasion; around 25,000 bees had landed on the 'spider cam' and some surrounded the Spaniard, stinging him on his forehead. It was a disturbing moment for Alcaraz, who tried to run away. The tournament had to call in a local beekeeper. A year later, he was able to laugh about it – when he looked up at the big screen inside the stadium and saw the spectators in their bee costumes, that instantly lifted his mood. Every time Alcaraz looked at the human swarm during the first set, it made him giggle, which he knew would put him in the mood for playing his best level. At the end of the match, which he won, Alcaraz walked over to those fans to take a selfie with them, as they had helped him and he felt they deserved it.

Carlos's on-court smiles don't necessarily mean he is happy, though. He might be smiling as a way of letting go of the nerves or managing the adrenaline surges you get in matches, says Kiko Navarro. Or perhaps Alcaraz is faking a smile, thinking that's the best way to go back to being his usual happy self. When Alcaraz is having an off day, Ferrero urges him to at least try to look happy. Smiling is the best way for Alcaraz to urgently elevate his performance. As Alcaraz once told three-time Grand Slam finalist Mary Joe Fernández: 'A lot of the time I try to have a smile on the court, but it doesn't mean I'm enjoying [the match] so much.'

Can forcing a smile trick his brain into feeling more positive? Santos believes that works for Alcaraz. But others who know Alcaraz well suggest it isn't as straightforward as that. 'When the smile comes naturally you can feel it and you can see it,' said Àlex Corretja. 'It's about the way he moves. When he's not moving well, and he's not feeling good and playing well, he's not capable of smiling because he's not enjoying himself.'

As Alcaraz observed when he was just 13 years old, everyone smiles in the good times but you must also smile during the bad times. But how you can tell when Carlos is genuinely joyful and when he's hiding behind the smile, trying to reset his head? If his opponents can work that out, that would give them an edge on court. In a tennis match, especially one as pressured as a final, smiling – whether it's genuine or fixed – can be a kind of superpower. If Alcaraz is feeling tense, he will remember the importance of showing his opponent that he's relaxed and enjoying himself (players notice these things, especially Novak Djokovic, who is always examining his opponent's face, looking at them across the net or on the big screen).

In Alcaraz's worst moments – and we will explore later in the chapter the times when he has lost his tennis mojo and some of his enthusiasm for travelling and competing – he can't even pretend. What some forget is that Carlos could be dealing with something off the court. 'The problem is that there are a lot of things going on in Carlitos's life and going on around him all the days,' says Alfredo Sarria.

'Sometimes if Carlitos isn't smiling on the court, it's not necessarily because of how he is feeling about his game; but it depends on things that happen around him, off the court. Sometimes he has some problems in his life away from the court and he doesn't have the solutions. People sometimes say that Carlitos lost a match because he doesn't smile, but it's difficult sometimes to smile, although you try. There are things that can be happening around you that stop you from giving your best in a match because your brain is also focusing on other things,' Sarria says. 'In an individual sport, all the attention is on you and how you're performing. People will always notice if you're in a bad situation, unlike with athletes in team sports. As a tennis player, you're alone on the tennis court and everyone is looking at you. If you don't have your best day, if you're not smiling today, everyone will notice.'

Alcaraz's agent, Albert Molina, doesn't smile much during matches. He can't. Not when Alcaraz takes the opening set easily. If the cameras were to catch Molina smiling in that moment, it might look like he is relaxing because he believes his client is sure to win, he once told *El Partidazo de COPE*. And if Alcaraz drops the opening set, Molina can't smile then either (not that he would be in the mood for grinning in that situation); people would say Alcaraz's agent doesn't care. There's almost no scenario on court when Molina can risk a smile. But while Molina keeps a straight, solemn face – and the others in the box, including Ferrero, are also looking serious – Alcaraz is free to smile and grin and even laugh as much as he wants.

*

One swing was it all it took to break the racquet. Getting the anger out would require a few more. Carlos Alcaraz, raging in the Cincinnati heat, kept on going, slamming his racquet down against the hard court four times in all. After the fourth swing against the cement, a surface as unforgiving for racquets as it is for tennis players' bodies, the frame was barely hanging together. A mess of shattered, twisted graphite. It was the summer of 2024, a previously happy time during which Alcaraz had already won both the Roland-Garros and Wimbledon titles and reached the Olympic singles final. Yet in this defeat in an early round to Frenchman Gaël Monfils he was as upset on court as most had ever seen him. Here, Alcaraz was playing against another of the sport's great entertainers, and it could have been one of those occasions when people celebrated the fun side of tennis. Instead, there was a very heavy moment: as dark and destructive as Alcaraz ever is.

Some in Spain – and around the world – used that moment to make an unfavourable comparison between Alcaraz and Rafa Nadal. How saintly Rafa didn't break a single racquet in all his years on the tour – perhaps in part because his uncle and long-term coach Toni had told him he would quit if his nephew ever did so. While Kiko Navarro, Alcaraz's former coach, was as surprised as many others were by Alcaraz's unexpected loss of control, he felt as though too much was made of it. Many people in Spain, especially those with a better understanding of professional tennis, were sympathetic towards Alcaraz, who apologized on social media for being so violent towards his Babolat frame: 'I'm human.' He had experienced a lot of nerves and it can be difficult to control yourself when your heart rate is high. Alcaraz's team and family would have had a chat with the player about why he'd lost control, according to Kiko: 'It's clear that Carlitos had a lot of pressure and he reacted like that but I'm sure we won't see him doing that many more times. He has matured a lot, and he knows it's not right, that he's an example for children.'

Álvaro didn't want his younger brother, so 'full of rage and anxiety' on court, to be alone in his room that night, where he inevitably would have spent the evening re-living the moment on social media, reading others' hot takes and over-thinking. Sometimes, Alcaraz has said, there's a puzzle in his head that he can't solve. In those moments, he doesn't know what he wants and that can be overwhelming. Álvaro invited Carlos to 'shoot some hoops' and to talk. People around Alcaraz talk gravely of 'the Cincinnati incident'. Around that time, Alcaraz had wondered whether he needed to stop playing tennis, and whether this was really what he wanted to be doing. 'Maybe I was losing the passion. I thought that going there and playing and feeling like that, I might as well not go and quit tennis,' he said in his Netflix documentary. Even thinking back to that day can make Alcaraz tearful again.

Old friend Antonio López doesn't imagine Alcaraz will be breaking many more racquets like that. 'People weren't used to seeing Carlitos doing that. What people don't realize is that athletes at that level have [a degree] of pressure and anxiety that is very difficult to contain. They work on it every day but sometimes they can explode. But, in his case, it was an isolated event and I don't think it will happen again many more times.'

Watching Alcaraz smile through his matches, you might be forgiven for thinking that he is more interested in having a good time than in winning. His smile can hide how ambitious he is, how badly he wants this. Behind the smile, there's a competitive spirit, and a will to win, that isn't as clear to see as it is with other players. 'When Carlos broke that racquet, that was the first time he showed he was human,' says former teenage Grand Slam champion Mats Wilander. 'Sometimes when you watch him, you're not sure if he wants to win because he's smiling so much. When he broke that racquet, people were realizing, "OK, we have this unbelievably talented and entertaining player and he really wants to win too." Maybe before then people hadn't seen Carlos's competitive side. I don't like it when players break racquets – it's a terrible look for the sport – but that moment showed that Alcaraz can be both fun and competitive.'

It might have been the first time that Alcaraz had destroyed a racquet since becoming a Grand Slam champion, but he broke a few frames during his younger years. Actually, more than a few. 'A lot,' Alcaraz has said. He was more of a hothead as a child – he would occasionally fling racquets, sometimes break them, and need a walk and a cry after matches. Looking back, Alcaraz feels as though he was almost a different person back then: he was frequently 'mad' and often complaining a lot; he didn't enjoy his tennis as much then as he does now. 'Carlos was more emotional on court when he was younger. I remember him throwing his racquet,' says his first coach, Carlos Santos. 'If a match didn't go his way, he would get angry.' López recalls many occasions when his matches against Alcaraz would see one or both of them raging: 'When we are little, we all have our moments of anger. Carlitos and I, it is true that we had very strong characters on the court, but it was normal at our ages.'

Navarro has seen Alcaraz smash a few racquets over the years. 'A very bad loser,' Navarro has said of a young Alcaraz, who was highly competitive at everything, even card games. When Alcaraz lost a tennis match, he would often take out his anger on his racquets. 'I got really pissed off,' Alcaraz has recalled. Navarro would know to give Alcaraz some space. He would wait for Alcaraz to calm down before offering his thoughts on the match and asking Alcaraz for his opinions. Recognizing that he was a little all over the place, Alcaraz sought psychological help as he could see that being able to control his emotions was one of the most important skills he'd need in tennis. Navarro also had honest conversations with Alcaraz about learning to manage his emotions – they spoke 'a lot' on that subject – but maybe, Navarro thought, hating losing was a good trait for juniors who aspire to become professionals. Alcaraz wasn't accepting of defeat.

Alcaraz wasn't upset for long, though. 'When Carlitos lost a match, he didn't have that bad feeling for more than ten minutes,' Alfredo Sarria says. 'People thought that Carlitos would feel bad for hours. But that's not correct. By the time Carlitos arrived at the changing room, he was another kind of person. He wanted to be happy. He had forgotten his problems. Of course, he always wanted to win every match he played. For him, it was easy to move on after a defeat.'

The story of a young, racquet-trashing hothead achieving serene superstardom is one we've seen before in tennis: Björn Borg, Roger Federer. Alcaraz is different. Alcaraz is more joyful than Borg, Federer or anyone else who has ever played this sport at the highest level.

While Carlos doesn't get as angry these days, some of that fire is still inside him and it occasionally comes out – as it did that day in America. Other times on the tour, Alcaraz has thrown his racquet, whacked his hand against a bag or smacked a ball out of the stadium. Alcaraz wouldn't be Alcaraz without the smile, but there's so much more to him than that. He's more complex than that. Alcaraz's range of emotions doesn't begin and end with pure happiness. Alcaraz may be more joyful on court than all the rest, but he isn't a smiley face with a tennis racquet. He's dealing with a lot: the stress from the high stakes, the nervous tension, others' expectations and not wanting to let down the people closest to him. Being smiley doesn't make him a soft touch or mean that he won't stand up for himself on the court; if he thinks that a line call was wrong, or that a ball bounced twice before an opponent played it, he will let the umpire know. If an opponent fires the ball at him when he is at the net, he might just respond with a glare rather than a smile.

He's an emotional man who sometimes cries in public, in happy moments – like he did after winning his first major – but also on sadder and more upsetting occasions. One of those was when he was doing a television interview with Àlex Corretja ten minutes after losing the 2024 Olympic singles final to Novak Djokovic. Alcaraz, who felt as though he had let the Spanish people down by not winning the gold medal, became so emotional that he started to cry. Corretja put his arm around the silver medallist to try to console him. 'Take your time, Carlitos,' Corretja said in Spanish and Alcaraz wiped his eyes with his T-shirt. 'I felt as though Carlitos was overwhelmed by the whole situation,' Corretja recalls. 'He had a complete meltdown. He was so emotional. It was very deep. In that moment, I was thinking, "OK, I'm live on TV but I'm next to a kid who is crying and I didn't want to push him and make him talk in that moment." I told him to relax and take his time. I had the microphone and I really needed to talk to the audience as well. I said we needed to give him some space.'

Mostly, though, Alcaraz is a smiley presence. Alcaraz's refreshing, fun-loving approach to life stops tennis from becoming grey and boring, and in the future might help him to keep playing for longer than he might if he was more serious. At the same time, Alcaraz has been inspiring other players, including older men who have been on the tour for longer than he has. Alcaraz has been showing those players – including Stefanos Tsitsipas, a former Grand Slam finalist – that it's possible to be ultra-competitive and very smiley at the same time. Tsitsipas was so taken by Alcaraz's positive energy, which he saw as enabling the Spaniard to become a better, more consistent player, that he told himself he wanted to be more like that, too; if the Greek subsequently felt and looked happier, that was in large part thanks to Alcaraz.

*

How does the smiliest of tennis champions avoid burnout? If Carlos Alcaraz is to feel good on the court, he must first feel good off it. He must be enjoying life away from tennis, which means having fun with his friends, family and team. That's not an indulgence; he says he needs that if he is going to function as an athlete.

Golf, which for many others can sometimes be a maddening sport, is one way for Alcaraz to clear his head and lighten the mood. Juan Carlos Ferrero is into speed. He loves motorbikes and cars. He's also into a slower pursuit: golf. It was Ferrero who introduced Alcaraz to the sport as a way to decompress and take his mind off tennis for a few hours. Alcaraz, Ferrero and the rest of his team are on the course whenever they have a chance; they play in pairs, which leads to even more laughter during a round. Alcaraz has been known to carry a golf glove in his tennis-racquet bag, saying it's there 'just in case' he has a chance to play.

One such opportunity came the evening before his opening match of the 2024 Wimbledon Championships, when he played a round at the Royal Wimbledon Golf Club and at one point was seen looking for his ball in the rough. As he said to another golfer on the course that evening: 'It never goes straight.' Two years after beating Casper Ruud in the 2022 US Open final, Alcaraz played some golf with the

Norwegian – probably the best golfer on the ATP Tour – and took the chance during their round to discuss the importance of having a life outside tennis. One of the reasons that Alcaraz loves competing at the Indian Wells tournament is that it's easy to play golf in the Californian desert, which might have contributed to him winning successive titles in 2023 and 2024. The Indian Wells tournament calls itself 'Tennis Paradise' but Alcaraz also thinks of the desert, with its many courses, as 'a paradise of golf'.

One of the greatest challenges for Alcaraz has been trying to stay mentally fresh throughout the season and keep the smile that allows him to bring his best level of tennis. That's hard for any player. But harder still when you bring as much energy to the court as Alcaraz does. Alcaraz's greatest fear, he has realized, is that tennis starts to feel as though it's an obligation, when he flies to a tournament thinking about ranking points and bonuses, and not what has always been most important to him: the pure joy of playing tennis.

There have been times – and this is concerning in someone so young – when Alcaraz hasn't felt motivated to get on a plane and fly thousands of miles to play a tournament. When he hasn't felt energized to be there and would rather be at home with his friends and family. That was how he felt after his early departure from the 2024 US Open, when there were still two or three months of the season left to play. Carlos wasn't in the mood for tennis, for all the practice and travel and everything that comes with being on the tour. Carlos didn't want to touch his racquets for a while. But what choice did he have? In a later chapter, we will look at how Alcaraz's motivation had dipped two years earlier after winning a first major in 2022.

As Antonio Cascales says, the tennis calendar is so full that players don't have the time to pause, reflect and maybe ask themselves: 'How am I doing?' Because the tennis calendar never stops, Alcaraz can't either, aside from a few days dotted here and there. There are times when the fun-loving, freestyling Alcaraz, who says he has tennis in his blood, suddenly finds the sport a drag. In his worst moments, he feels emotionally exhausted. Jet lag is the enemy for all tennis players; while some of his team have been looking for ways to speed up his adaptation to new time zones, which will improve his focus and concentration and reduce the chance of injury, there's no escaping the physical and mental effects of regularly moving across several time zones. Alcaraz must accept that the season runs until late November, culminating with the ATP Finals – an exclusive tournament to which only the leading eight men are invited – and a chance to end the year on a high.

'As you go from tournament to tournament, it's about the energy you need to deliver your best tennis. With Carlitos, as he's such an explosive guy, it's difficult for him to maintain the same energy throughout the year,' says Àlex Corretja. 'When he doesn't maintain that energy, you can tell his tennis is affected. I think he needs to select his calendar very well and not play too many events. His freshness, and the way he flows on the court, and the way he flies on the court, he will lose some of that if he plays more. If he plays too much, he will lose his essence. If you lose your essence, you might struggle. But he's learning.'

New York City has brought out some of the most dynamic tennis of Alcaraz's career. That's where he bagged his first Grand Slam, after all. The city has also been the setting for a couple of the most troubling matches of his life. In his own assessment, Alcaraz's attitude in his semi-final at the 2023 US Open was 'unacceptable'. He had played some loose points in the tiebreak to drop the opening set to his Russian opponent, Daniil Medvedev. That looseness wasn't what concerned him afterwards; the problem was what happened next, as he felt as though he 'gave up a little bit' in the second set, which he lost 6–1. You wouldn't expect an elite player at a Grand Slam to give anything less than their best effort, especially if they were the defending champion. In the end, though, Alcaraz went down in four sets. At 19, he had been on top of the world – the US Open champion and the new world number one – but at 20 he was showing signs of immaturity. Alcaraz thought about throwing his racquet on to the court that day but stopped himself. He knew he shouldn't approach a match in that way again. It felt like an experience he could learn from.

The trouble was, when Alcaraz returned to New York City a year later, to play in the 2024 US Open, he was fighting against himself as well as against his second-round opponent, a Dutchman called Botic van de Zandschulp who was then ranked 74 in the world. Alcaraz had barely had any time off over a productive summer during which he had won Roland-Garros and Wimbledon titles and reached the final of the Paris Olympics; so it would have been understandable if he had been suffering from some mental and physical tiredness. The US Open also came soon after what his agent Albert Molina calls 'the Cincinnati incident'. In New York, Alcaraz felt as though it was a rollercoaster in his mind; his mood was abruptly up or down – he didn't have the calmness he needed to think clearly on the court and to play the tennis he wanted to play. Alcaraz had felt as though he had learned some lessons from previous matches like this one. But, reflecting after this defeat – his earliest departure from a Grand Slam since the 2021 Wimbledon Championships – maybe he hadn't learned nearly as much as he'd imagined he had.

While Alcaraz isn't a controversial figure, he also speaks freely; and shortly after the 2024 US Open he was very strong on the schedule, saying, 'They are going to kill us in some way.'

Alcaraz made that remark at the Laver Cup, a non-mandatory team competition between Europe and the rest of the world. In the days that followed, Alcaraz knew that some people were talking about the exhibitions he played, saying that he didn't have to sign up for those events if he wanted more breaks between Grand Slams and the mandatory ATP events. His response was that playing an official tournament was different to appearing at an exhibition. Competing for ranking points, prize money and potentially a piece of history is going to take much more out of you than having some fun. You can't equate the two. Alcaraz's comment about the schedule 'killing' the players was quoted in the lawsuit filed by the Professional Tennis Players' Association (PTPA), which was cofounded by Novak Djokovic, against the sport's governing bodies in 2025. Alcaraz was unaware his words would be used in that way. No one had even told him about the legal action, which he didn't support (he said he agreed with some parts of the lawsuit and disagreed with others).

As a young tennis player, what's the cost of chasing your dreams? How much will Alcaraz sacrifice to be the best? In the beginning, Ferrero has noted, everything is fresh and exciting for a young player. But that feeling fades, and you must then find ways to stop the tennis life becoming monotonous. Juan Carlos Ferrero sometimes used to watch Rafa Nadal practising and wonder: after winning all those Grand Slams, how did he continue to train with that kind of daily intensity? Alcaraz doesn't have to be like Nadal to keep on having success. But when he's feeling low, he must somehow find the desire to get back on the road again; and when he's there, he must summon the energy to produce some more outrageous tennis.

He's searching – sometimes successfully and sometimes not – for the feelings and rhythm that will take him back to smiling and being joyful on court. Playing for a team can help. Alcaraz's first two events after the 2024 US Open were in team competitions – he represented Spain in the Davis Cup and Europe in the Laver Cup – and renewed his energy. Soon, he was once again happy to be travelling, training and competing. When Alcaraz took the title at his next singles tournament, in Beijing, which ended a challenging period in his young career, Ferrero was moved to tears. But that wouldn't be the last time that Alcaraz went through a difficult period, as after losing his opening match to Belgium's David Goffin at the Miami tournament in 2025, he said openly: 'Mentally, I'm screwed.'

Being an elite athlete, or aspiring to be one, doesn't mean you have to live like a monk and deprive yourself of all fun. You can still go out and even have a few drinks if you wish, even if that's very occasionally. When he was 18 years old, Alcaraz appeared on a Spanish television show, *El Hormiguero*, and said he had been 'tipsy' a couple of times and that his drink of choice when going out with his friends was gin with lemon. The presenter replied: 'Be careful with that, you might end up getting tangled up with the first one that passes by.' Before going out as a teenager, Alcaraz's parents would say to him, 'Don't come back too late,' and he knew that if he did there would be 'problems' (his word). His mother was often stricter than his father about his rare evenings out. Even if he tried to be quiet on his return to the apartment, he would always wake his parents up, so they would always know when he was getting home (generally earlier than all his friends were). Going out for a few hours was good for Alcaraz, though. Just for a bit, he felt like a normal teenager.

There were moments when it upset Alcaraz that he couldn't do everything his friends did. Having an occasional night out helped to silence the thought in his head that, by choosing tennis and a life of dedication and discipline, he was missing out on the fun and the abandon of being young.

A simple boy, some say of Alcaraz. But it's more complicated being Carlos Alcaraz than it first appears. Alcaraz needs to be happy, to have a smile on his face, if he is to play the tennis that will allow him to win many more Grand Slams. And yet the pursuit of that off-court happiness, and the time and the energy that goes into that, could be what endangers his chance of becoming the greatest of all time. It's a tension that we will explore later in the book: what was someone with ambitions of true tennis greatness, of winning more majors than anyone else in history, doing preparing for Wimbledon by 'getting wasted' in Ibiza? Is it possible to be a normal young guy, as Alcaraz sees himself, as well as a tennis immortal? That's the question, as yet unanswered, that shapes Alcaraz's world.

8

La bici, they call it in Spain, as the two zeroes in the scoreline look a bit like the wheels of a bike. Antonio López doesn't play so much these days – he spends more time coaching than competing now – but when he does enter tournaments in Murcia, people will half-recognize him: 'Are you the guy who once beat Carlitos 6–0, 6–0?'

The most one-sided defeat of Alcaraz's life – a loss he's now able to laugh about – was in a junior tournament in Totana, a town in Murcia about a 40-minute drive from his village of El Palmar. López was twelve at the time, so two years older than Alcaraz, which is a significant age advantage in junior tennis. That advantage was even greater because, as López recalls, Alcaraz was short for his age. López didn't hold back against his younger, smaller and weaker opponent. Over the space of five or six years, they would end up playing each other around sixteen times as boys, usually in a semi-final or final, and they would always go all out; that match was no different. 'Carlitos and me, our characters were both hard on the court in those days. We were always fighting on the court. We both wanted to win every match and if you were the one who lost you would get angry, for sure,' López says.

López, who was the number one junior in Murcia for many years, found that Alcaraz's 'clean tennis' allowed him to produce his best level, and he was faultless that day against ten-year-old Carlos. He would go on to win the first 14 of his 16 matches with Alcaraz, only losing a couple of times when he was 17 years old and Alcaraz was 15. 'Carlitos had grown up by then,' López says.

Alcaraz and López have stayed friends; they meet up every two months or so in Murcia. Between his own coaching commitments in his home city of Cartagena, and doing a second degree, López also occasionally travels to support Alcaraz at Grand Slams and other ATP tournaments around the world, such as in Rotterdam, Miami and Rome in 2025. He was also at Wimbledon in 2023 when Carlos won that title for the first time. If López is thinking about going to a tournament, he messages Alcaraz, who is usually able to give him some tickets (he says he wouldn't be able to attend otherwise because he wouldn't be able to afford the ticket prices). When López goes on those trips, he mostly travels with a group of the old tennis friends from Murcia and they try to be so vocal with their support for Alcaraz that he will be able to hear their cries of '*Vamos, Carlitos!*' above all the other crowd noise.

The wipeout in Totana has become an amusing memory for Carlos and Antonio. 'I had actually forgotten some of the details of that match. Carlitos remembers the match very well, though,' says López. 'Carlitos and I were talking one day, after he was playing on the tour, and he said to me, "Do you remember that time you beat me 6–0, 6–0?" That was so funny. Then Carlitos was playing an ATP tournament in

Argentina and he told the story of our match in an interview, calling me *cabrón*, which is kind of like a jokey insult between friends who are comfortable with each other [it roughly translates as "bastard"]. In the morning, every TV and radio station wanted to speak to me. I was famous for one day.'

López, still very much a curiosity in Murcia, is the only player to have ever beaten Alcaraz 6–0, 6–0. He tells the children he coaches in Cartagena about the time he crushed the future world number one – not because he is boasting but because he thinks it might motivate them. Hopefully they believe his story, because he thinks it's a powerful one. 'I'm saying to the kids that with some effort and some help from their coach, they can reach the things they dream about,' says López. Nine years after that match, Alcaraz was at the top of the world rankings.

There's another reason why López is an important figure in Alcaraz's story. As Alcaraz once remarked to López: 'You taught me how to play the drop shot.' Perhaps Alcaraz was half-joking when he said that. But maybe not. Their junior matches contained so many drop shots – on at least one occasion they must have hit more than 50 between them – that it must have encouraged Alcaraz to continue developing and playing that shot. 'If you had been in the crowd watching me play against Carlitos when we were juniors, you would have found it funny because we were hitting drop shots all the time,' says López.

Anyone can hit a drop shot, López thinks, but the skill – and what can make a drop shot so devastating – is knowing when to play it. Choosing the right moment in a rally is key and López says Alcaraz has that ability. Alcaraz's drop shots aren't premeditated; he's not typically plotting to hit one as he gathers himself for the next point. It's much more natural than that – he will play one when he is feeling it, when he has the confidence to go for it, though he recognizes he doesn't always judge it correctly and can sometimes introduce 'la dejada', as Spaniards call it, too early in a rally. For Alcaraz's opponents, it's almost impossible to read what he's about to do. But there's one very interested spectator who has a good idea. Maybe it's because he has played against Alcaraz so many times, and known him for years; but when López is in the crowd or watching a match on television, he can usually predict when Alcaraz is going to hit one. Supporting Alcaraz in the Rotterdam final in 2025, López was playing a game in the crowd with his cousin. López would say 'drop shot' if he thought Alcaraz was about to play one. He was almost always right.

*

This might sound odd but going for a high-risk shot relaxes Carlos Alcaraz. A drop shot is a risky option. That's why many players can be overly cautious about hitting one. Get it wrong and you can look silly. Play it at the wrong moment and it can look as though you've checked out of a rally. But if Alcaraz is feeling nervous, hitting a drop shot – or doing something else spectacular – helps him to relax into the occasion. Even when those shots don't work out, they're still worth trying as tennis feels fun when he's playing them. There are occasions, Alcaraz has said, when he produces 'disasters' with a smile on his face.

With Alcaraz, tennis is getting more powerful; it's also getting softer and more delicate. So, while Jannik Sinner once told Alcaraz to his face that he considers him 'a beast' on the court, he also said to the Spaniard during the same conversation – at the ATP Finals in Turin one year – that his drop shots were 'beautiful'.

Alcaraz can smack his forehand with as much power as anyone else in tennis. He could be faster than anyone else who has ever played this sport, with former Grand Slam champion Jim Courier saying it sometimes appears as though the Murcian is moving around the court on roller-skates. John McEnroe thinks Alcaraz's movement is key to his success. Some courtside photographers will tell you Alcaraz is the most dynamic and explosive tennis player to shoot since a young Boris Becker was diving all over the court in the 1980s. One likened Alcaraz to a bouncing ball. With Alcaraz, they are always guaranteed at least one great picture per match, which could be when he plays a tweener – hitting the ball through his legs with his back turned – or getting airborne when playing a backhand return. Others watch Alcaraz and think he moves like Spider-Man. But, for all that, Alcaraz's most damaging shot – the one his opponents dread, the one the crowds adore and the one his friends love to see – can be when he suddenly slows everything down and pops the ball over the net. The drop shot is Alcaraz's signature move, as it has been since he was a child.

Of course, you can't win matches on drop shots alone – you still need a strong serve and powerful groundstrokes to do that – but playing a short ball that an opponent can't reach is sending a big message. It's showing that Alcaraz can do anything, that he's in command of the space on both sides of the net. In the modern game, you can smack a 160kmh-plus forehand down the line for a winner, as he has done in Grand Slam finals and other big occasions. That's going to feel good. But winning a point with a drop shot will possibly inflict more of a psychological blow on your opponent, especially if you do that repeatedly. 'I guess if Carlos keeps winning over and over again with his drop shot, that could be humiliating for his opponents,' says Craig O'Shannessy, Novak Djokovic's former strategy coach. 'Everything that Carlos does makes opponents uncomfortable but players are going in knowing that if they're playing him, they had better be ready for his drop shots.'

You can, of course, hit too many drop shots; if you're always playing them, you're going to lose the ability to surprise your opponent – which is why Ferrero has said Alcaraz should moderate his use of them.

It was only an exhibition event, but when Alcaraz played against Frances Tiafoe in Puerto Rico in 2025 he hit one of his most outrageous drop shots: when returning the American's serve. There was so much backspin on the ball that it landed on Tiafoe's side and then bounced back over the net towards Alcaraz. Tiafoe could only smile and lean over the net in playful exasperation.

As his friend Antonio López says, Alcaraz's love of drop shots isn't new. Alcaraz's former coaches will tell you how a young Carlos dedicated a lot of time to making that shot even better, which was unusual as most young players tend to be most excited by whacking the ball. Turning the power right down and floating the ball over the net is often much less interesting for children. Alcaraz, though, has been practising the drop shot since he was seven or eight years old. 'Carlos practised his drop shot every day with me and that's why he's so good at it today,' says Carlos Santos, his first coach. 'I would give Carlos a target and he would hit drop shots with a whole basket of balls. I've never worked with another player who liked to hit so many drop shots. Most players, they're trying to hit the ball as hard as they can the whole time. But not Carlos – he wanted to play drop shots as well as big forehands.'

As a junior, drop shots were a natural part of Alcaraz's game, according to David Ayuela, his former captain in the Junior Davis Cup. Most children struggle playing the drop shot. But 'from a very young age', according to Kiko Navarro, the boy was able to play the drop shot extremely well, thanks to his technique, and they continued developing that shot. These days, Navarro says, Alcaraz's drop shots are nothing less than 'incredible'. He continues to develop them and on one occasion at the practice courts at an ATP tournament was happy to be filmed attempting the so-called 'Ultimate Drop Shot Challenge', with three different-sized wastepaper baskets or buckets – one small, one medium and one large – positioned in the service box for him to aim at.

Highly unusually, Alcaraz prefers hitting a drop shot with his forehand. O'Shannessy has observed how pretty much every other player – if not everyone else – favours their backhand. With their back turned to their opponent, it's easier to disguise that they are changing their grip to play a softer shot. Alcaraz does things differently, though. 'Almost everyone else hits a drop shot with a backhand down the line, as that's the easiest, but Carlos hits a lot with his forehand and he likes doing it inside out,' O'Shannessy says – meaning he plays that forehand drop shot from the backhand side of the court and hits the ball diagonally cross-court. 'Carlos has really [showcased] the forehand drop shot. Very few people were using it before him but he's specifically using it. Doing it off the forehand side is very unusual. He's definitely the best on tour at it.'

It's because Alcaraz hits the ball so hard that he can hit it so softly and win so many points. He has reflected on the idea that to have a fine drop shot you must first have a strong forehand, which allows you to push an opponent back beyond the baseline. 'Carlos disguises his drop shot really well. He sets it up by hitting a hard, powerful forehand first, or maybe two of those, and then he prepares exactly the same way, winding up as if he's about to hit a third,' O'Shannessy says. 'Carlos has shown the other guy, "I'm going to rip it, I'm going to hit it hard," and it looks as though he's going to do it again. He's sold it to the other guy, who's expecting another hard forehand. At the last moment, though, Carlos changes his grip and his backswing – he's so good at doing that – and plays a drop shot.'

Alcaraz's disguise is terrific, according to Paul Annacone, Federer's former coach, because opponents see 'the start of the big wind-up' before the Spaniard subtly softens his hand and plays the ball with a gentle touch.

Toni Nadal doesn't agree with those who suggest that the drop shot is Alcaraz's best stroke. 'Carlos's drop shots are, of course, very good but he can play those drop shots because of how well he hits his forehand or backhand. Carlos's forehand is so fast. When you hit the ball so hard with your forehand or backhand, as Carlos does, your opponent is normally going to be waiting at the back of the court for another fast ball,' Toni says. 'With his opponent expecting another big forehand or backhand, Carlos has the chance to play a drop shot.'

Alcaraz's speed allows him to play better drop shots. 'When you move as fast as Carlos does, you can get behind the ball and that's key. The problem for others is when everything is going too fast and you're not quick enough to get behind the ball, as then you can only push it back over the other side of the net,' Àlex Corretja says. 'Carlos is quick and that means he can choose what he does, and whether he wants to play another drop shot or not. Carlos has the touch. His feel is extremely high. He also has a huge forehand, one of the most powerful we've ever had in tennis. It looks as though he's about to hit the ball so hard and then – all of a sudden, and even without changing his grip – he just turns his wrist and places the ball in the other side of the court. It just drops over the net.'

As we've seen, Alcaraz is in love with tennis. But what he loves most of all, it seems, is the drop shot. If you're playing against Alcaraz you'll be expecting him to hit some, but that doesn't help you because what you don't know is when the droppers will come. Wondering when Alcaraz is going to hit another one can introduce worry and uncertainty in your mind while not allowing you to be any more prepared. All at once, Alcaraz's drop shots are completely expected and a total surprise. 'The opponent has to get ready for something and, with Carlos looking as though he's going to hit another powerful forehand, they get ready for that,' O'Shannessy says. 'His drop shots are almost impossible to cover.'

Garbiñe Muguruza says Alcaraz's opponents can't ever know when he will suddenly switch the power off. 'Carlos's drop shot is crazy. That's what I like most about his game. You don't see it coming,' says Muguruza. 'Carlos is playing so tough, so hard, so well and then he throws in his little thing, his drop shot, which his opponent never reaches. We call it a break of rhythm. You can be playing back and forth, back and forth, and then Carlos throws you a drop shot that you didn't see coming. Your legs are burned and you can't run anymore.'

Others might play a drop shot because, in tennis parlance, they're bailing out of a rally – because their legs are too heavy to continue rallying from the baseline, and their mind is tired too – but Alcaraz tends to play the shot when he's already in the ascendancy. Alcaraz doesn't play a drop shot out of desperation, because he can't think what else to do in a particular moment. He plays one when it feels like the best of his many available options. When O'Shannessy studied the data from Alcaraz's run to the title in Miami in 2022 – where the 18-year-old was the youngest champion in the tournament's history – he noticed that the Spaniard played more than double the amount of drop shots when he was serving than when he was returning. If anyone chooses to stand deep behind the baseline to return against Alcaraz, they're vulnerable to him playing a drop shot as his first shot after his serve. Usually, Alcaraz's opponents aren't retreating through choice, though; they're doing so because his power has forced them back. 'It's the power of Carlos's groundstrokes that pushes them back a little bit,' O'Shannessy says. 'That opens up the front of the court and he's smart enough to utilize that.'

Alcaraz will also play drop shots in moments you wouldn't expect him to at all. 'If Carlos wants to play a drop shot, he does it. It doesn't matter if it's a break point or not; if it comes to his mind, he does it,' says Corretja. 'He's young and he gets this feeling – and he's got this hand and he can do pretty much whatever he wants – so you need to let him fly. While letting him know that sometimes that drop shot is going to cause him trouble during a match.'

Other players don't want to risk playing the drop shot as often as Alcaraz does. 'It's such a hard shot, the drop shot,' says Muguruza. 'You must have such talent, such feeling in your racquet, and Carlos has that. The drop shot is very hard to train. Either you have that talent for it or you don't, and it comes naturally to Carlos. [Other] players don't dare to do it. It's scary to play. You want to keep playing the way you have been. You want to keep hitting the ball. You don't want to do something strange. But Carlos dares to do it and it's a weapon he can use when he's tired or when his opponent is tired. Novak has a good drop shot but Carlos's is better.'

Hitting a drop shot that an opponent can't reach is exhilarating for Alcaraz. It feels so good that he wants to hit another one very soon afterwards.

It's hard to reimagine tennis. Harder still when you're playing just as the sport's golden age of Djokovic, Federer and Nadal is coming to an end. And yet that's what Alcaraz has done. If tennis is no longer golden, perhaps with Alcaraz it's in the neon age: vivid, multicoloured, unmissable. Alcaraz's willingness to use drop shots at the most critical moments has changed tennis. 'What Carlos has done is a big deal,' says O'Shannessy. 'He has brought out the forehand drop shot on big points, such as in the tiebreak. He has been playing it when other players would shy away from it under the spotlight of a game point or a set point. Carlos was using it in those big moments. It's had an effect on the tour. Everyone's a bit more used to it now but when he first did it on the tour it was opening other players' eyes to how this is a legitimate play and not just a secondary thing that you'll do once a set. Carlos showed that drop shots are an integral part of the game. In today's power game, you've got the power groundstrokes, especially the forehand, and then you've got the complete lack of power, which is very effective as well.'

Deep into his thirties, and widely seen as the greatest of all time, Novak Djokovic has been adjusting his game because of a rival who is in his early twenties. 'Djokovic now plays more drop shots because he realized that Carlitos was hurting him with that part of the game,' says Emilio Sánchez. 'There are players who change the game, who leave a legacy for future generations. Carlitos is one of those players as he has been showing that in this super-fast era – the fastest-ever era in tennis – he is able to play with all the shots. Carlitos is incredible for tennis because he's fresh with a new way of playing. Younger players are going to try to follow him. If you watch the juniors, you will see that younger players are now playing way more shots and finding a way to do much more on the court. That's because of Carlitos.'

9

The next time Carlos Alcaraz is playing, close your eyes for a minute or two if you can and just listen (this will mean depriving your eyeballs of some of his shot-making but it should be instructive). You're not focusing on the sound of his shots or, if he's on a hard court, the squeaking of his shoes. You're listening to the crowd, because the spectators just can't help themselves. They know they're supposed to stay silent in the middle of a point, but when Alcaraz is playing they're making involuntary noises. Whoa! Ooh! Aah! Giant gasps (and thousands of spectators gasping at the same time is louder than you might think). And then, moments later, those noises again.

A tennis crowd watching Alcaraz play tennis sounds different than when anyone else is on court. It's a double breach of tennis etiquette. Tennis players aren't meant to have this much fun; tennis crowds aren't supposed to be collectively letting out these sounds during rallies. While spectators have oohed and aahed at Roger Federer, as well as at Rafa Nadal and Novak Djokovic, they have tended to do so at the end of the points, when you can make as much noise as you wish. But when Alcaraz is at his most compelling, you might get two, three, even four involuntary noises midpoint because people in the crowd can't control themselves.

'Carlos brings a unique energy to the court that you can really feel when you watch him play,' says Paula Badosa. 'It's this incredible mix of passion, explosiveness and pure joy that he exudes. He battles for every point, yet he plays with a sense of freedom and creativity that's hard to find. People really connect with that vibe. They can see how much he loves the game and the heart he pours into every shot, which stirs up emotions in them too. He makes tennis look both fun and intensely thrilling, and that's why audiences everywhere are completely captivated by him.'

Silence during rallies simply isn't realistic, not with all the hot shots. When Mats Wilander watches Alcaraz play, he can't help but be fascinated by the crowd noises. In all his years in tennis, he has never heard a crowd look and sound as emotionally invested in tennis matches as they do when they're watching Alcaraz. It's for this reason that Wilander, a seven-time Grand Slam champion, suggests Alcaraz might end up being the most important tennis player in the history of the sport. Maybe Alcaraz won't win as many majors as others do, but if he can excite crowds, and draw new people towards tennis, that's worth more to the sport, Wilander suggests. 'People are going absolutely nuts for Carlos,' the Swede says, noting that Alcaraz reached the top of the sport at exactly the right moment, just as the Big Three era was ending.

Alcaraz hasn't saved tennis – tennis hardly needed saving after that golden age – but his emergence has meant there was no 'lull' period.

Wilander says of this player who's been taking the sport to new places: 'Along comes Carlos Alcaraz and, with his smile and his personality and the way he plays, there's been no step down in celebrity status. People know they shouldn't react during points. But they are so surprised by what he is doing on the court, and the shots he's playing, they can't keep quiet.'

There's something else that the crowds struggle with when Alcaraz is on court: sitting back in their seats. Emilio Sánchez says spectators get emotionally involved because of the way Alcaraz plays tennis: 'Why does Carlos have such an emotional effect on the public? Why does he get people off their seats? It's not because of the smile. It's because of the shot he plays before the smile. I feel some are mistaken about the smile. The smile is great. But people aren't standing up to see him smile. They're standing up to see him play.'

As much as Alcaraz tries to win every match he plays, he also wants to have fun and to thrill the crowd. An aesthete as well as an athlete, Alcaraz is looking to hit 'rare, beautiful shots', as he once wrote in an essay for Eurosport. He's doing what he can to avoid tennis being monotonous. He knows which shots are going to get the crowd going – when he finishes a point at the net, plays a drop shot or hits a big winner. Most matches, there will be something rare and beautiful from Alcaraz's racquet and he will join the crowd in watching the replay on the big screen. That's not vanity, you must understand. It's just that seeing the shot again is fun, if not quite as enjoyable as hitting it was.

'Carlitos is like a kid in Disneyland,' says Àlex Corretja. 'Rafa was a warrior. Rafa had a different mindset. He was like the ultimate machine. He didn't care if he played well or felt good. He just wanted to win. With Carlitos, it's the opposite. Sometimes you feel as though he is there to have fun, though of course he wants to win. He's more like a child. Carlitos is a very professional kid; and it's not like he is fooling around, but he likes to have fun around the game. When Carlitos is fresh and free – when he is moving freely on court, and he's flying on court and he's got the crowd with him, and he's enjoying himself – then he's very dangerous.'

Alcaraz is scared of spiders, the dark and horror films – and of letting down the people around him. He was also so nervous during his driving test that his leg was shaking. What Alcaraz isn't fearful of is playing exhilarating, high-risk tennis. Every ten seconds or so, Andre Agassi has observed, Alcaraz tries to do something extraordinary. As Andy Roddick has said: 'You can't take your eyes off him while he's playing as he does all this crazy shit. He's able to pull off anything and therefore he often tries to pull off everything.' Brad Gilbert wrote a tennis manual called *Winning Ugly*; Alcaraz's playing is the antithesis of that. There are no ugly or dull points. Watching Alcaraz makes Andy Murray smile. Coco Gauff, a women's Grand Slam champion, has tried to channel Alcaraz's ability to play bold tennis and to keep on going for shots, sometimes even asking herself on court: 'What would Carlos do?'

What Alcaraz is often doing on court is both playing and hitting. Most young players just want to hit the ball, according to Sánchez. Alcaraz likes to play as well as to hit. The first time Sánchez saw Alcaraz on court – which was when the future world number one was a young boy playing junior events at Sánchez's academy outside Barcelona – he was shocked by how Alcaraz handled a racquet so 'properly'. Sánchez asked around, wanting to know more about the player's background. Sánchez thinks you can trace Alcaraz's playful side back to the games that he enjoyed as a boy, when you could aim only at the service boxes and not the whole court. That meant Carlos was practising using touch, slice, angles and trickery rather than just bashing the ball every time; he was developing the feeling that would be so useful for him as a professional athlete. When Carlos was a boy, if there were no spare courts or friends around, he would go to the practice wall to work on his volley and other parts of his game.

Alcaraz isn't afraid to play an all-court game today – and to be unpredictable – because he has been doing this for years. 'Carlitos was developing skills that the other players weren't because they were just hitting hard,' Sánchez says. 'Carlitos was playing rather than hitting. One of the biggest issues today is that players all hit too much. That's the big difference with Carlitos as he hits when he has to hit and he plays when he has to play.'

Alcaraz plays for himself first, and then for his team. But the crowd can't be far behind. He loves the reaction from the crowd. Which is why he'll sometimes put a finger to his ear after a big winner, inviting them to make even more noise. Carlos adores those moments when they scream his name, when they dance – why, even, he has said, when he sees them pulling funny faces. The energy from the crowd helps Alcaraz, and encourages him to be even more entertaining – and then the crowd get even more into it, with player and audience hyping each other up. And having famous faces in the crowd can further intensify Alcaraz's motivation to play good, entertaining tennis. When Alcaraz heard that actors Zendaya and Tom Holland were at the Indian Wells Tennis Garden, he was super energized for the 2024 final, which he won. Something similar happened when Tom Cruise watched Alcaraz in the 2024 Wimbledon final. If there were more nerves, they were good nerves. The same was true when he learned some Real Madrid footballers had come to see him play at the Caja Mágica facility in the city; as a fan of that team, he wanted to show them what he could do.

Alcaraz has been known to juggle backstage before matches to help him get his eye in. That seems apt. 'Carlitos can do everything on a tennis court – he can serve and volley, he can play drop shots, he can play hard,' says his friend Antonio López. 'He's not constant. He's always changing his style of play.'

One of the most enjoyable shots to play, Alcaraz finds, is when he hits a forehand hard down the line for a winner. There will be a roar from the crowd, and from Alcaraz, and then quietly he will be speaking to himself: 'All right, I'm at a good level right now.' He also loves to hit what you might call a flying backhand, when he gets airborne while swinging at the ball.

Of all the hot shots Alcaraz has played, the hottest, according to his coach Juan Carlos Ferrero, might be the outrageous forehand the then teenager hit when he was match point down against Alex de Minaur in their 2022 semi-final on the clay of Barcelona. Alcaraz shocked himself by making that shot; for half a moment, it seemed as though he had out-run the ball, which was behind him, but somehow he quickly rearranged his body to hit a forehand past the Australian. Another of Ferrero's favourites was Alcaraz's forehand passing shot – almost flicked, rather than hit, when he was running wide and when the ball was low to the ground – in an exhibition match with Tommy Paul in Mexico in 2023 (the American showed his appreciation with a small bow). As Wilander notes, Alcaraz is always doing something 'extra' on court; he's producing shots that others couldn't have even imagined, such as hitting the ball behind his back.

A strong imagination is key to Alcaraz's game, and to the spectacle. 'His imagination is beyond the normal thoughts of a young player,' says Àlex Corretja. 'You need a big imagination to play like Carlos. And if you imagine some nice things, can you then put them into practice? Can you play those shots in matches when you have all the pressure and when you're playing so much tennis over the year? Think about the speed they're playing at. And how he's still so imaginative. This is very difficult to do. Carlos is a genius because he does things at his young age that I don't think we have seen before. He's unique in the way he plays. Carlos is a very special human being and a very special tennis player.'

Alcaraz's all-court, aggressive game is a significant point of difference with Nadal, whose tennis was far more defensive (Nadal knows many people regard his game as defensive – although he doesn't share that view, he accepts he wasn't 'super-aggressive'). 'Rafa was a very defensive player – he was aggressive some of the time but mostly defensive – but Carlos is different,' says Garbiñe Muguruza.

Toni Nadal thinks there were some similarities between his nephew's game and the way Alcaraz plays. 'There's something that Carlos and Rafael both have and that's that they both play with big intensity. Carlos has unbelievable legs and Rafael was fast too,' Toni says. 'There are differences too. Rafael is a little more consistent as Carlos sometimes loses some control. Carlos has more shots than Rafael did. Carlos is a wonderful tennis player. He has everything. He has very good shots. He has so much variety.'

Sometimes it seems as though Alcaraz brings out his opponent's fun side. There's a feeling that Alcaraz's free and creative tennis – and the atmosphere his matches are played in – liberates his opponent to also play looser tennis. Alcaraz often finds opponents at their best. Before going on court, Alcaraz's opponents know that whatever happens, they're going to be part of a show – that there'll be a lot going on and the crowd are guaranteed a good time. Just as a reminder, that wasn't how Nadal's opponents felt before playing him – especially if a match was going to be on clay, and even worse if it was at Roland-Garros. Playing against Nadal was many things but few can ever have anticipated it would be fun.

'Am I a serve bot?' That was the question that Alcaraz wrote on a camera lens after winning an early round at the 2025 Australian Open, with 'serve bot' being the derogatory name for players with big, almost unbreakable serves and often very limited everything else.

Alcaraz had refined his serve during the pre-season for what he hoped would be a looser, more relaxed and more fluid action, in his search for greater accuracy. That remodelling of his serve involved the bizarre sight on the practice court of Alcaraz's second coach Samuel López holding up a small basketball hoop on the end of a long stick, presumably to help Alcaraz perfect his new ball toss. Another tweak Alcaraz had made was to add some lead tape to his racquet to make it 5g (0.18oz) heavier, because he had previously been playing with a racquet that was light by ATP Tour standards and felt he needed some extra weight behind his shots.

A couple of months later, in Indian Wells, Alcaraz was still joking about being a serve bot. As Alcaraz knows – and this is why his joke landed – he's about as far from being a serve bot as any tennis player competing on the tour today, or indeed any era. With all the hot shots, how can you not enjoy watching Alcaraz play? 'Carlitos is a gift for everyone,' says Corretja. 'If you like tennis, it's very difficult that you don't enjoy watching his style. Rafa's style of play was a bit rougher. Maybe you didn't like it so much as you thought it wasn't that smooth. I loved Rafa's game as he was epic every time. With Carlitos, every time he plays it's going to be fun and the new generation of fans love him as they identify with him and what he's doing.'

Even the ball kids, who are meant to be impartial, sometimes can't help but grin at Alcaraz's shots. Back when Alcaraz was just 16 years old – so a good while before he had established himself at the top of the sport, and three years before he achieved what you might call superstardom – he was attracting crowds. That's not supposed to happen to relative unknowns. But it seemed people were drawn to Alcaraz, with Ferrero noting that tennis fans were eager to watch him play. That would have been because of Alcaraz's game, which Ferrero thought exuded charisma, power and strength, and because of the way that Alcaraz moved, which was appealing to the eye. From a young age, Alcaraz had a presence on the court. He has always been very expressive on the court, Ferrero has said, and that 'resonates with people' far more than a player who is emotionally distant on the court and won't show a crowd how they're feeling. But that mostly would have been because of Alcaraz's colourful game, and how he has always been very comfortable showing off his fun side in front of large audiences.

'Playing on big stages motivates Carlitos,' says Kiko Navarro. 'Carlitos has always played very well when there were many people watching him and when he was under pressure; and for that reason I knew that he was a different player.'

Without being anything other than his natural self, and without doing anything other than playing his natural game, the Spaniard has become a hugely popular figure. Wherever he is in the world, Alcaraz is adored by the crowd. Federer used to experience something similar at every event he played, as did Nadal. But Alcaraz, as with so many other aspects of his career, has reached that status – loved in every city, even the ones he is playing in for the first time – much more quickly.

About the only time that he has encountered any hostility from a tennis crowd was at an indoor tournament in Paris in late 2021, where a few spectators booed him. But that was only because he had been playing against a French opponent, Hugo Gaston – and the Parisians, who love to feel as though they are a part of the occasion, probably didn't even really mean it. It wasn't real hostility. If they were being hard on the young Spaniard, it was only that special Parisian kind of pantomime menace. Playing a Frenchman in Paris was bound to be difficult. Alcaraz knew that. But he hadn't expected it to be quite so challenging. It was an unimaginably heavy day for Alcaraz, who cried into a towel. It wasn't easy to play tennis, he had discovered, when some of the crowd was against you. Not knowing how to deal with that situation hurt him. But that might have been the first and last time the atmosphere was like that in Paris for Alcaraz. In years to come – and especially when he won Roland-Garros in 2024 – he felt the love of Paris, just like he does in every other city.

If Generation Z are chronically online, there's something very Gen Z about Alcaraz's tennis – if his tennis is fun to watch live in the stadium or on television, it's also easy to clip and post on social media. If you don't have the time to watch his whole match, you can always snack on the best bits later. And Alcaraz's best bits aren't always the points or shots but casual moments of brilliance, such as when he caught a ball with his racquet at Wimbledon; a video of him doing that has been viewed more than 25 million times. 'TikTok tennis,' Barney Ronay from *The Guardian* calls it. Alcaraz understands that the spectacular points he plays will be viewed and shared online, which could persuade some who don't usually watch tennis to get into the sport.

What's exhilarating for spectators can be stressful for the people in Alcaraz's box. Alcaraz's physiotherapist, Juanjo Moreno, has worn a device that tracks his heart rate and his stress levels. Moreno has found that the data generated while he has been watching some of Alcaraz's matches suggests he was doing something very strenuous. What has made Moreno nervous has been when Alcaraz has been ahead in a match yet has done everything in his power to reach a ball. That has been when Moreno has asked: 'Is that really necessary?' But, as Moreno has noted, fighting for every point is part of Alcaraz's game. That adds to the entertainment Carlos provides every time he dashes and dances across the court.

*

Sometimes Carlos Alcaraz talks to himself during matches, asking himself what's more important: 'If I win or if I'm doing great things?'

As a spectator, you might ask a different question, which feels almost as urgent: what if, in the years to come, Alcaraz's matches end up being slightly less fun? They'll still be very entertaining, of course, as Alcaraz wouldn't know how to play boring tennis, but might they end up being a tiny bit less flashy and exciting than they were in the early years of his career? Some around Alcaraz think a change could be coming. That there's a chance he's going to adjust his game to a marginally more risk-averse style that might win him more Grand Slams, even if that means losing some of what makes him so original.

Some volatility is to be expected with Alcaraz. 'Carlitos thinks about tennis differently to how others do,' says close family friend Alfredo Sarria. 'He doesn't play tennis with the same structure that others do. He plays tennis the way he feels. Sometimes it's good and he's the best player in the world and sometimes he doesn't have the level and the results that people had expected of him. When you play like him, it's impossible to have stability in your results. When you play how you feel, sometimes it's going to be impossible to win.' Sarria adds: 'As the years continue, we think Carlitos is going to change how he plays and how he understands tennis, even though that is what makes him different.'

Has Alcaraz been having too much fun for his own good? Have there been moments when Alcaraz's desire to entertain – choosing the spectacular over the ordinary – has made his life more complicated or even cost him victories? Have there been times when he has perhaps been too willing to go for the shot that's going to get the great roar in the stadium and do big numbers on social media, rather than choosing the more mundane but more effective option? Rafa Nadal would never play shots that were 'unnecessary' if he could win the point by playing within himself, Andre Agassi has observed.

'While Carlos always wants to bring a show, that's very difficult to do,' Àlex Corretja says. 'Carlos's attitude on court is that he always wants to be enjoying himself on court. And that's never easy in a sport that is so precise and which can make you feel frustrated so many times. Sometimes Carlos needs to be practical. You don't always need to be putting on a show. Tennis isn't always a show. Tennis is a sport. It's Carlos's job. But he doesn't see it like that. He wants to see tennis as a game. Being creative is in his DNA. But his creativity sometimes crashes against players who are like machines.'

One machine-like player is Jannik Sinner. The Italian redhead has reflected how different he is to Alcaraz. The Spaniard 'brings the firepower and the hot shots', and involves the crowd, Sinner has said, before going on to describe himself as solid and calm. From his side, Alcaraz feels as though his rival plays every point at a very high level and very rarely misses. Sinner, for all his precision and poise, doesn't have the same flair and flamboyance as Alcaraz. 'It's like fire and ice,' Sinner has suggested.

In the 2025 Roland-Garros final, Alcaraz fought back from two sets down, including saving three championship points, to defeat Sinner, of which more later in the book. Even before that astounding match in Paris, Alcaraz had twice come from two sets to one down to beat Sinner at a Grand Slam and gone on to take the title. The first of those classic encounters was in the quarter-finals of the 2022 US Open, when Alcaraz came within a point of losing a match that lasted more than five hours and finished at 2.50am. Alcaraz hit the ball behind his back that night, just one of the entertaining points that he and Sinner played. The second occasion was in the 2024 Roland-Garros semi-finals. Sinner has also won some big matches against Alcaraz, such as their first Grand Slam meeting in the fourth round of the 2022 Wimbledon championships, and deep into ATP tournaments.

The Big Three were better tennis players because of each other; in the same way, Alcaraz and Sinner, who won a couple of Grand Slams each in 2024, have been challenging and provoking each other into improving. If one is winning titles, the other trains with a little more intensity, motivated by wanting to outdo their rival the next time they play. Alcaraz and Sinner have learned plenty from the matches they've played against each other, even including how you can take a different approach to tennis. Alcaraz has shown Sinner, who in Juan Carlos Ferrero's analysis has 'long arms and deep shots', how to win matches by using every part of the court and every shot. Sinner, meanwhile, has been illustrating what's possible when you play solid tennis. Alcaraz needs to recognize, Corretja says, that it's fine to just be solid sometimes. Solid wins matches. 'Someone like Sinner, he's a solid player and by being solid he wins. Carlitos needs to understand that solid can be good enough.' Later in the book, we will look again at Alcaraz's semi-final against Sinner at Roland-Garros in 2024, a match that showed the Spaniard the joy you can find in suffering. (The rivalry was put on pause when Sinner served a three-month doping ban in 2025 for testing positive for the anabolic agent clostebol the year before. Sinner's lawyers reached a settlement with the World Anti-Doping Agency that he had received no performance-enhancing benefit and that the substance had got into his body only through a team member's negligence. When Sinner was suspended, people kept asking Alcaraz whether he would make the most of that opportunity to move above the Italian in the rankings, and he found that unsettling: it was 'killing' him, he has said.)

Emilio Sánchez says Alcaraz's playful nature can cost him matches. 'Rafa was always on a mission. He treated a tennis match like a war.

He wanted to push his opponent into a corner and to make him feel as though he had no chance,' Sánchez says. 'Carlitos is playing with his opponent like you might play with a dog. He's moving them around, he's inviting them [to play shots] and he's giving them space. Sometimes when that happens in the key moments of matches, when Carlitos is playing with his opponent, he ends up losing. Carlitos plays shots that no one else plays. Roger Federer had an amazing game but he didn't play some of the shots that Carlos plays. Playing is Carlitos's biggest asset but sometimes when he plays too much it can be his biggest weakness.'

Alcaraz's problem sometimes? He has too much game, Sánchez says. For most of Nadal's career, according to Sánchez, the Majorcan was committed to his patterns of play: that's what made him 'super-consistent and super-persistent'. Sánchez wonders whether Alcaraz should consider being more disciplined. 'Carlitos has everything in his game but sometimes, because he's young, he makes the wrong choices. He has too much game. Sometimes in some big moments he has been overdoing it. When Carlitos becomes more pattern-orientated, doing what he does well in the key moments, he will become more effective and the others are going to struggle more because he has more game.'

Andy Roddick thinks Alcaraz would benefit from sometimes feeling bored on court, as a consequence of playing more consistently while Paul Annacone, Roger Federer's former coach, believes Alcaraz could become slightly more conservative in years to come: 'I have always felt the more options you have the more challenging it is to make the right decisions, particularly when you are younger. He loves to play, and you can see the joy he has when he executes all the various options.

As you mature and get more experienced, you learn. I think Carlos will always be electric and have an appetite for risk, but I do think we will see less as he evolves.'

The difficulty here is Alcaraz has said how playing within himself doesn't feel right.

The worst feeling for Alcaraz isn't losing a point after going for his shots. It's playing timid tennis – being careful and overly conversative, almost defensive – and losing a point. He wouldn't be playing his natural game and that would be upsetting. If that ever happens, if he feels as though he was holding back in any way, he will ask himself: 'Why didn't I take the risk?' If he gambles, plays a more attacking shot and it doesn't work out, at least he will know that he has given his all. There's a reason Juan Carlos Ferrero encourages Alcaraz to keep being aggressive on court; that's when he's at his best. In the biggest moments, when other players get tight and play careful and measured tennis, Ferrero wants Alcaraz to go for his shots. Alcaraz is urging himself to be bold: 'Go for it, go for it. You're going to make it.'

One of the most remarkable aspects of Ferrero's work with Alcaraz is how he has coached a player who has a very different game style to his. Antonio Cascales, who has advised both players, has observed that Ferrero's game was 'more solid' and 'more organized' while Alcaraz is 'more creative'. Yet Ferrero hasn't tried to turn Alcaraz into a new version of himself; he has based his guidance on Alcaraz's game and personality. As we will see in a later chapter, when Alcaraz won Roland-Garros in 2024, he did so without playing his usual kaleidoscopic tennis; and maybe, some around him thought, he was all the better for having realized you could be a Grand Slam champion without putting on a show. Ferrero had been telling Alcaraz that he didn't always have to play his most spectacular tennis.

Opponents don't know what Alcaraz is going to do next. Most of the time, he doesn't either. Playing on instinct and joy are, Alcaraz has said, fundamental to his game. Take those away and he thinks his tennis wouldn't be the same. Playing with patterns, within a framework, would risk Alcaraz losing what makes him different and what gives him an edge. The two are connected, it would seem: playing with any kind of constraint – tactical but probably also ideological – could have a negative impact on his happiness and how he feels about his game. Jim Courier, a winner of four Grand Slams, said the difference between Spain's most iconic tennis players was that while Nadal was a natural-born warrior, Alcaraz is a natural-born entertainer. Does Alcaraz want to resist playing his natural game?

But Alcaraz has also said how improvising isn't always the most effective approach for him. That doing whatever he feels like in the moment – whether that's getting to the net or playing a drop shot or another option that's aggressive or inventive or fun or even all three – isn't always for the best and sometimes doesn't work for him. There have been times when it has felt it would have been best to follow 'a strategy or a pattern', he told the *Louis Vuitton* podcast. However, Alcaraz went on to say: 'At least I did what I felt, and I had fun with it – that's the most important thing.'

Maybe there will always be a tension there, between wanting to have fun and wanting to win.

Alcaraz isn't against change. Since joining the tour, he has already adjusted how he operates. In the past, he would sometimes use too much energy between points, getting the crowd involved and screaming, *'Vamos!'* But Carlos was noticing that he didn't always have the same energy towards the end of matches, so he resolved to become calmer between points. To hold back where possible. That was especially important in Grand Slams, where matches are played over five sets and you need to conserve as much energy as you can.

There's no doubt that Alcaraz has been looser and freer on the court than any other multiple Grand Slam champion in tennis history. But what's better for the future of tennis? That Alcaraz continues playing this way and potentially wins fewer Grand Slams? Or that he restrains himself a little and is more successful at the majors?

'The joy that Carlos has comes from the way he plays. They go hand in hand,' says Mats Wilander. 'He's having fun because he's hitting drop shots and he's smacking the forehand and then he comes up with this crazy shot selection that no one is expecting. I'm watching and thinking, "What on earth . . .? What are you doing now? Why would you do that?" For us who are in the game, do we want him to be more controlled? For him to win more and be more controlled? It's unbelievable that Alcaraz has won majors while keeping playing like that. If he polishes his game and his shot selection, he will win more. But he will be less amazing and less of a draw. People might end up saying, "Oh, Alcaraz didn't hit any drop shots today." '

Wilander suggests fans are more interested in how Alcaraz plays than in how many majors he lands each year: 'As long as Alcaraz wins once in a while, maybe once every other year, they are going to come in herds to see him play.'

10

Carlos Alcaraz can be vulnerable: he's very comfortable speaking openly to his friends and telling them how he feels. 'Carlitos always talks to us without any problem, since he has a lot of confidence with all of us and he doesn't mind opening up,' says Antonio López. If Alcaraz has a disappointing defeat at a tournament, his old tennis friends – the ones in the WhatsApp group chat he's part of called 'Open Promesas', or 'Open Promises', named after the junior tennis circuit in Murcia that they all used to play on – will often get together to help him take his mind off his career for a few hours. 'When Carlitos comes home to Spain from some bad tournament, we usually make some plans so all of us friends can be together and we can be relaxed and help him forget what has happened.'

That's after the trips that haven't gone so well for him. But there was also the fortnight in New York City – the splashy, life-changing fortnight – when Alcaraz had his big breakthrough and it took him some time to process what he had done, and what it all meant. For a young player, success can sometimes be as challenging as setbacks and failures. That's especially true when you have achieved something unprecedented, when you've taken yourself – and the sport – somewhere new, which is both wonderfully exciting and potentially destabilizing. Aged 19, and on top of the world – as the 2022 US Open champion and the new world number one – Alcaraz was asking himself: 'Where do I go now?'

It was a reasonable question, given that he had already accomplished what he had been dreaming of and working towards since he was a small boy, or, as he put it, 'from the beginning of everything'.

Funny how Juan Carlos Ferrero had been suggesting to Alcaraz some months before that he shouldn't feel as though he needed to be in a hurry. It would be better, Alcaraz's coach was saying, to live in the moment and not to feel you had to get ahead of yourself and the process. But, as Rafa Nadal has reflected, things happen fast if you're not a normal guy. In Nadal's view, the Big Three aren't normal guys and Alcaraz isn't either. Everything about Alcaraz was fast in New York; his speed around the Arthur Ashe Stadium and the speed of his ascent. He was the first teenager to win a Grand Slam men's singles title since Nadal at Roland-Garros in 2005, as well as the first teenager to be the US Open men's singles champion since Pete Sampras in 1990.

Starting the 2022 season at number 32 in the rankings, Alcaraz had given himself what he had felt was an ambitious target for the year, which was to finish inside the top 15. But everything happened so quickly for Alcaraz that he surprised even himself. By September of that season, with a victory over Casper Ruud in a US Open final that was also a straight fight with the Norwegian for the top ranking, he had become the youngest world number one since the official computer rankings were established in the 1970s. No teenager had ever been that high before. The previous youngest number one was Lleyton Hewitt, an Australian who had been 20 years old when he first reached the top.

Tennis is a more physical game today than it ever has been. It's never been faster or more explosive or demanded so much of its athletes. You would think that would have made it harder, not easier, for teenagers, who might still be growing, to rise to the very top. But Alcaraz – the quickest player in tennis, who underwent a radical physical transformation after moving to the Ferrero Tennis Academy – did something that the likes of Björn Borg, Boris Becker and Pete Sampras couldn't.

It was 'strange', Garbiñe Muguruza says, that Alcaraz got to number one as a teenager. Strange as in unusually, shockingly good. 'I feel like in the women's game there's less of a physical difference between the teenagers and the older players,' says Muguruza. 'The men's game is so physical and many of the players are in their mid- to late twenties and they're strong and mature. You see the teenagers can be strong too, but I feel as though the physical part – being strong enough – plays a big role.' Only a select few can tell you what it feels like to be number one (and only Alcaraz knows what it's like to have been the youngest number one in history). If and when you get to number one, you feel as though that number is everything, according to Muguruza. 'No one remembers who the number two was but everyone cares about the number one. It's just so hard to get there. It's unique to say you were on top of the world and you had the number one spot. It's like, wow.'

Roger Federer was 22 years old when he reached the top. For some years, he blocked Nadal from getting to one in the rankings – the Spaniard was 21 when he made it. Novak Djokovic was older, 24, when he was first officially the best tennis player in the world. Some would suggest Alcaraz had been fortunate, as Djokovic hadn't played the 2022 Australian Open and US Open because he hadn't been vaccinated against Covid, and the Serb's Wimbledon victory that year was worthless when it came to the rankings (the men's tour had removed Wimbledon's ranking points in response to the All England Club barring players from Russia and Belarus after the invasion of Ukraine). But none of that should detract from Alcaraz's moment and diminish what he did. He had played some astonishing tennis in New York, and in the months before that, and deserved to rise so fast. No asterisk was required for Alcaraz, who beat Ruud in four sets, after saving two set points in the third set that could have seen the Scandinavian move ahead by two sets to one.

Here was a teenager with acne on his cheeks and stardust on almost every shot he played that fortnight: if Alcaraz's victory looked ridiculous from the outside, it felt almost unreal to the champion himself. The morning after beating Ruud, Alcaraz went online to look at the updated ATP Rankings, just to be sure that this was right, that he really was the number one.

Becoming the world number one is a strange feeling but also a satisfying one, Ferrero thinks. Nineteen years earlier, when Alcaraz was a four-month-old baby, Ferrero had also put together a strong run in New York to become the world number one for the first time. Being at the top is a huge moment for any player, but some moments are bigger than others and Ferrero's elevation didn't quite have the same order of magnitude; he had got there by winning his semi-final against Andre Agassi but had then lost the final to Andy Roddick in straight sets. Ferrero had left New York as the runner-up rather than as a champion, which tends to kill the mood somewhat. He was also older, at 23, and a more understated personality both on and off the court than baby Carlos would turn out to be.

A first Grand Slam title naturally brought Alcaraz enormous joy; falling on to the court after winning the championship point, he had barely even hit the ground before he was crying happy tears. That evening, he partied in a Peruvian restaurant in Manhattan's Upper East Side and the next morning he was at Times Square with his trophy. For a few days after that, he still felt giddy – as he should have done. It's a beautiful story, Alcaraz has reflected since, about a small boy pursuing his dream and becoming the number one.

But this was a dream that came with some complications, the kind of complications that Alcaraz couldn't possibly have envisioned as a child. Becoming the US Open champion was the start of a challenging, even unsettling time for him; he has spoken of going through 'a bad period'. Alcaraz didn't feel the usual joy and energy when he was on court; it was difficult for him to deal with feeling so flat and 'shut down' so soon after the most fabulous moment of his young life.

You could tell something was up with Alcaraz; the happiest man in tennis wasn't smiling as much as he used to, or as much as you'd perhaps expect him to in that moment. It was trying for Ferrero to see Alcaraz like that. A bad time after winning a Grand Slam? That sounds, as Alcaraz said in an interview with *Vogue* magazine, like something he'd made up. But he had enjoyed himself a lot after winning the title in Flushing Meadows and then when he returned to competition – by which point he probably still hadn't processed what had happened – he felt consumed by the stress.

Some wondered whether Alcaraz was possibly distracted during that time. Some new people had appeared in Alcaraz's life, Antonio Cascales has noted. Did those newcomers not understand the demands of being a tennis player and that Alcaraz, even after winning a first major, needed to give the sport his full focus? Carlos finds it hard to say no to people, according to his older brother Álvaro. That could have been a concern during that period. As Ferrero said a few months after Alcaraz's US Open victory, the athlete was capable of becoming one of the best tennis players in history, but 'many things can happen'. 'He's young. There are a lot of things he doesn't see,' Ferrero told *Vogue* magazine. 'We all know what the risks are: partying, getting distracted, not concentrating on tennis. When you've got the opportunity to meet the rich and famous it's easy to get disoriented.'

Soon after Alcaraz won the US Open, Cascales says, the new champion returned to work: 'Of course, the interviews and the celebrations can take some time; but the week after, he was back on court, practising as normal.' Going back to the academy, and seeing all the people who had helped him become a champion, was a proud moment for Alcaraz. But being back on court was one thing. Alcaraz needed to be fully focused when he was there. Cascales has also said that, for a while after becoming the US Open champion, Alcaraz lacked some of his usual calm in training. But Alcaraz couldn't stay distracted for long. Ferrero, who was as strict as ever, wouldn't have stood for that.

A while after his run in New York City, when Alcaraz was reflecting on how he had felt in the aftermath of becoming a teenage Grand Slam champion, he realized his ambition had unconsciously 'dimmed a bit'. The error you can make as a young player is imagining that winning a first Grand Slam will resolve everything in your head and in your life. That you'll be happy forever and it will all make sense. Unfortunately, that's not how it works. It was only after landing that first major that Alcaraz understood just how difficult it can be to stay motivated, and to keep working to become a better player. Once he was a Grand Slam champion himself, Alcaraz had an even greater appreciation for what the Big Three had done, staying energized for years when it would have been all too easy to coast. Staying that hungry was almost impossible, Alcaraz thought.

In the Spanish countryside, Ferrero is doing what he can to stop players at his academy wasting time on their phones (which is why they must keep them locked away when on court or in the gym). He doesn't like how today's youth 'don't have moments of emptiness, of reflection, of rest'. 'They're constantly looking at the screen, and it's hard to balance that with elite sports,' Ferrero told *El Mundo*. 'I hope it doesn't get worse, because if it does, we'll all end up looking like zombies.'

But was the academy's most celebrated player wasting time on his phone in that period after his US Open victory? Alcaraz uses social media a lot anyway. Probably more than he should, he concedes, though he feels it's a powerful and important way of communicating with his fans and keeping them informed about where he is and what he has been doing. Alcaraz sees many of the comments about him and occasionally replies to fans. Most of the comments are positive and supportive. But if he is going through a rough patch, if he's not winning tournaments, he's aware that people who don't know what he is feeling, and who have no idea of the impact their words are going to have, start offering their opinions online. If Alcaraz sees those 'bad' comments at the wrong time, he can find them hurtful and upsetting – he knows of some athletes who have been so disturbed by what others are saying about them that they have deleted their social-media accounts and called their psychologists. What's needed here, Alcaraz told Molusco TV, is for everyone to have more empathy.

Maybe it's unrealistic to think that Alcaraz, the first star of the 'TikTok tennis' age, is ever going to stay off his phone. But phones and social media make life trickier to navigate for young athletes. 'It's way harder being a tennis player now than it was when I was on the tour,' says Àlex Corretja. 'If we had had social media when I was playing, we might have been bigger stars than we were as you can reach more people around the world. But at the same time, it would have been way more demanding. With social media, you're everywhere. You feel you have to give fans something that they haven't seen before. That means some personal stuff, some practice stuff and physical training. If you have millions of followers, people expect content from you because otherwise they're going to be saying that your feed is boring and you don't want to feel as though you're boring,' Corretja says.

'I don't think it should be part of athletes' jobs to share their lives with everyone. It has to be something fun and you should be sharing it because you want to. You shouldn't feel as though it's mandatory. I don't like that athletes feel as though they have to share their professional and personal lives. I don't agree with that.'

Corretja retired in 2005. When he was competing, players would read more, listen to music and watch films in their hotel rooms. 'It was way easier for my generation to be on our own. You played, you did the interviews and then you went to your hotel room. It was much easier to be focused. Now there are so many distractions which make your life more complicated,' he says.

Alcaraz's return to the ATP Tour wasn't so smooth. He travelled to Kazakhstan to play his first ranking tournament since becoming the world number one and US Open champion only to lose his opening match to David Goffin, a Belgian lucky loser (meaning he had lost in the qualifying rounds but found his way into the draw when another player withdrew). It was the first time all season that Alcaraz had lost a match in straight sets. In a quiet end to the year, Alcaraz wouldn't win another title, or reach another final, in 2022. He also didn't play at the season-end ATP Finals in Turin because of an abdominal muscle tear; though he did make a brief appearance on court for a ceremony in which he received the trophy for being the year-end number one, after being the youngest in history to achieve that. Alcaraz would also miss the next Grand Slam, the 2023 Australian Open, after injuring his leg while training, though that longer absence from tennis gave him more time to think and process.

'Basically, it can suck being the new kid on the block,' says Mats Wilander, who, as one of the very small number of men who have won a Grand Slam as a teenager, has some insights into how Alcaraz might have been feeling after the US Open.

Wilander was 17 years old when he took his first Roland-Garros title, in 1982, and speaks from experience when he says it's not always so fabulous being a fresh face in tennis, even if it looks that way from the outside. 'When you're winning, you shut yourself off from the world. Your world becomes very small. And because it's small you kind of lose touch with reality. At some point, maybe after a few years of playing well, you're going to come back to earth. Then when you're not young anymore and you're not playing so well, you realize that you've lost touch with reality,' Wilander says. 'You might have had a few years when you were kind of excluded from everything because you're the guy. That part isn't that easy to deal with and there should be advice for young players. You think, "Shit, what happened? I don't have as many friends as other people do. I don't know if I can trust everybody." That's the part you have to be careful of.'

Being a teenage Grand Slam champion isn't always healthy, says Wilander; in his experience, early success can be a problem for a young player: 'It's a dangerous thing when it happens too soon too fast.'

That's what can go wrong. Fortunately for Alcaraz, it sounds as though he has avoided isolation by ensuring he continues to spend time with his old friends in Murcia. Losing touch with reality is not an accusation you can level at Alcaraz, the most down-to-earth of champions. Listening to Wilander, you get a sense of how well Alcaraz seems to be handling his new status inside and outside tennis. 'For Carlos, I hope that winning came at the right time for him. So far it looks as though he's handling it unbelievably well,' Wilander says. 'The expectation on Carlos has come so quickly. Becoming the world number one at 19 is uncharted territory. I hope it works out for him. I think it will because he seems so grounded and the people around him seem so grounded. And they're having a good time too. There's no anger in the box.'

*

How did Carlos Alcaraz – at a time of great change and upheaval – manage to reset and rediscover his love for tennis? 'When you win your first Grand Slam, that's very hard to manage and you need support from the people around you,' says Antonio López. 'Carlitos was getting that support from his family and his team.'

That team stayed the same, which doesn't always happen in these moments. In the swirl after a first major, when so much else is changing, some continuity is important. But that's often where new champions go wrong, ditching their coach soon after the Grand Slam breakthrough. They think – usually wrongly – that they no longer require them (and perhaps didn't even need them in the first place). Alcaraz didn't do anything as self-destructive as that; several major titles later, he appears to admire Juan Carlos Ferrero as much as he has always done. 'There have been so many cases in tennis when players have had some success and have then changed everything. They have lost their drive and their respect for their coach,' says Emilio Sánchez.

'It's lucky Carlos hasn't done that and he keeps enjoying working with Juan Carlos. You can see the admiration that Carlos has for Juan Carlos – that's clear every time Juan Carlos is talking on the court. As a player, what your coach says is so important, as many times when you're on court you don't see what's happening. The way that Carlos follows and understands what Juan Carlos is saying, that's a magical thing for as long as it lasts. If the moment comes that Carlos loses that admiration for Juan Carlos – if it feels flat and he doesn't want to keep listening to the same voice – he won't be able to learn anymore and his results will stop growing.'

As Sánchez says, the player–coach relationship can be a challenging dynamic: the player hires the coach and the coach then tells the player things they might not want to hear. But Alcaraz has shown that he still wants to listen to what Ferrero has to say, that he still believes that he can improve by following his advice. 'Having a desire to learn is absolutely the number-one thing,' says Sánchez. 'You need to always keep wanting to be the best. And learn to be the best. You're going to be working for hours every day with your coach and if you don't have that respect and that willingness to listen to and accept what your coach says, it's going to be a problem. It doesn't matter how much you have been winning; the moment you think you don't have to keep learning, another player will come along and you will be pushed aside. You will become afraid and you won't win anymore; you'll become a loser.'

Contrast Alcaraz's story with that of Emma Raducanu, who won the 2021 US Open women's singles title as a teenage qualifier and soon afterwards chose not to extend her arrangement with Andrew Richardson, who had been her coach in New York. The Brit has had a number of coaches since then. 'I'm really happy that Carlos has a solid team that is helping him and protecting him so much,' says Garbiñe Muguruza. 'We've seen the example of Raducanu, who was very successful but has had a weird environment, changing a lot, people not clicking. With Carlos, there's been a solid team since he started. They're all going in the same direction, with no changes or barely any. If there are changes, they are adding people to make the team even better. You have two up-and-coming and talented players in Carlos and Raducanu and they handled winning a first Grand Slam very differently.'

As Ferrero was telling Alcaraz after he became the US Open champion, there was work to be done. In that moment, some would have been telling Alcaraz he was already doing everything well. Ferrero felt as though he was there to introduce some reality, to keep Alcaraz grounded by telling him that he still had plenty of weaknesses. How the teenager had to improve almost everything, including his consistency and approach to tricky moments in matches, which required greater maturity. This was no time for complacency or self-satisfaction. Yes, Alcaraz was a Grand Slam champion and the world number one at 19, but that didn't mean that he was a complete player. Far from it. When Alcaraz became a Grand Slam champion, Ferrero thought the teenager was operating at only about 60 per cent of his potential. And when Alcaraz reached number one, Ferrero was telling him that the focus could no longer be on moving above anyone else in the rankings but he would have to keep pushing himself nonetheless.

Something else stayed the same: Alcaraz kept on speaking to Isabel Balaguer, the psychologist he had been working with since 2019.

Winning the US Open as a teenager doesn't necessarily mean you'll go on to win a bunch more majors very quickly. But despite the challenges after winning that tournament, and then a quiet period, Alcaraz hardly went through a slump; less than a year later, he would be holding a Grand Slam trophy again – this time, on a less familiar surface: grass. Not only that, but his opponent in the Wimbledon final would be the greatest of all time: Novak Djokovic. While it took Alcaraz a while to adjust to winning a Grand Slam title and becoming the number one, it's not as if his tennis fell away. And there would be even more Grand Slam success in 2024; he would have four major titles just after turning 21. 'It's not like Carlos won the US Open and then he disappeared for a while,' says Muguruza. 'I can see he has kept performing at a high level since winning the US Open.'

Nineteen was 'too young' to become a Grand Slam champion and the world number one, Àlex Corretja suggests. 'It was a big thing and Carlitos was still a teenager. He was too young and it wasn't easy for him to deal with that. But I think he dealt well with everything. He won another Grand Slam in 2023 and then had a tremendous season in 2024, winning two more and reaching the final of the Olympics.' Ferrero's former coach José Perlas has a similar view: 'Historically, it's not easy after winning a first Grand Slam. There's too much expectation. It's difficult to repeat and win another one. But Carlos has been winning Grand Slams faster than other people. It's not really a problem. We're really happy with him. He's easy with these things. He's very natural and he's managing.'

People talk too much about how hard it can be after winning a first major, says Toni Nadal. 'Both Rafael and Carlos won their first Grand Slam titles when they were 19 years old and they both did so at their first tries, in their first major finals. A difficult moment after winning a first Grand Slam? I don't think so. People talk a lot. It was a very simple moment. And, in fact, it's a little easier for you as a tennis player after winning a Grand Slam; then at least you already have one, and that gives you more confidence to go out and get the next one,' Toni says. 'If you're Rafael or Carlos, you win that first Grand Slam at 19 and then when you're 20 years old, you're going to think you can win again. Same when you're 21 and so on. No, it's not so tough after winning a first Grand Slam title as a teenager.'

Once in a while, the palace informs Carlos Alcaraz's agent, Albert Molina, that King Felipe would like to speak on the phone with Alcaraz and the athlete finds a quiet room to take the call. Every day – because they're relentless and because there's nothing like the same protocol for these interactions as for a conversation with the Spanish monarch – Alcaraz's admirers contact him through private, direct and unsolicited messages on Instagram.

'You can't imagine just how many messages Carlitos gets from girls – it's a lot,' Alcaraz's old friend Antonio López says. 'Sometimes the girls say good things in their messages and sometimes not.' When Alcaraz is out with his friends, he gets plenty of female attention. 'For every boy, it's good if a girl wants to talk to you,' López says. 'Carlitos needs to stay focused on tennis but in his relaxed moments he tries to meet girls. He has been saying he has been looking for a girlfriend and probably he is meeting girls.'

Alcaraz can be proactive, with Rafa Nadal noticing the Murcian often 'likes' pictures that women from Majorca have posted of themselves on social media. One of the challenges for Alcaraz – whose first crush was on a Spanish influencer – is knowing whether he can trust the new people in his life, both female and male, and whether they potentially want to be friends only so they can use his fame for their own ends. 'Some of the people around Carlitos, they aren't the best,' says Alfredo Sarria. 'Things around you start to change when you become a star. You can have a problem if you don't know whether the people around you are actually your friends, and genuinely want to help you, or they are only there because of your new status. It's difficult for Carlitos and his family and his manager to know whether someone is trying to get close to him to use that to their advantage, maybe to earn some money or become more popular. Sometimes it's difficult for Carlitos to see this. He has tried to start making decisions in his life. But, for the most part, the decisions have been taken by his family.'

Alcaraz turns to his brother Álvaro for guidance on who he should trust (and who to keep his distance from). 'Knowing who to trust and who he can't trust is one of the biggest problems for Carlitos since he became famous,' says López. 'There are lots of people who want to meet Carlitos and to spend time with him and it's not always easy to recognize who is only doing that because they want something from Carlitos and who genuinely cares about him. In those moments, you need help from your family and your team to talk about these things. Álvaro helps with this.'

A possible challenge is that Carlos, with his friendly and open nature, finds it difficult to say no to people. What makes Alcaraz's agent nervous is the possibility that someone might take a photo or record a video of Alcaraz that could look bad out of context. Molina's not concerned about Alcaraz's close friends photographing or recording him with their phones. His worry is about others who might be around the athlete in social settings, such as when Alcaraz went to Ibiza for a few days between Roland-Garros and Wimbledon in 2023 and 2024 to forget about tennis for a bit. Alcaraz threw his racquets in his room and didn't want to see them again for a few days. One video that emerged from his 2024 trip was Alcaraz and his friends singing Queen's 'We Are the Champions' in what appeared to be a late-night karaoke session in a bar or club. Molina would like Alcaraz to be aware that while most people he meets are decent and trustworthy, there will always be a few who aren't.

But Molina doesn't want to turn Alcaraz, who is so engaging and personable, into a fearful and paranoid young man. Filling his head with fear would do more harm than good, Molina told *El Partidazo de COPE*. Ultimately, Molina believes, Alcaraz is going to have to learn to tell the difference between true friends and people who'll try to take advantage of him.

Whether in hotels or anywhere else, Molina does what he can to shield Alcaraz from opportunists. Callers can't assume they will get through. That's unless they're the King of Spain. When the palace contacts Molina and says the king would like to speak to Alcaraz, Molina of course passes the message on. One such occasion was after Alcaraz won the Miami title in 2022, when the teenager was possibly more nervous talking to the monarch than he had been playing the final.

Some public figures – such as Spanish footballers and Florentino Pérez, the president of Real Madrid football club – have Alcaraz's number. Others must try going through Molina, and they're rarely successful. Sometimes when people contact Alcaraz directly on Instagram, he isn't sure how to respond – or whether to respond at all – and he will ask Molina for advice on how to handle the situation. Some things, though, are best left unsaid between player and agent – Molina is aware he doesn't know about every female friend that Alcaraz might be messaging and calling (Alcaraz once said it was difficult as a tennis player to find a girlfriend, because you have to travel so much). Those communications aren't managed by Molina.

When you become a celebrity, other famous people might try to befriend you, perhaps over social media. 'Carlitos isn't the kind of person who has changed a lot. But everyone who becomes famous changes something because there are often other famous people who want to be your friend,' Sarria says. 'With phones and social media, it's easier than in the past for other famous people to contact you. Carlitos has started to play golf and he has had the opportunity to play golf with other people who are famous too. As a star yourself, you start to have famous friends. But for Carlitos it's important to spend time – to go out for lunch or dinner – with the people he has been friends with his whole life.'

*

Carlos Alcaraz can draw a crowd even when he tries to keep it casual and low-key in his personal life. When he went to watch one of his brothers playing padel in Murcia, so many fans gathered around him that he spent half an hour posing for pictures and signing autographs.

Antonio López has never seen Alcaraz decline a request for a photo or an autograph.

In López's words, Alcaraz wants to do 'normal things', such as going to the cinema or a restaurant. But Alcaraz must be sensible about how he goes about being normal, according to López: 'Carlitos tries not to stay somewhere if many people can see him.' Alcaraz knows that if he's out in the centre of Murcia he will attract a lot of attention, so he doesn't tend to do that. If he's going to a restaurant, he will try to park as close to it as possible so that he doesn't have to walk too far on the street. There would be little point in Alcaraz trying to hide his face with a cap, López says, as he would be quickly spotted (though when the friends were together in Rome in 2025, Carlos did wear a cap and sunglasses when they were out in the city). There are days when Alcaraz wishes he could just walk around like a normal person, without anyone spotting him, but he accepts that's impossible now (there are also days when he enjoys people recognizing him when he's going about his day).

There was the time – witnessed by one of his former teachers, Laura Caballero – when Alcaraz was driving through El Palmar and noticed that some boys on the street had recognized him and were asking him to pose for photos. Alcaraz found somewhere to park and stayed there until everyone had the picture they wanted.

Unless he is eating or training – because these activities must be protected from interruptions – Carlos will instantly say yes to any requests for autographs or photos. If he is having lunch or on the practice court, he'll be sure to give people some time afterwards. Often when Alcaraz finishes a practice session at a tournament, he'll pick up a marker pen and sign some balls that he'll hand to watching children or throw into the crowd. Alcaraz doesn't regard himself as being in any way superior to his fans; he sees himself as being on the same level, which he thinks helps him to connect with them as human beings.

At the country club, the place where he learned to play tennis, Alcaraz can mostly go about his business without too much fuss; as much as he enjoys his interactions with his fans, it would be tiring if he was forever signing his name and posing for pictures. He practises in the mornings, when most of the members are working or at school, and there might just be a handful of juniors around who have travelled to train in El Palmar. If he's between exercises in the gym, and he knows the person who has approached him, he might chat with them, but he tries to be professional when training and then accessible once he has finished.

As Carlos knows, if he went anywhere else to train, there would be a crush of fans. In El Palmar, the locals are interested in what Alcaraz is doing but he doesn't feel crowded. 'When Carlitos is training at the country club, people are relaxed around him as they are used to seeing him,' says Carlos Santos. Alcaraz also uses the country club for shoots for his sponsors, which is why you might very occasionally see him walking around in high-fashion outfits that have been selected for him by stylists. A long black coat, for instance. He once did a shoot in his tennis clothes on one of the clay courts in the evening sunshine and there was a large group of children at the country club at the same time, but they didn't care about Alcaraz's shoot – they continued roller-skating around the football pitch.

Being as famous as Alcaraz can be exhausting. 'One of the good things for Carlos is that he's a very natural kid. A very simple kid. But, at the same time, it's very difficult to be simple when you're such a big star around the world,' says Àlex Corretja. 'I feel as though Carlos is still enjoying being famous but that he is starting to understand how demanding that can be, in all aspects. Not just in the tennis world but in the regular world. Carlos has got a great family and a great team around him, and he has been handling it well, but he is realizing how tough it is to be a big star at such a young age. Carlos can't walk around any part of the world without being noticed and that's very tiring. I don't think too many people in the world will understand just how demanding it is to be that famous. Only the other huge stars of this world will know. I'm thinking here about rockstars and big football players.'

If you're as recognizable as Alcaraz, there's always a risk you will be pestered by other guests when you're doing ordinary things like browsing the breakfast buffet in your hotel. That can drain you of energy. That's why Albert Molina tends to book Alcaraz into smaller and more secure and private hotels during tournaments, rather than one of those mega-hotels with hundreds of rooms, a large lobby and lots of guests who might approach Carlos when he is ordering his omelette.

One of Molina's strengths is forecasting when Alcaraz might encounter some challenging moments. 'Albert has an ability to see the problems in the future,' says Alfredo Sarria. 'Carlitos and the family have a good relationship with Albert. Albert is dealing with partners who want to do different activities – the rules around those activities are very strict – and he's also handling the media. It's not easy. We feel as though he has the best experience to be doing this role and has known Carlitos since he was 12 years old.'

Fame like Alcaraz's – when you're a global figure – means you get to star in your own three-part Netflix documentary series. It also means you can walk on court at the 2025 Indian Wells tournament with a temporary tattoo on your arm showing the date of *My Way*'s upcoming release, knowing that people will take notice. Alcaraz clearly hadn't been put off by what some in tennis called the 'Netflix Curse', after all the players who were in the *Break Point* documentary series that aired just before the 2023 Australian Open either missed that tournament through injury or lost early.

While Alcaraz felt as though the public had got to know him on the court, he wanted to show what he was like off the court, including where he is from and 'who my people are'. That would give fans a better understanding of the 'crazy' life he was living. For much of the 2024 season, starting at the Netflix Slam exhibition in Las Vegas in early March, Alcaraz was followed and filmed by a Netflix crew of six people (sometimes just two or three, if the moment demanded a smaller crew). Many players would have found that potentially awkward and uncomfortable, and maybe even distracting – how can you act naturally when a camera is always there? But it didn't seem to have disturbed Alcaraz during a year in which he won four titles, including a couple of Grand Slams.

'I don't think Rafa Nadal would have done a Netflix documentary when he was at his peak,' says Emilio Sánchez. 'He wouldn't have done that because of his personality and because that would have put him off his preparation for tournaments. That Carlos was able to do that documentary with Netflix and still keep on winning, that's amazing to me.'

Alcaraz had more editorial and creative control over his Netflix documentary than he ever could over what the media and others write about him online and in print. Almost inevitably, there have been some minor controversies along the way, such as when Alcaraz attended a bullfight in Murcia a few days after the 2023 US Open. That drew condemnation from animal-rights group PETA, who sent him an open message on social media: 'Bullfighting is torture, not culture. There's nothing entertaining about stabbing and torturing animals – and the majority of young people in Spain reject bullfighting as the bloodsport it is. Please reject this cruelty today. Tennis is sport; animal abuse is not.' Others in Spain attacked Alcaraz for going, too, with one insider in Spanish tennis noting: 'Some people took the opportunity to criticize and insult Carlos.'

Some of the comments after Alcaraz broke a racquet in Cincinnati in 2024 were a touch sensationalist. It seems to Garbiñe Muguruza, who has been through this herself as a Grand Slam champion and a world number one, that you must understand that some in the media are waiting to burn you – and that you should try to view that as a good thing.

'In Spain, the media will love you at the beginning. But you pay a price for all the attention and positivity. You create a certain standard and the expectation that you have to deliver every time. In my experience, the media can help you but they can be your enemy sometimes. But that's how it works with the media,' Muguruza says. 'I always thought that the more the media challenges you, it's because they see more potential in you. They expect more from you. That only comes from being great at something. If they don't expect much from you, they'll say, "She lost but it's OK." You have to love it when they write negatively about you, because of the expectations they have for you. You have to think, "Ah, they see me winning and they see that I should be up there." You're then telling yourself, "Come on." '

Alcaraz could go through the same experience. 'That hasn't happened yet with Carlos. The media is still building, building, building. There might be a year when he's injured. I'm sure that will happen. That's normal. Or there might be a little drop in energy. Or a tough swing of tournaments. The media will be there, waiting for that,' Muguruza says. 'The media have been tough on Rafa, in all those years when he was injured or when his tennis wasn't as aggressive. They burned him many times. Then the story can be that he came back from the dead. Well, he was never dead in the first place. But you know how it is. We need to be smart and the media helps us so much. You just have to learn how to navigate it.'

There will always be noise: when Alcaraz isn't winning titles, people are going to talk. But he has realized that rather than engaging with that debate, he must keep focus on what he and those around him are saying about his game and how he moves forward.

The expectations from the Spanish media and fans can weigh on players. 'Spain has a real passion for tennis, and the expectations are high, especially after all the success we've seen from players like Rafa,' Paula Badosa says. 'The fans are incredibly enthusiastic and supportive, but it can get a bit overwhelming at times – those expectations can weigh heavily. The media is always on top of every match, which adds a lot of pressure to consistently deliver great performances. I'd say the fans are proud and fiercely loyal, but patience isn't always easy, especially since Spain has been used to such high standards for so long.'

Alcaraz feels more comfortable than most speaking freely, in private and in public. Other players seem to choose their words with greater caution when doing interviews. Alcaraz, meanwhile, doesn't seem to have much of a filter. 'Carlos is going to tell you if he likes something or not. He hasn't become a robot yet. The media can be tough sometimes and you can find yourself thinking about every word you say. Everything is thought out,' says Muguruza. 'But Carlos has managed to continue being refreshing and natural.'

Some suggest Alcaraz's openness is one of the reasons for his popularity. One person who has known him for years says Carlos tells you what's going on in his head without stopping to think about the consequences. He's smiling and he's joking and making people feel as though he's like them or their son or grandson; people feel a connection to him. There's a group of women from Murcia who like to travel to watch Alcaraz when he is playing tournaments in Spain because they almost look at him as if he's their own son.

Now more than ever, tennis players can control what the public thinks of them. 'If you have a bad match, you just write on social media, "What a tough day, this was a terrible match". Right away you're moving on. People move on too. They don't stay stuck in something,' says Muguruza. 'If people are giving their opinion on something, you're able to clarify many things. You can show your personality, such as the music you like and the clothes you like to wear. You can also show your training, and the dynamic in your team. That's great. That's where social media helps Carlos. The new generation of players are active on there and he does that very well. Now players have much more control of how others perceive them. Before social media, if you really wanted to say something, you had to go somewhere and say it; and now players can just go on social media.'

While Alcaraz became a global figure after winning his first Grand Slam, he had already been adapting to his fame for a while before that. 'It looks as though it happens from one day to another but it's not like that,' says Muguruza. 'You start playing on small courts and then you go to stadium courts and then centre courts. Everything is fast but with a process.'

Fame can be a fun ride, Muguruza says: 'You're thinking, "OK, I'm more recognizable now." Then you're thinking, "OK, when I go to the courts, people clap for me." You are playing on bigger and bigger courts and you're thinking, "Nice!" You kind of get used to it. You get used to the fans. These are nice things. You don't suffer from it. You suffer if you have a bad year and you're thinking, "Man, I'm not finding the solutions. This sucks." Other than that, everything is really positive. You're getting sponsors, you're getting the attention, you're getting the love.'

*

Returning from Rotterdam to Spain one February morning, having spent the weekend in the Dutch city watching his friend Carlos Alcaraz winning the indoor title, Antonio López flew economy class. He was sitting in the ninth row. He was closer to the front of the plane than Alcaraz, who was three rows further back. López has known Alcaraz for more than a decade and he doesn't think that success and fame have corrupted his friend one bit. 'Carlitos is still the same guy that I met all those years ago. He's humble,' says López. 'He's a normal guy from a normal family, who have helped him to stay humble. It doesn't matter about the money or luxury cars or buying many things. On the way home from Rotterdam, he was happy travelling economy class on that plane, just like a normal person.'

Note that when Alcaraz's foundation put on an exhibition in Murcia in late 2024 and early 2025 – which included photographs and objects from his career, such as a net from Wimbledon – it was called 'Los Pies en La Tierra'. Feet on the ground. 'Fame hasn't changed Carlitos,' says López. 'Carlitos is really funny. He's always making jokes with people. He's always laughing. He always has a smile on his face. When we're together as a group, we laugh and we talk about a lot of things, like football or politics, all the things. I can't see any change in Carlitos. He's just the same.' All that has changed is that Alcaraz can now afford to pick up the bill for the group's lunches and dinners. 'The times I've had a meal with Carlitos, I've never paid,' López says. 'He's generous too.'

Alcaraz was still a child, and an unknown in the wider tennis world, when his then coach, Kiko Navarro, started advising him on how to behave in the future as a star player. When Alcaraz travelled to junior tournaments, small crowds would sometimes gather, even at practice sessions, which doesn't happen too much in junior tennis. Was this a small preview of what Alcaraz's life might look like in the future? Navarro thought it was and he wanted Alcaraz to be ready. Often, when there was dead time on a flight, a train journey or a car ride, Navarro would initiate a conversation with Alcaraz about the importance of avoiding ever becoming arrogant or entitled. 'I had those conversations with Carlitos because I felt as though he was going to be a great player – and I wasn't wrong. When Carlitos was playing as a child, he was the centre of attention and people were already beginning to know him. They really liked his way of playing,' Navarro says. 'That's why when we were travelling, I liked to take the opportunity to have those conversations with him.'

When Navarro was coaching Alcaraz, he found him to be a very simple person who was happiest when he was at home with his family and friends. Alcaraz hasn't changed. 'One of the things I'm most proud of with Carlitos is how he is. I love that even though he is a world star, he still keeps his feet on the ground. It's not easy to deal with everything that has happened in such a short time. I always told Carlitos that he should always stay the same person and I'm very proud that that is the case,' Navarro says. 'Obviously his life has changed but he is a simple and humble boy and he loves being in Murcia and seeing his childhood friends. He believes that's good for him.'

It's always a pleasure for Kiko when he bumps into Alcaraz at the country club; they will give each other a big hug and they'll talk. 'We had many years together, many trips, many hours on the court, many moments together and we'll never forget that,' Navarro says.

Rafa Nadal credits Alcaraz's family for Carlos being 'a great kid, a great guy'. 'That's why Carlos is the way he is – the values you receive at home, and the way you are educated, is the way you show up,' he told Andy Roddick.

Between tournaments, Alcaraz wants to be with his family – particularly his mother and younger brothers, as they don't often travel with him. It doesn't matter how rich or famous you become, Alcaraz thinks, you mustn't forget your roots (and you're not going to do that if you're still sleeping in your childhood bedroom).

Continuing to live in El Palmar, surrounded by his family, has enabled Alcaraz to handle fame. It helps Carlos that his family are still the same, according to Alfredo Sarria: 'Their lives are similar to how it was before Carlitos became a star – they are busier now than before but they have the same friends and they're trying to do the best for Carlitos. His mother and father are wonderful people. They are a wonderful family.' While Alcaraz's parents now have more demands on their time, as they have relationships with their son's commercial partners as well as with politicians and dignitaries, they ensure that they still spend time with their old friends and the families they have known forever.

Alcaraz's old English teacher Laura Caballero agrees that the athlete's family have allowed the tennis player to stay grounded: 'His mother worked in IKEA. His roots are very humble. He's also one of four brothers. I think his family have helped Carlitos to stay the same – he still has the same feeling inside.'

Star power and humility can be a rare combination in elite tennis players, or in any athletes.

When Emilio Sánchez attended the 2024 Miami tournament – having been invited by Alcaraz and his team – he saw the young champion was still the same guy he had been before winning any Grand Slam titles. 'Carlitos is super humble and has a good way about him. I took my son with me and Carlitos came over to say hello. All that success isn't easy to manage. I've seen so many players who have had success and have then found themselves in difficulties. This can depend on the culture of where they are from, as well as their personalities, but players often change when they have success. Carlitos hasn't changed at all,' says Sánchez. 'Carlitos is from a very humble family. They're super nice to everybody.'

When Alcaraz sees another player being 'so rude', he has said, he asks himself: 'What happened with this guy?' Nothing matters more to Alcaraz than being a kind, good person, he told the *Louis Vuitton* podcast. Alcaraz was influenced by the Big Three; he saw them behaving well while still doing great things on the court and he aspired to be the same: 'I really want to be like those guys.' What the Big Three showed Alcaraz's generation, Nadal has said, is that you don't have to 'hate' your opponent to produce your best tennis. That you can combine a competitive spirit with a genial off-court approach (though it's unlikely that the biggest rivals are ever going to be best friends). 'I know that Carlos is a very nice guy,' says Toni Nadal. 'All of Carlos's family, including his father, are very correct. But maybe Carlos has seen how Rafael has had the respect of many people in Spain because of his values and his humility. Rafael showed him how to do that.'

One rare example of Alcaraz being inconsiderate, for which he was admonished by his agent Albert Molina, was when he was late for an event because a lunch with friends had overrun. As Molina told Alcaraz, that showed a lack of respect for others and he couldn't tolerate that.

Some other players like being around Alcaraz because of his positive energy, which is what they might need when they're away from home for several weeks. In the locker room, Alcaraz is known for his decency; this explains his popularity among other players and why there appears to be little to no jealousy towards him for being so successful, wealthy and famous at such a young age. When Alcaraz's career is over, he wants others to think of him as being a good person – as someone who was normal, natural and happy around other players, the fans and the ball kids. That's more important to him than being a good athlete. He messaged Jack Draper when the Brit was missing tournaments because of injury. And when Draper retired from their fourth-round match at the 2025 Australian Open, the Spaniard wrote on a television camera lens: 'You will be where you deserve. Get well soon, Jack.' A small act, but a generous one nonetheless, and it wouldn't have gone unnoticed by other players.

Alcaraz is known for his good manners. Again, small things, but telling all the same: he thanks the person who cleans his practice court or who hands him a bottle of water. People close to Alcaraz say he is willing to say sorry when he does something wrong. It's not unheard of for a player to lose to Alcaraz and then post on social media, congratulating him on his victory and saying something along the lines of: 'I really think you are an amazing person.' Just try to imagine, say, John McEnroe and Jimmy Connors expressing those kind of thoughts after a match. But Alcaraz attracts that kind of warmth.

The first time that Alcaraz and Jannik Sinner played at an ATP tournament – at the Paris Masters in 2021 – the Italian said something at the net that gave some indication as to whether that rivalry would be one of warmth and respect or something colder. Alcaraz had won, but Sinner almost looked happy as they embraced – and whispered in his opponent's ear: 'I hope we play a couple more times.' Alcaraz couldn't hear him at first, because of the noise of the crowd, and Sinner said it again. You can actually trace their rivalry back to 2019, to a second-tier Challenger tournament in Alicante in Spain, when a 15-year-old Alcaraz beat a 17-year-old Sinner on the clay. But when the stakes have been a lot higher, when they have played on the ATP Tour or at the Grand Slams, their competitiveness has been good-natured.

Their cordial relationship was evident in December 2023, when Sinner travelled to Spain to practise with Alcaraz in preparation for the next season. Likewise, after the 2024 Beijing final, in which Alcaraz beat Sinner in three sets, the players and their teams shared a private jet from there to their next tournament in China.

At the highest level of sport, there's a limit to how friendly you can be with another player. Alcaraz's friendship with Holger Rune goes all the way back to their junior days, when they both played in a tournament in Majorca and subsequently played doubles together at Les Petits As. While there was initially a language barrier, as Alcaraz's English wasn't so strong back then, they got on well. Now they have both established themselves on the ATP Tour – Rune has been in the top ten – and can communicate easily in English, they're still friendly, but the Dane once said he had never been out for dinner with Alcaraz. Rune doesn't want to open up to Alcaraz, or be honest about his game, as there would be a risk of such information being used against him in their next match. Rune would never, for instance, tell Alcaraz he had had a bad day.

Alcaraz is different on and off the court, says his first coach, Carlos Santos: 'When Carlos is on court, you can see he likes putting on a show; but then after the match is over, he becomes more reserved.'

But gone are the times when Molina would be telling Alcaraz something and a young Carlos would just nod. These days, as Alcaraz has his own opinions, there are occasions when he doesn't just silently agree with what his agent is telling him. Alcaraz will listen – people around him say that he's a good listener – and then he might suggest to Molina that there could be a different way of going about things. Given the amount of time they spend together – Molina goes to 90 per cent of the tournaments that Alcaraz plays and they're together almost all day – it's hardly surprising that they disagree occasionally. Alcaraz can be stubborn when he has an idea in his head, according to Molina. In those moments, Molina likes to give Alcaraz five minutes just to think things over. Often, but not always, Alcaraz will come back to Molina and say: 'You were right.' Any disagreement tends to be smoothed over quickly as Alcaraz knows Molina is there to help him, not to make life trickier.

Alcaraz has grown up, then. But Molina doesn't feel as though Alcaraz's character has changed much since he first started representing the player when he was 12 years old. Somehow Carlos is still the same easy-going young man, still happy, still straightforward, just a bit more mature. Reassuringly, Molina can see Alcaraz still likes to smile, laugh and keep it light. He's still grounded and modest. One of Alcaraz's strengths, Molina has said, is his ability to normalize extraordinary things. That's just as well, because extraordinary things keep happening in Alcaraz's life. Staying so grounded – even when he has so many adoring fans around the world – makes Carlos's life a lot simpler.

12

Carlos Alcaraz had bought a sports car as a surprise present for his father. And his dad, even though he had said for many years that he wanted that car, wasn't thrilled about it.

Spending money isn't as easy for Alcaraz as you might imagine it to be. His annual income has been estimated at more than US $42 million (£31.5 million) making him the world's highest-earning tennis player. Just so long as we're only counting active tennis players as some in the industry will tell you that Alcaraz's boyhood idol, Roger Federer, earns double or even triple what Alcaraz does, even though he retired in 2022. If Alcaraz is still some way off Federer's level, he's doing OK for himself, thanks to the deals brought in by his agent Albert Molina, and the team at the International Management Group agency. Just one of Alcaraz's contracts, with his clothing supplier Nike, is potentially worth as much as US $200 million (£150 million) over ten years. And yet, despite his riches, he has hardly been spending freely and living a life of excess.

'Carlitos doesn't have much time to notice that he has a lot of money,' says Alfredo Sarria. 'He can only spend money when he's having lunch or dinner with his friends and sometimes on clothes and shoes but not on much else. If Carlitos wants to go on holiday, there are some resorts that pay him to go there.'

It's believed that with his endorsement deals with Rolex and BMW, Alcaraz receives watches and cars as well as cash. Alcaraz's family have been building a new home near the country club in El Palmar, that's for all six of them – the parents and the four brothers – but he doesn't buy much that is just for himself, aside from golf clubs and sneakers. Sometimes Alcaraz can't even spend money on dinners with his friends. Restaurants in Murcia occasionally invite Alcaraz and his friends to have dinner – and there's no bill to pay at the end of the evening. There have been at least two occasions, according to Alcaraz's old friend Antonio López, when a group of them have been invited to a restaurant in the city and they didn't have to pay a single euro for what they ate and drank, with the owner waiving the bill (out of friendship and admiration for Alcaraz, and maybe also because it won't do the restaurant any harm if word gets out that he likes to go there).

If Carlos is thinking about buying something expensive – such as a pair of limited-edition, US $2,000 (£1,500) shoes to add to his sneaker collection – he tends to run it past his parents first, as his father looks after his money. 'If Carlitos likes something and it's expensive and he's thinking that maybe his family won't approve of him buying it, he will ask them,' Sarria says. 'Carlitos might say to his parents: "If you notice something going on with my account, that's because I'm going to buy some shoes and they're $2,000." His parents will probably say,

"Really, $2,000 for some shoes?" When Carlitos says something it's because he knows his family are going to say to him, "Carlitos, why are you asking? For us, it's not the correct decision. When are you going to use this?"'

But there was one occasion when Alcaraz didn't consult with his parents and he purchased something several times pricier than shoes: the luxury car for his dad. 'Carlitos's father had always said – he had been saying this since he was young – that if he had money in the future, he was going to buy an Aston Martin,' says Sarria. 'And then one day Carlitos arrived with an Aston Martin for his father. It was a surprise. But when his father saw the car, he asked Carlitos, "When am I going to drive this car? And where? Here in El Palmar with my neighbours and my family and the people who see me every day here? No, I already have a BMW because they are your partner." Carlitos's father doesn't want people looking at him, which they would do if he was driving an Aston Martin around the village. The Aston Martin is in a car park most of the year because no one is going to drive that anywhere around El Palmar. Carlos doesn't want Carlitos to be spending money on these kinds of things. Maybe they're going to sell the car soon because they're not going to use it.'

There's another car that has been on Alcaraz's mind: Alcaraz would love to own a Lamborghini, his friends say. 'Carlitos, like many young people, really likes sports cars. He has said that he would like to buy a Lamborghini but not at the moment, maybe in the future,' says López. 'Carlitos has really thought about [driving a Lamborghini] and when he's older he will buy it.'

*

When he was at primary school, Carlos Alcaraz achieved decent grades in English, usually getting a seven or an eight out of ten in tests, according to Laura Caballero. And that was despite missing lots of lessons because he was away at tournaments. Of all the subjects Alcaraz learned in the classroom, English would potentially have the greatest impact on his future life as a tennis player and, in particular, his ability to charm crowds, raise his profile and make money off the court. Caballero will be pleased her old student continues to work on his English. Alcaraz has invested time and effort in pursuit of his goal of speaking perfect English, including working with a tutor and through watching television series in English, such as *Suits* with Meghan Markle (*Suits* also made Alcaraz think that if he hadn't become a tennis player he would have liked to have been a lawyer).

Alcaraz's English – which he practises informally by speaking to players and anyone else he can chat to – is noticeably better than Rafa Nadal's was in his early years on the tour. Lola Jiménez Rivas, who was Alcaraz's English teacher at senior school in El Palmar, has been pleasantly surprised by her former pupil's progress. 'Carlos's grades weren't that high. He was an average student. It was difficult for him as he missed so many lessons because of his tennis training,' Lola says. 'When I watch his interviews, I can hear how he has improved a lot. Carlos has enlarged his vocabulary and worked on his grammar. He must use English more frequently on the tennis tour. I'm really impressed, and surprised, by how good his English is.'

Becoming fluent will allow Alcaraz to showcase more of his personality in media interviews and demonstrate his ability to film commercials in English; all of that will make him more attractive to companies who are looking for a global ambassador. Speaking English is considered crucial for those global partnerships, which pay considerably better than national or regional partnerships. Within tennis, people say one of the reasons Federer earned more than Nadal off the court was the perception that the Swiss was more comfortable speaking English.

One of the phrases you hear a lot in the tennis marketing world is: 'You need to have the right passport.' If you're from a wealthy country with a strong tennis culture, and if you're from an English-speaking country and you're a natural English speaker, you will have more opportunities. No one does better off the court than an American player who is winning lots on it. As someone in the tennis industry notes: 'Spain isn't the best market but it's also not the worst.' Alcaraz can't change his passport – and wouldn't want to – but he has been making himself as appealing as possible by winning titles and improving his English.

When a player is coming up, and when they need the money more urgently to fund their travel and coaching costs, it's very tempting to agree to smaller deals. But doing that means, as one insider put it, 'blocking that space out' – if the player's status rises quickly, they'll be unable to capitalize as they're already committed to those smaller contracts. As you might expect, Alcaraz's sponsorship portfolio was initially more focused on the Spanish market, with deals with Spanish companies or global brands that were mostly using him in Spain. But that has started to shift, as one insider observes: 'It's typical for young players to be used locally or regionally and then expand into global deals as they ascend to superstardom, and I think you're already starting to see Carlos be used more across Europe and internationally.'

Alcaraz's love of the NBA has done him no harm in building his profile in the United States. He collects Nike Air Jordan sneakers; and for the media rounds after winning the 2024 Roland-Garros title he changed into a Michael Jordan T-shirt. He's also close with basketball player Jimmy Butler, who described him as 'a really good friend, my brother, *mi hermano*'.

Even without speaking fluent English, Alcaraz has already been the off-court number one. The youngest-ever men's world number one at the age of 19, Alcaraz was just 21 years old when he reached the top of another significant tennis list: *Forbes* magazine's annual assessment of the world's highest-earning tennis players. Even for someone who had had an agent before he was a teenager, that was an astonishing rise both on and off the court. In the 12 months ending in August 2024, Alcaraz won just over US $10 million (£7.5 million) in prize money. But that was the smaller portion of his income: according to estimates from *Forbes*, he earned US $32 million (£24 million) from off-court deals. That included sponsorship deals as well as appearance fees for playing in exhibitions and tournaments.

It was in 2022, the year that Alcaraz won his first Grand Slam, that a growing number of brands began to contact his management company about possible partnerships. Winning multiple Grand Slams is always going to attract people's attention, but if you do so when you're still young and in a short space of time, as Carlos did, you're going to be able to negotiate much higher rates with sponsors. Tennis is all about timing. How you time your shots and when you sign your deals, including renewals. If you're able to do so soon after winning a major, as Alcaraz has with some of his contracts, that's going to push the numbers up even higher. Besides winning a lot, Alcaraz has plenty more going for him, including his sunny personality and his looks – plus, as one tennis insider put it, he has 'the cool factor', which other players don't necessarily have.

Another consideration, according to some in tennis, is that Alcaraz has shown he is willing to consider the commercial opportunities that are presented to him. To earn as much as Alcaraz does off the court – approaching US $1 million (£750,000) a week, according to *Forbes* – you need willpower as well as star power. 'A lot comes down to how interested a player is in the off-court work. It's key with Alcaraz that he seems to relish the limelight,' says an influential figure in tennis. 'He's willing to do appearances and commercials and really put himself out there. As tennis is a year-round sport, some players don't want to commit the time to the off-court stuff. They would rather just focus on training and playing. If you want to be a marketing star, you have to carve out time in the schedule. If you want to be successful off the court, you get as much out of it as you put into it.'

Alcaraz wouldn't ever agree to anything that could disrupt his preparations for tournaments.

Albert Molina ensures Alcaraz's commercial activities fit into his tennis schedule, with the contracts making clear how many days or hours the athlete will be available for shoots and creating other content, along with the number of social-media posts he'll do or appearances he'll make.

When Max Eisenbud was managing Maria Sharapova during her playing career, he wouldn't allow her partners to do photoshoots the week before tournaments, during the events themselves and then for three or four days afterwards, when she would be tired. In a typical year, that left around 16 days to fit in all her shoots and other commercial activities. That approach informed the way he worked with Li Na and Emma Raducanu, too; and given his role as head of tennis clients at IMG, you might suspect it has also shaped how the agency looks after Alcaraz. There are dead spots in the calendar when Alcaraz gives his sponsors time; one week in December 2024, for instance, he did several shoots at the country club.

Alcaraz's sponsors tell you that the athlete is a joy to work with; and they can see he hasn't been going crazy with the money they have been paying him. 'You don't see many shiny things in his life. I don't want to say Carlos has a normal life because what is a normal life? But when he goes to a shoot, he says hi to everyone,' says Babolat's Jean-Christophe Verborg. 'He brings energy and is always happy, even on a three-hour shoot, which can be slow. He's really humble. When Carlos sees you – and Rafa was like this too – he always comes over to say hi. His parents are the same. They're always thanking us. Carlos pushes me and my team to be even better. You can feel that he really appreciates what we do and we don't want to miss anything.'

Only if Alcaraz keeps on winning – and that means winning Grand Slams – will he continue to earn such large amounts of money. Some of Alcaraz's contracts, such as the ones he has with Nike and Babolat, are longer, but a long-term deal in tennis is usually for three years.

If Alcaraz doesn't keep picking up major titles, his portfolio could look different in time.

As is the case with most tennis players, Alcaraz's biggest contract is with his clothing sponsor. But his contract with Nike is likely built around a series of performance-related bonuses and possibly even reductions. In their dealings with tennis players, Nike typically pay a relatively small annual guarantee that can then be topped up with bonuses for winning majors or that are tied to the athlete's position in the year-end rankings. If Alcaraz is going to earn in the region of US $200 million (£150 million) from his Nike deal – that's the figure that has been circulating, though it has never been confirmed by the sportswear company or by the Spaniard – it's possible he will need to score multiple Grand Slams every season and finish each year as the world number one. But according to one insider, if he drops out of the top ten those numbers will head towards zero very quickly. To keep Nike happy, to keep them paying large sums, Alcaraz must continue winning a lot of majors.

A tennis player's racquet deal is also structured around performance, though not usually to anything like the same degree as a clothing contract tends to be. In 2023, Alcaraz signed a seven-year extension with Babolat, taking him to 2030, by which time he will have been with the same racquet brand from the age of ten until his late twenties – and then after that maybe even beyond. If Alcaraz's deals are typical of how the industry usually operates, his contracts with his other partners will guarantee most of the money, though there could be bonuses for winning a major or being the year-end number one.

With the looks to cross over from tennis into fashion, Alcaraz was the first tennis player to be an ambassador for Louis Vuitton, with the French fashion house even creating a personalized trunk for him and selling near-identical ones for €150,000 (£127,200) each. He has also modelled for Calvin Klein. According to people in tennis marketing, fashion deals don't usually pay as well as other commercial partnerships but can be valuable for brand positioning as they get an athlete out there while framing them in a new way. Such as when Calvin Klein photographed Alcaraz in some briefs and put him on giant billboards and pushed him on social media. The time Alcaraz has spent working with Louis Vuitton and Calvin Klein could prove to be well invested in the long term, if it positively changes people's perception of him and adds to his appeal and value.

Some think Alcaraz's agents are still trying to establish what sort of brand they want to build for him, and the type of sponsorship portfolio that fits with that. If Federer always stood for luxury, and his agent built a portfolio for the Swiss that was almost top-to-bottom luxury, how about Alcaraz? 'I don't think there's anything that's synonymous with Carlos yet,' said a senior figure in tennis marketing. 'Is he a tech guy? Or a performance guy? Or a luxury guy? I think they're still developing Carlos's personal brand. We'll have to wait and see how they position him.'

*

Carlos Alcaraz earns significantly more from appearance fees – whether at exhibitions or ATP tournaments – than any other player, according to someone who regularly speaks to agents. Appearance fees make up a large portion of his earnings. Alcaraz's celebrity, along with his willingness to travel, has seen him play in a good number of exhibitions, including one at New York City's Madison Square Garden and one with Rafa Nadal that was streamed by Netflix. His fee for playing in an exhibition, which is often just a day of semi-serious tennis, with perhaps a few media appearances and other elements, is believed to be around US $1 million (£750,000) – though sometimes, such as when he's played in Saudi Arabia, the figure has been higher.

Alcaraz has acknowledged that he'd be lying if he said that he played in the Six Kings Slam – an exhibition tournament held in Saudi Arabia in 2024 – purely for fun and hadn't cared about the money. This has never been confirmed but it's said he was paid a guaranteed fee of US $1.5 million (£1.1 million) for the event, which was offering the largest champion's prize in tennis history: US $6 million (£4.5 million). For context, that is considerably more than he received for winning each of his two Grand Slam titles that season, at Roland-Garros and Wimbledon. Over the course of the 2024 season, Alcaraz won just under US $10 million (£7.5 million), so he travelled to Saudi Arabia in October that year knowing that a good week could have earned him close to that figure again.

Mostly, Alcaraz doesn't think about dollars or euros when he plays tennis; his focus is on enjoying himself. But the Six Kings Slam wasn't a regular exhibition. A cinematic, five-minute-long promotional video released in advance had higher production values than some movie trailers and gave some indication that the nature of this event was very different to anything else Alcaraz has played in (another sign was the Saudis giving Rafa Nadal a racquet made of gold). But, as Alcaraz said, doesn't everyone work for money? Isn't that just life? Unfortunately for

Alcaraz, it was Jannik Sinner – who suggested he *wasn't* in Riyadh for the money – who ended up taking that prize after beating the Spaniard in the final.

Appearance fees aren't allowed for the Grand Slams or the biggest ATP tournaments; but, according to some in the industry, the price secured by Albert Molina for Alcaraz to compete in smaller ATP events is sometimes as high as seven figures. 'When you see him playing some ATP 250 or ATP 500 tournaments [the two lowest categories on the tour], you know he's getting paid,' said one insider. Generally, though, Alcaraz's fee for playing in an exhibition will be higher than what he would receive for a competitive, sanctioned event. In the coming years, the portion of Alcaraz's earnings from appearance fees may dip if he is able to increase his endorsement portfolio and wants to reduce his schedule; there may come a time when his body starts to tell him that he should be playing less tennis.

13

Everything felt off. Carlos Alcaraz was playing some shaky, anxious tennis on his Wimbledon practice court; it's very possible he had never previously had a worse pre-match warmup, and he perhaps hasn't had a more unsettling one since. His doctor, Juanjo López, was watching and he couldn't think of a practice session when the 20-year-old, who was on court with his older brother Álvaro in London that day, had made so many mistakes.

Wimbledon's gorgeous, Alcaraz's father thinks. But it can also be a place that makes the family nervous (and not just because Carlos was once told by officials he would have to change his underwear for his next match as his colourful briefs were visible through his whites, which was a breach of the tournament's fabulously strict on-court dress code). All day, even before having (a small) breakfast, Alcaraz had been on edge; that afternoon he would be playing in his first Wimbledon final. Alcaraz would have sensed how his team – who had been sharing a rental house with him close to the All England

Club – were also uneasy. Alcaraz was so tense he ate very little. His team could also only pick at their food. Everyone had a feeling in their stomachs, the doctor thought, that Alcaraz was so close to achieving a tennis dream and yet, at the same time, was so far away from it – after all, he would be playing Novak Djokovic for the 2023 title. Alcaraz told his psychologist, Isabel Balaguer, how he was feeling as the final drew closer: 'I'm incredibly nervous.'

You might wish to think of Balaguer as the Carlitos Whisperer. One Spanish newspaper, *El Mundo*, once suggested that Balaguer looks after Alcaraz's soul, which sounds about right. As you might expect, she does that work privately, whether in person or remotely. A professor at the University of Valencia, Balaguer isn't sitting in Alcaraz's player's box at every Grand Slam final or big moment, ready to pump her fist in television close-ups. You might not have previously known her name, or what she looks like, or even been aware of her existence. But Alcaraz considers Balaguer, who has been his psychologist since 2019, to be one of the major reasons why he has had so much success so early in his career. Preparing for the Wimbledon final, Alcaraz wished to speak to Balaguer. He thought that would help; she would have some advice on what he could do to soothe his soul before it was time to play.

Head, heart, balls, Alcaraz's grandfather always says. In that moment, Alcaraz had to get his head right. This wasn't the emotional state he wanted to be in before playing Djokovic and so, two hours before walking out on to Centre Court, he put his headphones on, lay down on a physiotherapist's treatment table inside the gym for half an hour and closed his eyes. He appreciated it probably looked as though he was asleep but, with the calm music in his ears and breathing slowly, he was doing whatever he could to control his emotions before the match began. While that's not a technique Alcaraz uses that much before matches, he had done something similar earlier in the fortnight to help him deal with his nerves before playing his old Danish friend, Holger Rune, in the quarter-finals.

Alcaraz has often listened to 'Eye of the Tiger', 'Heart on Fire' and other rousing music from Sylvester Stallone's *Rocky* films before going out to play, even singing them loudly with his team in a car on the way to a match. The music makes him think of the training scenes in the films; and picturing those moments is always inspiring and motivating for him. Sometimes he just streams the films – during a rain delay at a tournament in America, he was seen watching *Rocky* on his phone. There have been other moments, even before big matches at Grand Slams, when Alcaraz has danced in the locker room or gym beforehand, perhaps pausing to play some keepie-uppie with a tennis ball. But there's no doubt that the moments before the 2023 Wimbledon final needed a gentler, more relaxing playlist.

Just an hour or so before the final started, Djokovic was playing board games with his team, seemingly untroubled by the prospect of playing yet another Wimbledon final. Djokovic's calm somehow added to the tension within Alcaraz's entourage (Roger Federer had been doing that to opponents for years, freaking them out with his backstage serenity before finals).

Before the swirl and the chaos, calm is needed. When Alcaraz feels at peace in the hours before a match, he is more likely, he finds, to be at his most explosive on court. Tennis players can be superstitious types and Alcaraz is no different. It's not unheard of for him to keep going back to the same restaurant during a tournament, even eating with the same people and asking them to sit in the same seats. When Alcaraz wore a nasal strip throughout a tournament in Rotterdam in 2025, that was partly down to it helping him to breathe more easily, as he had arrived with a cold. But, as the week continued and he felt better, wearing the strip became less about aiding his breathing and more about wanting it there until he'd won the title, which he did. There was a reason Alcaraz had a beard when playing at Wimbledon in 2023: friends were telling him to shave but he felt as though his facial hair was bringing him luck.

Ferrero was trying to keep Alcaraz off his phone. He advised his player to stay away from anything that was being said about the final. Best to shut out the noise and to attempt, as much as you can, to have a more relaxed approach.

As Rafa Nadal says, anyone who tells you they're not nervous before playing a tennis match is lying. Naturally, Alcaraz still felt some nerves when going out to play – and it would have been very odd if he didn't – but at least he had been able to stop the pre-match tension from overwhelming him. López, who was sitting with the rest of Alcaraz's team, found Centre Court to be a beautiful yet intimidating place, he wrote in his book *Hábitos para ser el Número 1*. The doctor imagined being out there on the grass himself, all alone – very alone – and watched by the thousands inside the stadium and the millions tuned in to the live television coverage and he couldn't conceive of being anything other than consumed by fear. How could you even hit a single shot into the court in that situation? López considers Alcaraz to have phenomenal mental strength.

Alcaraz had won his first major in the absence of Djokovic, who had been unable to enter the United States and play at the 2022 US Open because he had chosen not to be vaccinated against Covid. But if Alcaraz was going to win Wimbledon he would have to go through the GOAT (the Greatest of All Time). Looking over the net at Djokovic only added to the psychological pressures of Alcaraz's first Wimbledon final. When Alcaraz faces Djokovic, he tries not to think about how many Grand Slams the Serb has won or how many hundreds of weeks he has spent as the world number one, or any of the other numbers and records, because if he did that, he probably wouldn't be able to play at all. But it was harder to push from his mind what had happened a little over a month earlier in Paris. Playing Djokovic in the semi-finals of Roland-Garros, which was his deepest run yet in Paris, Alcaraz had felt a tension he had never known before; and what was going on in his head brought on such terrible cramps – first in his arms and then in his legs and every other part of his body – that he was left broken and uncompetitive. He won only two games in the last couple of sets.

Alcaraz had had cramps before at the Grand Slams – such as when he beat Stefanos Tsitsipas in the third round of the 2021 US Open – but never like the ones he experienced against Djokovic in Paris. Alcaraz was embarrassed that day. 'It hurts,' he said in his Netflix documentary. 'You fucking hate to be seen like that.' Was there a chance that was about to happen again in London? To fortify himself on Wimbledon's Centre Court, where Djokovic hadn't lost since 2013, Alcaraz had brought pickle juice – which he would drink between games – but possibly the most crucial intervention was the pre-match conversation with his psychologist, who would help him to be in the right state of mind. Alcaraz had a very slow start, losing the opening set 6–1, which alarmed some of his supporters inside Centre Court, but that didn't throw him; he responded and raised his level. In the end, Alcaraz and Djokovic would settle the final in a fifth set, and the Spaniard didn't get cramp.

There are almost no grass courts in mainland Spain. For a Spanish player, adapting your game to grass can take a while, often years. And Alcaraz had had very limited time on grass going into the summer of 2023. As a boy, Alcaraz had often learned best through watching. Visual learning helped him as a 20-year-old to speed up the process of acclimatizing to the lawns: he watched videos of Roger Federer and Andy Murray, looking at how they moved and played on the surface, and that knowledge was useful when playing a warmup tournament at the Queen's Club in London, which he won. Alcaraz's aggressive game was also key; his transformation into a grass-court champion would have been slower if he wasn't so attack-minded. 'Carlos is very aggressive. And that's why I think he has managed to play so well so early on every surface,' says Garbiñe Muguruza. 'He has the game that allows him to adapt very quickly.'

As a Spaniard, if you win Wimbledon, you instantly become a god, or a goddess. 'In Spain, you grow up hearing people say, "Roland-Garros, Roland-Garros." When you're practising, the coaches are always going, "Come on, think that you're playing the championship point at Roland-Garros." You grow up hearing about the clay, about Nadal and the other past Spanish champions. For Spaniards, Roland-Garros is usually the one. Grass courts are very rare in Spain. But Wimbledon is the most prestigious tournament we have in tennis,' Muguruza says.

'If you win Wimbledon, you're a god, basically. You've won the hardest event. Winning Roland-Garros is like a dream come true as you become a legend, but it feels more familiar. Wimbledon feels more exotic. You think, "Wow, I won Wimbledon on grass, on the royal grass land." If you win Wimbledon, you've made it – it's very special.'

If the hours before your first Wimbledon final make your nerves fizz, they are nothing compared to the moment, in late afternoon, when you find yourself trying to serve for the title. Alcaraz's hands and legs were shaking, which made it hard for him to be as technically precise as he needed to be. But he dealt with everything to become Wimbledon champion for the first time. With his second Grand Slam title, Alcaraz had moved ahead of his coach, Juan Carlos Ferrero. He would later appear for his champion's media interviews in a white bucket hat, which almost made it look as though his Sunday in England had been close to a laidback, Wimbledon–Glastonbury crossover. But playing that match had been far from relaxed. In those moments, Alcaraz can't start playing timid tennis. He must keep going for his shots, just as he has done all match. Alcaraz is urging himself on: 'Go for it. If you miss it, you miss it. Don't hold back. Don't regret. Play positive. Go aggressively. Play your game.'

People outside tennis were taking more notice now. Will Smith, who had won a Best Actor Oscar for playing Serena and Venus Williams' father Richard in *King Richard*, sent a message of congratulations, which thrilled Alcaraz.

*

Isabel Balaguer started working in this space – the psychology of elite tennis players – before Carlos Alcaraz was born. In 2002, the year before Alcaraz came into this world, Balaguer wrote a chapter on the psychological demands of playing tennis for a book on the psychology of a range of sports.

Some coaches aren't that keen on having a psychologist in the team as they think they know the player better than anyone else does. Juan Carlos Ferrero, though, can see how much value there is in having Balaguer involved. Ferrero's willingness to embrace psychology is informed by his experiences as a player, when he worked with psychologists and found it beneficial. A psychologist can help to prevent a tennis player 'getting lost', Ferrero once told *The New York Times*. According to Ferrero, Alcaraz speaks to Balaguer about his experiences, along with how to manage his life and stay calm and grounded. Alcaraz is comfortable speaking to Balaguer about his concerns and doubts and fears. He's an easy-going character who can talk to anyone. What puts him even more at ease is that he has been working with psychologists since he was a small boy, going back – as we have seen – to when he was drawing pictures of himself as a future Roland-Garros champion.

When Carlos was young, his father had recognized the value of his son having the psychological training to help him become a tennis champion. 'His father was always concerned and placed great importance on working on this aspect in his son's development,' says Alcaraz senior's close friend Alfredo Sarria.

At first, Alcaraz had been part of the group sessions that Josefina Cutillas ran. The idea behind those sessions, which she tried to make as playful as possible, was to introduce the young players to how athletes might go about training their minds to play sport. When it became clear that Carlos was technically superior to his peers, and knowing that competing at a higher level would come with greater demands, he and his parents thought it would be useful for him to have more personalized psychological tuition. He started having individual sessions with Cutillas, during which they spoke about what Alcaraz could do to play at his best – including how to stay focused and how he could deal with the pressure on him – as well as the expectations he had. Alcaraz's mind was like 'a sponge', Cutillas told *El País*; he was absorbing everything she said.

As if to illustrate his modern approach to tennis, Alcaraz is open about how psychologists have helped him throughout his career. To talk about having a psychologist isn't an admission of weakness, or even anything close to that; it's merely a statement of fact, just as you might say you have a fitness coach to improve your body. Alcaraz is appreciative of how psychologists have helped him during his career. Cutillas is grateful he has spoken so freely about the work they have done together.

Without Balaguer, Alcaraz has thought, his tennis life would have been much more complicated, maybe even impossible. Some adjustment was necessary when he first started having some success and the public began to recognize him when he was walking down the street. But, as with so many other aspects of his life, Alcaraz was able to talk it through with Balaguer, who could offer advice and give him some mental tools for managing it all.

*

A lot of tennis players almost dread playing the biggest points. The stakes are high and one moment, one error, can destroy several hours' work (or days, weeks, months or even years of work, depending on how you want to look at it). It's to Carlos Alcaraz's great advantage – and Juan Carlos Ferrero noticed this before the young player had won his first major – that he savours those moments when the match could move violently for or against him.

As we saw in an earlier chapter, Alcaraz will play drop shots and make other risky moves when playing a break point, a set point or even a match point. In keeping with his grand ambitions, Alcaraz prefers tennis when it's big. The largest points and the grandest stages, such as the US Open's Arthur Ashe Stadium and the largest courts at the other majors. When Alcaraz is 'playing for something big', as he once put it, there will of course be nerves and tension, but he has shown he can cope with this better than most other players. If that's one part of tennis psychology that Alcaraz excels at, though, he knows there are others he must continue to work on, such as trying to reduce the ups and downs in his matches.

Alcaraz has long admired Rafa Nadal for his ability to maintain his intensity in matches – it didn't matter whether it was the first game or he was two hours deep into a match, as he was always just as competitive. Alcaraz, meanwhile, can have periods in matches when he loses focus a little. He's aware his level can be very high and then, not long afterwards, a lot lower. There have been matches when he's felt he was in the ascendancy and relaxed too much, leading to a drop in intensity and less effective movement. That has made him lose a few matches.

Sometimes there are concerns before Alcaraz even gets on court: he knows when he has 'a big problem'. It's when he's spending too much time before a match thinking about his opponent's game. What he should be doing, he believes, is focusing more on himself and the tennis that he's planning on playing. The dangers of becoming too consumed by an opponent were evident on the day he played Jack Draper in the semi-finals of the 2025 Indian Wells tournament. Going into the match, Alcaraz was potentially just two more victories away from winning that title – which is sometimes and very unofficially called the fifth Grand Slam – for the third year in a row. But pretty much from the moment Alcaraz woke up in the desert, he had his British opponent on his mind. Alcaraz was uneasy all day and that tension didn't fade when he got on court, where his run came to an end.

There's no physical contact in tennis, of course, but some of Alcaraz's confidence on court can be attributed to Ilia Topuria, a mixed martial artist. The Spanish athletes met at the Madrid tournament in 2024, as part of a promotional stunt where Topuria playfully and very gently showed Alcaraz some of his moves before lifting the tennis player up and carrying him around the 'octagon'. But the greatest value in their interactions that day was the private conversation they had, and the connection they established; seeing how assured Topuria was before every fight inspired Alcaraz to not doubt himself and he gained a greater understanding of who he is and what he has to offer. Thinking of Topuria, and the fighter's self-confidence, has helped Alcaraz to 'dust myself off at times', he has said. Topuria clearly believes in Alcaraz – he bet US $50,000 (£38,000) that his countryman would take the 2023 Wimbledon title, winning almost US $250,000 (£188,000) in return.

Even with a mixed martial artist for a mentor, the occasional negative thought is going to find its way into your head. But, for the most part, Alcaraz can think positively. He doesn't doubt himself as much as other athletes do. In the middle of a match, a mistake doesn't destabilize

Alcaraz as it might other players. Even if he is losing heavily, he always thinks he is going to win. One of the reasons Alcaraz loves tennis is that a match can change in an instant; that 'until the last point, anything is possible'. From a young age, Josefina Cutillas thought, Alcaraz showed an unshakable belief in his tennis and what he can accomplish (in the next chapter, we will explore just how ambitious he is). Losing a match isn't going to throw him off. After a quick reset, he will go back to working towards his next goal.

As a tennis player, you're in your head most of the time, even if the sport has recently relaxed the rules about mid-match coaching. Coaches speaking to their players was previously prohibited but is now allowed and even celebrated and exploited to give broadcasters more content; at the 2025 Australian Open, Ferrero and other members of Alcaraz's team sat in a court-level pod in the Rod Laver Arena where they could pass on their thoughts. Even so, for the most part, a tennis player is essentially alone on court. And you're not just taking on your opponent. As Cutillas once told *La Razón*, when Alcaraz plays, he's facing himself and his inner voice. If he is going to play his best tennis, he must find a way of shaping the dialogue in his head. He can use words and phrases that will help him to control that dialogue and to ensure he is focused and doesn't allow himself to be distracted by whatever is happening on court.

Just as a young player learns how to serve or to hit a forehand, they can also start early with discovering ways to manage the emotions they will feel on the court. Frustration and anger are unavoidable when playing tennis; and Cutillas spoke to Alcaraz about how he could deal with those emotions. The earlier he became familiar with doing that, the better. According to Cutillas, when Alcaraz walks out to play, he has the ability – and this is rare – to leave behind whatever is going on outside the court.

*

During his school days in El Palmar, Carlos Alcaraz's friends would worry about an exam for days beforehand. Then, once the test was over, they would switch to obsessing about whether they had passed or failed. Alcaraz, though, didn't over-think exams. If he had been away for a while, missing a lot of lessons because he had been travelling to tournaments, his teachers would sometimes offer him the option of taking the test on a later date, which would give him more time to absorb more of the topic in question. But, according to Laura Caballero, Alcaraz would want to do the test on the same day as everyone else; and, she says, 'would always pass with good marks'. Alcaraz would barely mention an upcoming exam and after finishing a paper would hardly talk about it again, if at all; that was done and he was moving on, even if others weren't.

What worked for Carlos the schoolboy works for Alcaraz the athlete. He generally moves on quickly from his victories and defeats, not letting a big win or an unexpected defeat dominate his thoughts and his mood. For all his energy on a tennis court, and the excitement or even mania he can provoke in spectators, Alcaraz has an emotional balance that sets him apart from many others. Rather than having an extreme reaction to what happens on the court – and being too up or too down for days after a match – he's usually able to be calmer and more measured about it. In the first few moments after a defeat, Alcaraz often won't feel like talking to anyone, and he has sometimes found himself thinking, 'everything is shit', he once said. Other times, losing a tennis match leaves him wanting to 'destroy everything', and those are the occasions when it will take him a while to calm down. But after most defeats, Alcaraz will be feeling more positive again within 20 minutes. Sometimes Alcaraz doesn't even need a few minutes to process a defeat – he will walk off the court instantly feeling good because he is proud of how he played despite losing.

If he's feeling raw after a defeat, it can help Alcaraz if he remembers that he often learns more from a loss than from a victory. It's not easy playing so many tournaments in a year, but after a defeat Alcaraz can put a positive spin on the busy calendar; today might not have gone as well as he would have wanted but next week will bring a new opportunity to play well and have better feelings on the court.

During his playing career, Juan Carlos Ferrero wasn't very good at processing defeats. The losses hurt him too much and for too long. He spent too much time thinking darkly about each setback, rather than analysing what had happened and what he could do in the future to address failings and avoid defeat next time around. Ferrero has helped Alcaraz to be better at dealing with defeats than he ever was. Alcaraz's friends agree that he knows how to learn from his defeats, which is an important skill. 'When Carlitos loses a match, he is probably a bit angry but later, when he is more relaxed, he will learn from those defeats,' says one friend. It's a balance – taking what you can from a loss without letting it drag you down.

Some thought Alcaraz's defeat in the 2024 Olympic final weighed heavily on him for some weeks and months. But the reality is that, although he cried during a television interview after losing to Novak

Djokovic in Paris, within half an hour of the match finishing, he had calmed down and was thinking more clearly; he realized that winning a silver medal was a fine achievement (that defeat wasn't an easy moment for him but it's not as if the result took him days or weeks to get over, which can occasionally happen).

Dwelling on the past isn't that interesting for Alcaraz. He's mindful, with an ability to live in the moment and focus all his energy on what he is doing right now. He's also a propulsive character, looking to the future and what's next.

14

They were talking slot machines, casinos and dancing fountains. Carlos Alcaraz was in Las Vegas, sitting in the back of a black van with a tennis elder, Andre Agassi. Travelling along the Strip and around the city, they spoke about gambling and the fountains outside the Bellagio casino, which Agassi thought looked as though they were almost dancing. Alcaraz was in Las Vegas for the first time to play in the Netflix Slam exhibition match against Rafa Nadal and Agassi, who was raised in the city and still lives there with his wife, Steffi Graf, was showing the Murcian around. In Las Vegas, Agassi was saying, you can go out to do some grocery shopping – maybe buy some eggs at the store – and then pop into a casino for some gambling.

It was a van ride that combined sightseeing and small talk with some big truths from Agassi; a winner of eight Grand Slam titles, he was passing on some of his wisdom about what you can accomplish as a tennis player if you just back yourself (Agassi has found that as an athlete you often become wise just as your body starts to go). There's something outrageous, absurd and irrepressibly ambitious about Las Vegas, of course. How can somewhere with a half-size, imitation Eiffel Tower be regarded as anything else? You don't build that, and everything else along the Strip, without some belief. Without, as Alcaraz's grandfather might put it, some *cojones*. Agassi always compares tennis to Las Vegas, he told Alcaraz. 'If you believe it, if you dream it, you can do it,' Agassi continued as they passed some more mega-casinos. 'I call it the can-do spirit, like you on a tennis court.'

That was March 2024. Just 20 years old, Alcaraz had already won two Grand Slam titles. The conversation with Agassi would have only reinforced Alcaraz's belief that he could do something special in his career, as if winning a couple of majors while still only 20 hadn't been spectacular enough already. Alcaraz won't remember any of Agassi's eight Slams. Agassi's last major came at the 2003 Australian Open, a few months before the Spaniard was born. But Alcaraz knew that Agassi was someone worth listening to. Ten months after their conversation in Las Vegas, Alcaraz would change into a pair of retro Agassi Nike shoes on court after his matches at the 2025 Australian Open at Melbourne Park, which looked like the sneakerhead's way of showing his respect to a former great (Alcaraz also wore some retro John McEnroe shoes after his appearances at the US Open one year).

Carlitos – Little Carlos – is dreaming big these days. And he knows it. He appreciates that what he is chasing might be beyond him, that it could be 'impossible', but he feels as though you must dream big. While still in his early twenties, while still in single figures for Grand Slams, Alcaraz is already thinking about becoming, as he puts it, 'the best in history'. Alcaraz has been very open about his dreams; he hasn't hidden what he hopes to achieve, and Novak Djokovic – who has won more Grand Slam singles titles than any other man and is almost universally acknowledged as the greatest of all time – has been taking it all in.

Djokovic admires the ambition of a young rival he calls 'Titanito' or 'Little Titan'. He likes how Alcaraz looks at himself and concludes: 'Hey, I've got the goods.' Djokovic also believes that Alcaraz isn't being unrealistic, that it's possible he could end up winning more Grand Slam titles than he did: 'Carlos could already be the next guy.' But Djokovic, speaking to *GQ* magazine for an interview published in 2025, did wonder whether it was maybe a little early in Alcaraz's career for him to be talking about chasing history. Djokovic, for all his greatness, didn't start thinking and talking like that until much later in his tennis life. But no one is suggesting that Alcaraz should stay quiet about the history he is chasing. Juan Carlos Ferrero has also been bold with his public statements about what might be possible, once saying he would love to see Alcaraz winning 30 Grand Slams.

Alcaraz has managed something impressive that's almost as hard as winning majors: expressing those grand ambitions without sounding arrogant. It's an unusual and welcome combination – the self-belief to think you could out-perform every other tennis player in history, together with the smile and the charm to keep other players onside and for the public not to think you're getting ahead of yourself.

*

In tears again (and they were sad tears rather than the happy kind). Feeling weird. Doubting whether he would ever feel normal again. The awful, gathering anxiety.

You don't make tennis history, as Carlos Alcaraz now knows, without sometimes going through some physical pain. Without feeling, as he put it, 'really shitty'. And that brings on 'mental distress', as Alcaraz described the weeks leading into Roland-Garros in 2024, when he had a forearm injury, having first felt a sharp pain at the Indian Wells Tennis Garden in California, that was making him question himself. What chance did the 21-year-old have of taking a first title at Roland-Garros, where he had grand plans of becoming the youngest man in history to win majors on three different surfaces, if he couldn't even hit a forehand properly? Carlos hadn't even played three of the biggest tournaments during the European clay-court swing – in Monte Carlo, Barcelona and Rome – and those absences had made him cry. The only event he'd played on that surface before Roland-Garros was in Madrid, where he'd hit his forehand more softly than usual out of concern he would damage his arm again. Sitting in the box watching Alcaraz, the 2022 and 2023 champion at La Caja Mágica, play his quarter-final in 2024, Juan Carlos Ferrero whispered to Albert Molina: 'If we win the tournament with this forehand, Albert, I swear I'll get drunk, OK?' Ferrero wouldn't go out partying: Alcaraz would lose that match to his Russian opponent, Andrey Rublev.

Doctors were telling Alcaraz his arm would be fine, and he was doing everything he should have been, but it didn't seem to be getting any better. Still aggravated by the injury, he was asking himself whether he would ever be OK again and whether he would go back to hitting a tennis ball 'normally'. That brought on 'a lot of anxiety', he told Molusco TV; and it was another one of those periods when he needed to speak to his psychologist, Isabel Balaguer.

For a few days after cancelling his appearance at Rome's Foro Italico, which would have been his last tournament before Roland-Garros, Alcaraz didn't even touch his racquet. He had barely played during the European clay-court season. Going into Roland-Garros, Alcaraz was still uncertain about his arm and what he might be capable of on the Parisian clay—which, with its slow, high bounces and punishing rallies, is often the most physically demanding of the Grand Slams. What if a match went to five sets? He didn't know how his arm would hold up. Ferrero, who felt as though Alcaraz had a mental block or weakness about going all-out, was urging him to increase the intensity on the practice court. But still Alcaraz continued to play at less than full power, in training and in matches. Alcaraz, with a sleeve on his arm, couldn't get the injury out of his head: would he ever whack a forehand at top speed again?

While Alcaraz didn't feel any pain in the first five matches he played, he was still being cautious, still playing within himself. This wasn't the usual Alcaraz, who needs a full-power forehand if he is going to bring all his other creativity to the court. Something had to change. It was before he played Jannik Sinner in the semi-finals that he decided he would be going all out with his forehand against the Italian. 'If I hurt myself, if it's painful, then let it be here,' Alcaraz was saying to himself. Don't be scared, Alcaraz thought, telling himself to trust the rehabilitation work he had done and to try to forget about the injury. Sinner was moving Alcaraz around to see whether the Spaniard was in more pain when hitting the ball from certain areas of the court. After losing the opening set, Alcaraz resolved to hit the ball harder with his forehand, and that adjustment got him back into the match. But a twist was coming: for the second year in a row, he was cramping in a Roland-Garros semi-final, and he lost the third set. But this time, Alcaraz decided, would be different. Alcaraz, even though he felt as though he wasn't moving at his best or always thinking clearly on the court, was going to play through any pain and adversity. There was a voice in his head expressing what he might have said to his opponent, and which he articulated very clearly through the way he played against an opponent who was also cramping: 'Jannik, if you really want to beat me, you're going to have to take me out on a stretcher.'

Walking on to Court Philippe-Chatrier at Roland-Garros, Alcaraz had often found himself thinking about all the great matches that have been played on that rectangle of clay, some of which he had watched on television as a boy after running home from school. He had also thought about the past champions, including the Spaniards who have won La Coupe des Mousquetaires, the Musketeers' Cup. The quick historical recap in Alcaraz's head would have intimidated many other players. It excited and energized Alcaraz, though, who told himself: 'I want to be part of the history of this tournament and the history of this court. Let's do it.'

When a young Alcaraz drew himself as being the Roland-Garros champion, had he imagined he would have to suffer so much for the trophy? Winning his first two Grand Slam titles hadn't been easy, but he went through even more adversity in Paris. In both his semi-final against Sinner and in the final against Alexander Zverev, Alcaraz trailed by two sets to one down before coming back to win.

The five-setter with Zverev wasn't pretty or comfortable viewing. But maybe, as some around Alcaraz have observed, playing an odd, fluctuating final without much of his usual rhythm and colour and polish was no bad thing (he had been leading 5–2 in the third set and this match would have felt a lot easier if he hadn't lost the next five games). Just as he had done against Novak Djokovic in the 2023 Wimbledon final, Alcaraz was shaking with nerves as he prepared to serve for the title against Zverev. But once again he found a way of dealing with those nerves.

The tournament had demonstrated that Alcaraz didn't always have to play spectacular tennis. 'Carlitos struggled big time in the semi-final and final,' Àlex Corretja says. 'He suffered so much. And yet he ended up winning. That was a big thing.' If ever there was a tournament that showed Alcaraz you can find joy in suffering, it was that one. Reflecting on their semi-final, Sinner had seen Alcaraz's mental strength that day. In Corretja's analysis, Alcaraz learned an important lesson at that tournament. That you can't hope to be the Roland-Garros champion just by hitting winners. You need to be willing to go through some hardship if you're going to have a chance of lifting that trophy. Maybe that was a lesson that could be applied everywhere and not just to Roland-Garros. Alcaraz didn't always have to play 'incredible' tennis to win Grand Slams, Juan Carlos Ferrero thought; Alcaraz was trying to play at a high level and would sometimes benefit from 'slowing down a bit'.

Historically, Alcaraz hasn't done anything slowly. Lifting the trophy in Paris was another reminder that Alcaraz was, and is, so much more than what some people had called him for years: the 'Second Rafa' or the 'Next Nadal'. The previous youngest winner of majors on the three different surfaces? Nadal, who had been 22 years old when he completed the set. Alcaraz had got there even faster. He had out-Rafa'd Rafa. Only 21 years old and Alcaraz had already demonstrated he could excel on hard, grass and clay courts. While he had grown up on clay, he had known from a young age he couldn't spend all his time training and playing on that surface. Being a great tennis player means doing well on all surfaces, not just on the one you spent much of your childhood on. Most of the tournaments in professional tennis are on hard courts, after all. These days, Alcaraz often feels more comfortable on hard courts than he does on clay; note how his first Grand Slam victory came at the US Open and his second on the grass of Wimbledon – clay was the last surface he won a major on.

In the back of a car driving through Paris, a triumphant Alcaraz told Molina he felt like climbing to the top of the Eiffel Tower and then hanging off it, like King Kong on the Empire State Building. Later that evening, Carlos was sitting in the back of another vehicle with his brother Álvaro and Molina that was taking them to a restaurant in the city popular with the fashion set when he informed his agent he would be 'drinking' his dinner. When Alcaraz said to Molina, who was seen in the Netflix documentary looking a little horrified, that he would be 'pulling an all-nighter' and 'I'm going hard tonight, Albert', it was perhaps only half said in jest. In that moment, Molina might have preferred it if Alcaraz had gone ahead with the King Kong-style celebrations. Molina informed Alcaraz he would be 'banging on your door at 11am' to ensure he was up for the day's media activities as the new champion.

On arrival, Alcaraz walked into the restaurant holding a replica of his trophy. Soon almost everyone in the restaurant was on their feet, singing, waving sparklers and swirling napkins in the air. Alcaraz celebrated with champagne, wine and pizza.

*

From Paris, the party continued in Ibiza, which created some tension within the team (given how much time is dedicated to this trip in Carlos Alcaraz's Netflix series, this might well be the most scrutinized holiday in tennis history and maybe even sporting history). Alcaraz doesn't travel to Ibiza for the sunsets; he goes there, he has said, 'to get wasted'.

Juan Carlos Ferrero made his views clear to Alcaraz; he didn't think the Murcian should have been having a few hedonistic days on the island when he had just three weeks to prepare for Wimbledon. Albert Molina was also against Carlos going clubbing, as were other members of Alcaraz's team. But Alcaraz could remind them he had partied in Ibiza the year before and that had hardly damaged his tennis on the grass in London; on his return he had won an ATP tournament at Queen's Club, followed by a first Wimbledon title. Ferrero wasn't against Alcaraz enjoying himself, but felt as though his player should have been picking a different moment in the tennis calendar to let loose: 'Carlos, now is not the time.' To which Alcaraz responded: 'No, it is because I need it.'

Alcaraz craves those moments when he can forget he's a tennis player; he feels as though they give him the mental freshness he needs for a long year on the tour. Ferrero, meanwhile, believes a small part of Alcaraz's brain should always be reminding him he's an athlete. Ferrero would much rather Alcaraz disconnected by playing some more golf. But he couldn't stop Alcaraz from going to Ibiza once again. Ferrero tells Alcaraz hard truths. And Alcaraz wants his coach to be straight with him. He appreciates that Ferrero, Molina and others are trying to protect him. But Alcaraz is of an age when he wants to make his own decisions; if he messes up, at least it will be because of a choice he has made, whether or not to party in Ibiza, attend a Formula One race or go on any other trip he feels as though he needs.

Ultimately, it was a holiday that made Ferrero think that he and Alcaraz have very different approaches to 'work and sacrifice'. Ferrero was left questioning whether Alcaraz had the discipline to achieve his ambition of becoming the greatest tennis player in history. To be the best, Ferrero has said, Alcaraz must be willing to be 'a slave' to tennis, because otherwise you must come to terms with the fact you're not living up to your potential. And Alcaraz, while he says he's in love with the sport, and it brings him joy, won't ever be enslaved by tennis.

Being away from home, and his wife and children, doesn't get any easier for Ferrero, but he has been happy to travel to help Alcaraz become the best player he can be. Molina, meanwhile, is always away for his birthday, which falls during Wimbledon, and for many years has missed seeing his children grow up so he can be there for Carlos. Others around Alcaraz are making personal sacrifices to support the player's shot at greatness, setting up the question: how much is Carlos willing to give up in pursuit of his tennis dreams?

Being around Carlos has changed how physiotherapist Juanjo Moreno views life; he has become happier and more easy-going. Ferrero, though, still seems to have the same views on life, including a strong work ethic, and he said in the Netflix documentary he wasn't sure whether he could continue coaching Alcaraz if expectations ever dropped. Molina tells Alcaraz that, while he might wish to think of himself as a typical young man, he isn't. Molina also believes that if Alcaraz ever loses his joy for tennis, he could walk away from the sport (and the agent would be devastated if in years to come Carlos tells him that, while he achieved so much during his career, he wasn't happy).

Alcaraz isn't as disciplined as Rafa Nadal, who has said that if you ever feel as though you're sacrificing too much, you'll burn out: maybe Rafa was always willing to sacrifice a little more. Carlos also isn't Novak Djokovic. Alcaraz is not going to be as self-disciplined as the Serb, who does things like setting an alarm on his phone to go off after he had gone a whole year without eating chocolate. Before Djokovic does anything, he will ask: 'How will this help my tennis?' In the way he approaches tennis and life, Alcaraz is closer to Roger Federer, a creative spirit who always took care to have a good time along the way, than he is to the other two of the Big Three. Alcaraz enjoys life. Maybe, he has mused, he enjoys life more than he should. While, in so many ways, Alcaraz is extraordinarily disciplined, he's not sure whether he is willing to do everything he can, which would mean denying himself certain joys and pleasures, for tennis greatness. 'I'd choose happiness over massive success,' Alcaraz has said. 'Because happiness is already success. And it's not an easy thing to find.'

*

For a tennis player, Paris and London must seem as though they are separated by more than just the English Channel, or a couple of hours on the Eurostar. Going from the burned orange of the Roland-Garros clay to the emerald green of the Wimbledon grass is to feel as though you are leaving one world and entering another, a shift in colour scheme that signifies how very different tennis is about to look and feel. Switching from the slower, higher bounces of clay to faster, skiddier grass, you're having to re-learn much of what you know about tennis, including how you move and think. With only three weeks between the European majors, you hardly have much time to remodel your game, and even less if you have spent some of that period getting 'wasted' in the Mediterranean.

Winning Roland-Garros and Wimbledon in the same year, which is sometimes known as the Channel Slam, is one of the hardest feats in tennis. We know that because so few men have done it. Going into 2024, only five men in the post-1968 Open Era had previously achieved the Paris–London double in the same season: Rod Laver, Björn Borg and the modern, golden trio of Rafa Nadal, Roger Federer and Novak Djokovic. Any time you win Wimbledon you make some tennis history, but victory for Carlos Alcaraz that summer would feel even more momentous because of what he had already done in Paris.

To add to the historical feel, Alcaraz ended up playing Djokovic in the Wimbledon final – the second consecutive year that they had faced off for the golden trophy with a pineapple on top. They wouldn't play another five-setter, as they had done in 2023, but Alcaraz's straight-sets victory wasn't without its psychological challenges and dangerous moments. Leading by two sets to love, and serving at 5–4, 40–0, Alcaraz had three championship points. It appeared he was just moments away from beating Djokovic, who was wearing a grey knee brace: he had had a knee operation just weeks before Wimbledon and some, including his own wife, Jelena, had been unsure whether he would even play on the grass. But Alcaraz couldn't convert those three chances – he wasn't helped by a spectator screaming out when he was about to hit the ball at 40–30 – and he was taken to deuce and then lost his serve.

That was a dangerous moment for Alcaraz, who just a minute or so earlier had pictured himself holding the Wimbledon trophy again. Getting your serve broken like that can break you in other ways. It would have been very easy, given everything that was on the line, to have spiralled mentally. Alcaraz could have thought he had missed his chance against this 'beast' of an opponent, who was trying to win an eighth Wimbledon title and to extend his Grand Slam collection to 25 titles. Alcaraz had been through some tough moments earlier in the fortnight, such as when he had been two sets to one down against his friend Frances Tiafoe in the third round, but this was on a different level: a mini disaster in a Wimbledon final against the greatest of all time. The last thing you want to do against Djokovic is to let him back into a match that you should have already won. When Djokovic broke Alcaraz's serve, Juan Carlos Ferrero got up from his seat for a better view of Alcaraz, to check on him. Alcaraz was in the corner of Centre Court, towelling himself down. He was fine. Still thinking clearly, Alcaraz was telling himself – because he knew that playing careful, timid tennis could have been self-defeating – to keep on attacking Djokovic: 'I have to go after him.'

Somehow – and this was a moment that showed the importance of the work he had done with his psychologist – the Spaniard held it all together. He showed his resolve. He showed going to Ibiza hadn't been the catastrophe some had thought it was. He also showed his teeth, smiling in the tiebreak as he prepared for his fourth championship point, which was the one he converted. As Alcaraz always tells himself, finals aren't for playing in – they're for winning. Victory over Djokovic meant Alcaraz had won his first four Grand Slam finals.

Alcaraz is friends with Álvaro Morata, who was captain of Spain's men's football team that summer. Shortly after winning his second Wimbledon title, Alcaraz phoned some of the Spanish footballers to wish them luck and to send them 'all my strength' for that evening's final of the European Championships in Berlin.

In a busy, joyous few hours, Alcaraz was doing all the post-final media interviews, as well as getting ready for the Champions' Dinner at the Raffles Hotel in central London (swapping his Wimbledon whites for a dinner jacket) and getting himself to the venue. That meant watching the final on a phone at first, switching to a television in the home he had rented in Wimbledon and then following the last few minutes on an iPad in a car on the way to the party. Driving to the hotel, they passed a pub and he could see the drinkers celebrating England's equalizer. When his car arrived at the venue, Alcaraz didn't immediately get out but waited to see whether Spain's late winner was disallowed for being offside (it wasn't, completing what was a fine day for Spain's athletes on the lawns of England and Germany).

With four majors, Alcaraz had already won more than three-time Grand Slam champion Andy Murray, whose career had been celebrated with a retirement ceremony on Centre Court during that Wimbledon. More significantly, Alcaraz was winning majors at a faster rate than the Big Three. At 21 years and 2 months, Alcaraz was ahead of Nadal (who had three majors at that age), Djokovic (one) and Federer (none).

In his early twenties, was Alcaraz a better player than the Big Three had been at that age? Andre Agassi, who wrote in his memoir *Open* how he 'hated tennis with a dark and secret passion', has sounded very excited about this young Spaniard's game. About Alcaraz being athletically unmatched, including by being so quick around the court. Agassi thought Alcaraz could have been putting more revolutions per minute on the ball than Nadal's topspin forehands. Alcaraz could have had better defensive skills than Djokovic, according to Agassi, who also suggested that Alcaraz's touch and feel were already at Federer's level, and maybe even higher.

'We can all agree that Carlitos is better than the Big Three were at his age,' says Àlex Corretja. 'Rafa was solid and strong at that age. Novak was the same, he was growing. Roger was good but he had some tough places, like when he was playing a backhand up high. Mentally he was struggling sometimes. Carlitos is better than them at his age. He has huge potential.'

If you believe in evolution, as Mats Wilander does, Alcaraz plays better tennis than the Big Three ever did: 'Carlos smacks the ball so freaking hard. The way he moves, the way he slides, is creating a sensation. He's at another level of athleticism.' If you just look at the physical part of tennis, Alcaraz is already superior to Djokovic, Nadal and Federer, according to Wilander; but he notes that's only 20 per cent of tennis and the rest is mental and psychological. If peak Alcaraz played any of the Big Three in their prime, there would be so much psychology involved, Wilander said, that it would be hard to predict a winner.

Alcaraz has had a very strong start to his career but he recognizes that he has to keep going—because that's how he will give himself a chance of 'sitting at the same table as the big guys' at the end of his playing days. Sometimes even Alcaraz forgets that he's still young, that he still has time to work on his tennis and improve. Ultimately, what matters is that he feels as though he is maturing and heading in the right direction; that he's getting closer to being the player he wants to be. 'Carlos has a wonderful future ahead of him,' says Toni Nadal. 'He's so young. He's one of the best players in the world. He has a long time ahead of him to win many Grand Slams and big titles. We have to see what happens in the next few years.'

Just four years after winning a match at a Grand Slam for the first time – at the 2021 Australian Open – Alcaraz arrived at Melbourne Park in 2025 for his first chance to become the youngest man in the Open Era to complete the Career Grand Slam. The Spaniard, who was still only 21 years old, went as far as the quarter-finals, where he was stopped by Djokovic. But that still left two more opportunities, as victory in 2026 or 2027 would still make him a younger winner of all four Slams than Nadal, who was 24 years old when he completed the set. For comparison, because comparisons are inevitable, Federer was 27 when he achieved the Career Grand Slam while Djokovic was 29.

Perhaps in one way, Alcaraz has already achieved tennis immortality, or something very close to it. He did that by putting his heart into it, as he described it, and winning what was possibly the greatest match ever. When Carlitos met Jannik Sinner for the 2025 Roland-Garros title, it was the first Gen Z Grand Slam final, contested by two men born this century. Together they produced five hours and 29 minutes of absurdly entertaining tennis, with Alcaraz recovering from two sets down for the first time in his career, including saving three championship points, to win the longest ever Roland-Garros final. Every minute was compelling. No

TikTok video could possibly capture the emotions and the shot-making and the general absurdity of what the Gen Z athletes created on Court Philippe-Chatrier, which was decided in a fifth set match tiebreak. 'Unreal,' Àlex Corretja says, and you feel as though others in Paris, as well as many of those watching from around the world, couldn't process the tennis that was being played on the clay court. It was unreal because Alcaraz never doubted himself, not even when defeat appeared to be a certainty.

Even before Alcaraz beat Sinner to retain his Roland-Garros title, Wilander had been saying that the best tennis matches he had ever seen were when Carlos faced Jannik: the Swede had never witnessed tennis played at that speed and that level before. But the 2025 Roland-Garros final was beyond any match Alcaraz and Sinner had played previously. Was Alcaraz's victory also above Nadal's win over Federer in the 2008 Wimbledon final, which until June 2025 had been almost universally seen as the greatest of all tennis matches? Very possibly. Were the 15,000 spectators more into Alcaraz versus Sinner, more invested and energized, than any crowd at a Grand Slam final had ever been before? Again, very possibly. Just a month after turning 22, Alcaraz had won his fifth Grand Slam title in his fifth major final, bringing history and hysteria, which he promises to do again and again in his tennis career.

Whether or not Alcaraz goes on to win more majors than anyone else, or becomes the best in history, he is already changing the sport. He is showing you can bring joy and positive energy while playing tennis that's more fun and colourful than anything that has come before. As a spectator in the stadium, or watching at home on your television or phone, you can't help but smile yourself. Happy tennis, Alcaraz calls it.

ACKNOWLEDGEMENTS

With his happy tennis, Carlos Alcaraz has showed that you tend to do your best work when you're enjoying yourself and it has been a pleasure collaborating again with Trevor Davies, my editor at Octopus (the first book was *Searching for Novak*). I'm also grateful to Rimsha Falak and the rest of the team at Octopus for their excellent work on this project, as well as to Monica Hope for editing the book. Huge thanks to my agents Nick Walters, David Luxton and Rebecca Winfield from David Luxton Associates for the coffees, support and encouragement along the way. On my research trips to Spain, I appreciated the warm welcome from everyone at Real Sociedad Club de Campo Murcia and around El Palmar, including in Victor's café, and the team at the Ferrero Tennis Academy couldn't have been more helpful. Thanks also to everyone else I interviewed for this book, as well as to Fernando and Rocio for their support and translations. I was delighted when I heard Garbiñe Muguruza was interested in writing the foreword; her insights as a former world number one and Grand Slam champion from Spain add a lot to this book.

SOURCES

Books:

- *Alcaraz: La forja de un campeón* by Carlos Santos
- *Hábitos para ser el número 1* by Dr Juanjo López
- *Open* by Andre Agassi
- *The Secrets of Spanish Tennis 2.0* by Chris Lewit
- *Unstoppable* by Maria Sharapova

Newspapers, news agencies, magazines and digital publications:

- *El Mundo*
- *El País*
- *Esquire*
- *Fisio*
- *Forbes*
- *GQ*
- *La Opinión de Murcia*
- *La Razón*
- *La Verdad de Murcia*
- *Marca*
- *Murcia Plaza*
- *Plaza Deportiva*
- *Reuters*

- *Sports Illustrated*
- *The Daily Mail*
- *The Guardian*
- *The New York Times*
- *The Sunday Times*
- *The Times*
- *Vanity Fair*
- *Vogue*
- ATP
- BBC
- Clay Tennis
- ESPN
- Eurosport
- Tennis Majors

Television, documentaries, radio and podcasts:

- *'Academy Life': Juan Carlos Ferrero Tennis Academy*
- *Announcing Alcaraz*
- *Carlos Alcaraz: My Way*
- *Double Bagel*
- *El Hormiguero*
- *El Partidazo de COPE*
- *Más allá de la red — Beyond the Net*
- *Louis Vuitton [Extended]*
- *Served with Andy Roddick*
- *The Netflix Slam*
- *Trans World Sport*

- *Young Guns: The New Tennis Titans*
- HEAD
- Molusco TV
- Tennis Channel
- Tennis TV

PICTURE CREDITS

INDEX

By the same author

Available in paperback, eBook and audio now.

C CASSELL